The Neoconservative Imagination

The Neoconservative Imagination

Essays in Honor of Irving Kristol

Edited by Christopher DeMuth and William Kristol

The AEI Press
Publisher for the American Enterprise Institute
W A S H I N G T O N, D. C.
1995

Available in the United States from the AEI Press, c/o Publisher Resources Inc., 1224 Heil Quaker Blvd., P.O. Box 7001, La Vergne, TN 37086-7001.

ISBN 0-8447-3898-0 (alk. paper)
ISBN 978-0-8447-3899-4 (pbk.: alk. paper)

The AEI PRESS
Publisher for the American Enterprise Institute
1150 17th Street, N.W., Washington, D.C. 20036

Contents

Contributors

IRVING KRISTOL was born in New York City in 1920, graduated from the City College of New York in 1940, and served as staff sergeant in the armored infantry in Europe in World War II.

He was managing editor of *Commentary* magazine from 1947 to 1952, cofounder of the British magazine *Encounter* and its editor from 1953 to 1958, editor of the *Reporter* from 1959 to 1960, executive vice-president of Basic Books from 1961 to 1969, and professor of social thought at the New York University Graduate School of Business from 1969 to 1988. Since 1988, he has been John M. Olin Distinguished Fellow at the American Enterprise Institute.

Mr. Kristol is a founder of two of the most important policy journals of the postwar era, *The Public Interest* and *The National Interest*. He has been coeditor of *The Public Interest* (first with Daniel Bell, more recently with Nathan Glazer) since in its founding in 1965 and publisher of *The National Interest* (edited by Owen Harries) since its founding in 1985. Since 1972, he has written a regular monthly column for the editorial page of the *Wall Street Journal*.

CHRISTOPHER DEMUTH is president of the American Enterprise Institute. He served as administrator for regulatory affairs at the U.S. Office of Management and Budget and executive director of the Task Force on Regulatory Relief during the Reagan administration and was previously lecturer at the Kennedy School of Government and director of the Harvard Faculty Project on Regulation. His articles on government regulation and other subjects have appeared in *The Public Interest, Harvard Law Review, Yale Journal on Regulation,* and *Wall Street Journal.*

WILLIAM KRISTOL is chairman of the Project for the Republican Future. During the Reagan and Bush administrations, Mr. Kristol served as chief of staff to Education Secretary William Bennett and to Vice President Dan Quayle. Before moving to Washington in 1985, Mr. Kristol taught at the John F. Kennedy School of Government of Harvard University and at the University of Pennsylvania. His writing in political philosophy and American politics has appeared in journals such as the *University of Chicago Law Review, Commentary,* and *The Public Interest.*

ROBERT H. BORK is the John M. Olin Scholar in Legal Studies at the American Enterprise Institute. He was the solicitor general of the United States, 1973–1977; acting attorney general, October 1973–January 1974; circuit judge, U.S. Court of Appeals, District of Columbia Circuit, 1982–1988; and President Reagan's nominee to the Supreme Court, 1987. Judge Bork's books include *The Antitrust Paradox: A Policy at War with Itself* and *The Tempting of America: The Political Seduction of the Law.*

MARK GERSON, a 1994 graduate of Williams College, wrote his senior thesis on neoconservative thought. His articles have appeared in *Commentary, First Things, Policy Review, Steve Hawes' Fantasy Basketball,* and *Beckett Basketball Monthly.* He teaches history at St. Mary High School in Jersey City, New Jersey. Mr. Gerson will attend Yale Law School in 1995.

NATHAN GLAZER is professor of education and sociology emeritus at Harvard University and coeditor of *The Public Interest.* He has taught at the University of California at Berkeley, Bennington College in Vermont, Smith College, the Salzburg Seminar in American Studies, and the École des Hautes Études en Sciences Sociales in Paris. He is the author of numerous books and articles including *American Judaism; The Social Basis of American Communism; Beyond the Melting Pot* (with Daniel P. Moynihan); *Affirmative Discrimination: Ethnic Inequality and Public Policy; Ethnic Dilemmas, 1964–1982;* and *The Limits of Social Policy.*

OWEN HARRIES is the editor of *The National Interest*. Educated at the University of Wales and Oxford, he taught at the University of Sydney and New South Wales for twenty years. He was the director of policy planning in the Department of Foreign Affairs and personal adviser to Prime Minister Malcom Fraser in the late 1970s and Australia's ambassador to UNESCO in 1982–1983.

MICHAEL S. JOYCE is president and chief executive officer of the Lynde and Harry Bradley Foundation. He was previously executive director and a trustee of the John M. Olin Foundation. In 1978–1979, Mr. Joyce was director of the Institute for Educational Affairs and, from 1975 to 1978, director of the Goldseker Foundation. He is a contributing editor to a textbook series in the social sciences and author of numerous research studies and articles.

H. J. KAPLAN spent twenty-five years in the U.S. foreign service in Europe, North Africa, and Asia and ten years as a business executive. He was a member of the American delegation to the Vietnam peace talks and was editor in chief of *Geo* for four years. The author of several novels and translations and of numerous magazine articles, he is now retired and living in Paris.

LEON R. KASS is Addie Clark Harding Professor in the College and the Committee on Social Thought, the University of Chicago, and adjunct scholar of the American Enterprise Institute. Author of *Toward a More Natural Science: Biology and Human Affairs* and of *The Hungry Soul: Eating and the Perfecting of Our Nature,* he has written widely on ethical and philosophical issues raised by biomedical advance and on the ethics of everyday life, making use of biblical stories.

MICHAEL NOVAK, the 1994 Templeton laureate, holds the George Frederick Jewett Chair in Religion and Public Policy at the American Enterprise Institute. He is also AEI's director of social and political studies. In 1986, Mr. Novak was U.S. ambassador to the Experts' Meeting on Human Contacts at the Conference on Security and Cooperation in Europe. In 1981 and 1982, he led the U.S. delegation to the United Nations Human Rights Commission in Geneva. In 1994, besides the Templeton Prize for Progress in Religion, Mr. Novak was awarded the Wilhelm Weber Prize in Essen,

Germany, and the International Award of the Institution for World Capitalism in Jacksonville, Florida. The author of more than twenty-five books, he is also a cofounder and the publisher of *Crisis* and a columnist for *Forbes.*

NORMAN PODHORETZ has been the editor in chief of *Commentary* since 1960. He is the author of six books including *Making It* (1967), *Breaking Ranks: A Political Memoir* (1978), and, most recently, *The Bloody Crossroads: Where Literature and Politics Meet* (1986).

EARL RAAB has been an adjunct professor of Jewish public policy and the director of the Perlmutter Institute for Jewish Advocacy at Brandeis University since 1989. He is the executive director emeritus of the Jewish Community Relations Council of the San Francisco area. Mr. Raab's numerous publications include *Jews and the New American Scene,* with Seymour M. Lipset.

PHILIP SELZNICK is professor emeritus of law and sociology at the University of California at Berkeley, where he is affiliated with the Jurisprudence and Social Policy Program. A fellow of the American Academy of Arts and Sciences, he is a senior scholar at the Woodrow Wilson Center for Scholars. Mr. Selznick's research centers on the interplay of moral and social theory. His most recent book is *The Moral Commonwealth: Social Theory and the Promise of Community.*

WILLIAM E. SIMON is president of the John M. Olin Foundation and chairman of William E. Simon & Sons, a private merchant bank. His varied career in business and finance has taken him from Salomon Brothers, where he was a senior partner, to the founding of several successful international financial ventures, to the boards of more than thirty leading business corporations. During the Nixon and Ford administrations, he served as deputy secretary of the Treasury, administrator of the Federal Energy Office, and, from 1974 through 1977, secretary of the Treasury. He has served on the boards of trustees of many major policy research institutes, including the American Enterprise Institute, the Heritage Foundation, the Hoover Institution, and the Hudson Institute. He is the author of two bestselling books, *A Time for Truth* (1978) and *A Time for Action* (1980).

IRWIN STELZER is a resident scholar and the director of regulatory policy studies at the American Enterprise Institute and an honorary fellow of the Centre for Socio-Legal Studies, Oxford. He has been the director of the Energy and Environmental Policy Center at Harvard University, an associate member of Nuffield College, Oxford, and an associate member of the Advisory Panel of the President's National Commission for the Review of Antitrust Laws and Procedures. He is a political and economic columnist for the *Sunday Times* (London) and the *Boston Herald*.

JAMES Q. WILSON, former president of the American Political Science Association, is James Collins Professor of Management and Public Policy at UCLA. For twenty-six years, he was Shattuck Professor of Government at Harvard University. His extensive publications include *The Moral Sense, Bureaucracy, American Government, Thinking about Crime, Varieties of Police Behavior, Political Organizations, The Investigators, Crime and Human Nature* (with Richard J. Herrnstein), *City Politics* (with Edward C. Banfield), and *On Character.* He is a trustee and chairman of the Council of Academic Advisers of the American Enterprise Institute.

PEREGRINE WORSTHORNE'S career as a journalist has spanned almost fifty years, beginning on the *Glasgow Herald* after the Second World War. His five years on the *Times* included a spell in Washington. Sir Peregrine joined the *Daily Telegraph* in 1953 and moved to the *Sunday Telegraph* as deputy editor in 1961. He was named editor in 1986. From 1989 until his retirement in 1991, Sir Peregrine was editor of the Comment section, to which he still contributes a weekly column. His autobiography, *Tricks of Memory,* was published in 1993.

Preface

The essays in this volume were written by Irving Kristol's friends and intellectual compatriots for his seventy-fifth birthday, January 22, 1995. They include memoirs and reflections by some of his oldest friends, touching on his life and thought from his youthful days on the anti-Communist Left through his emergence as the founder and leading exponent of neoconservatism in the 1970s and down to the present. Several of his colleagues have contributed studies of issues in political economy, religion, and culture, prompted by Kristol's own work on these subjects. The final essay is by a 1994 graduate of Williams College, representing the newest generation of Kristol's students and disciples. The book also includes a collection of passages from Kristol's writings and a bibliography of his published work through the end of 1994.

Since his first published essay more than fifty years ago, Irving Kristol has written with rare insight and prescience on topics ranging from politics to literature and from economics to religion, while editing several of the most influential intellectual journals of our time and serving as mentor and career shaper to hundreds of journalists, intellectuals, and academics. The specialization of knowledge in the twentieth century has made it virtually impossible for even the most gifted thinker to cut so broad a swath; those who try usually lose depth and influence in proportion to their breadth. What is most striking about Kristol, however, is not that he is an effective generalist in an age of specialists but that his wide-ranging work exhibits strong intellectual unity; he not only crosses but combines disparate fields of inquiry and does so in a way that deepens our understanding of each field.

The combining principle of Kristol's thought is a refined application of the old idea of the primacy of politics—politics taken in its broadest sense as the confrontation of general ideas about what is good and desirable and the need to make practical choices in contingent circumstances. Kristol thus regards all social phenomena—economic theories; legal doctrines; government policies; conflicts between nations and ideologies; the organization of commerce; fashions in art, music, and literature; even matters of faith and family—as interrelated. Despite his brief collegiate career as a Trotskyite, Kristol has never been a Marxist; he has always been struck by the power of ideas in politics, convinced that ideas shape action even when the actors do not recognize it. He is strongly inclined to judge ideas by their practical consequences, but he recognizes that ideas are autonomous and that a body of thought may grow and flourish independently of its consequences—even the most clearly observable and disastrous consequences. Much of his work has, indeed, been devoted to marshaling intellectual resources to counteract the damage done in modern times by intellectuals. Kristol respects and defends the everyday practical perspective of ordinary men and women, and uses this perspective not to buttress the status quo but to illuminate the most fundamental intellectual issues.

Kristol's ability to meld the practical and the abstract is surely key to understanding his largest and most sustained project: the founding of neoconservatism out of his progressive disillusionment with modern liberalism—a project that began with concrete objections to the "unintended consequences" of specific liberal policies and grew into a fundamental critique of liberalism itself as based on a mistaken conception of the nature of man. It is also the key to his success, famous among friends and colleagues, as an editor and leader of strong-minded intellectuals and counselor to men of action as well as men of thought.

Philip Selznick, in his essay in this volume, calls Kristol's position "moral realism." This is as good a label as any, but, as Selznick would be the first to agree, no label can adequately capture the power of Kristol's approach to matters of life and morals as conveyed by his writings. The Kristol essay is never reductionist or formulaic: it respects the multifariousness of life while providing a coherent perspective on the issue at hand. That is why his matter-of-fact pronouncements so often prompt philosophical reflection, why his acute observations on the headlines of the day so often suggest lasting conclusions.

In his preface to *On the Democratic Idea in America* (1972), Kristol writes:

> I had to discover for myself, uneasily and fumblingly, many things which a serious student of political philosophy— someone soundly versed in Aristotle's *Politics*, for example—might have known early on. But since there are so few students of political philosophy from whom one can learn these days, I should like to think this effort at self-education was perhaps not entirely wasted and that others may possibly find something instructive in it.

Kristol's modesty, usually covered over by his wit and bravado, here peeks through. But he has identified one reason so many readers have found his writings so instructive—because they derive from, and in fact embody, the author's own self-education. Put another way, Kristol's conclusions often seem so "right" because they are based on observation and reflection rather than mere research (as his friends know, he will read and ponder on a subject for months, but when it comes to writing his milieu is the desktop cleared of all but yellow pad, pencil, and ashtray). In an early essay, Kristol writes that "important social theories convince us by their self-evidence." To this we would add that the self-evident proposition does not write itself but rather comes at the end of a strenuous intellectual journey led by a thinker of wisdom and courage.

Irving Kristol's work speaks for itself, as, we hope, do the affection of his friends, the respect of his colleagues, and the love of his family. On behalf of all of them, we present this volume to him as a token of our appreciation and esteem.

Christopher DeMuth
William Kristol

The Neoconservative
Imagination

PART ONE

Essays and Memoirs

1

A Man without Footnotes

Nathan Glazer

A few of us can say that we have read (almost) everything Irving Kristol has written for publication, all the way from contributions to *Enquiry* in the 1940s to his columns in the *Wall Street Journal* in 1994. In between, there have been many articles in *Commentary, Encounter,* the *Reporter,* the *New York Times Magazine, The Public Interest,* and a variety of other journals, contributions to books, and three books of his own. We can't be sure of just what *is* everything. When I asked Irving if he had a list of his writings, he responded with disdain that he keeps no bibliography of his writings, he leaves that to the scholars, who do indeed keep coming up with pieces he has forgotten.

A copy of what must be one of his earliest pieces of published writing, an essay on Lionel Trilling in *Enquiry,* an obscure radical journal published in New York between 1942 and 1945, was given to me by a documentary filmmaker who was making a film on Irving and had researched his writings. Irving had forgotten it, but on reading it I was struck by a remarkable consistency in his central ideas reaching back fifty years to the time when Irving had just left off being a Trotskyite and still thought of himself as a radical. It seems that no major alteration in Irvings's view of man and politics had become necessary as he moved from radicalism to a position as one of the most eloquent defenders of capitalism. (But recall, only *Two Cheers for Capitalism,* as he titled his second book.)

The essay in *Enquiry* is in form a review of Lionel Trilling's book, *E. M. Forster,* published in 1943. Irving begins by referring to a Trilling essay of 1940 in *Partisan Review* that discussed T. S. Eliot's *Idea of a Christian Society.* In that essay, Irving writes, "Mr. Trilling publicly announced his strategy.... [H]e subjected the liberal-socialist ideology to a vigorous and pointed chiding." There were two distinct chidings. On the one hand, Trilling was "angry with the left for having surrendered its traditional moral vision, and at the same time accused it of allowing this vision to blind it to the true principles of humanism. It was all done with such noble vehemence as to blur any hint of incompatibility."

Yet Irving does not really take Trilling to task for this incompatibility: he seems to approve both sides of Trilling's criticism of the liberal-socialist ideal. First, Trilling wrote, in contemporary radical thought, means have taken over from ends: "The noteworthy quality of Eliot, contrasted to Trotsky, is his belief in morality as an end, not simply as a means, as an ever present shaping ideal, not a set of prescribed tactics." Irving has no argument with this criticism:

> This critique of radicalism partakes of the normal religio-ethical tone so consistently set forth by men like Maritain, Niebuhr, Dawson.... Such an appeal cannot help but be effective in these days when an ideal is at best a momentary, individual vision, and the raw stuff of politics is so pervasive and unyielding. It offers a way of penance and justification, all the more attractive for having so few definite programmatic implications.... It encourages frank self-analysis and excites the moral faculties—two very good things.

But then there is the other side of Trilling's criticism: radical philosophers seem to expect that (to quote Trilling) "man, in his quality, in his kind, will be wholly changed by socialism in fine ways that we cannot predict: man will be good, not as some men have been good, but in new and unspecified fashions." So, on the one hand, Trilling objects to the lack of an ultimate, guiding moral ideal—perhaps indeed, a *religious* ideal—though Irving here, with his references to Maritain, Niebuhr, and Dawson, may be pushing Trilling further than he would be willing to go. On the other hand, socialism and radicalism expect too much from politics, from reform, from indeed revolution—they will not, cannot, change man in his essential qualities. The "moral realism" of Forster and Trilling, Irving writes, is better: "It foresees no new virtues.... It is non-eschatological, skeptical of proposed revisions of man's nature, content with the possibilities and limitations that are always with us.... Dodging the sentimentality of both cynicism and utopianism, it is worldly, even sophisticated."

Irving thus accepts both parts of the criticism, whatever the possible contradiction between them if one extends them too far. And he quotes, approvingly, Forster's "two cheers for democracy; one because it admits variety, and two because it permits criticism. Two cheers are quite enough." That is all that any political ideal warrants.

Irving was ready to give only two cheers for socialism and radicalism; more than thirty years later, he was restrained enough in his enthusiasm for capitalism to title his 1978 book *Two Cheers for Capitalism*. I don't know to what extent Irving still thought of himself as a radical when he wrote this essay (*Enquiry* called itself "a journal of independent radical thought," and from one passage he seems to be writing from within the tradition of "radical political thinking"), but this half-century later there is nothing in this piece that Irving, I think, would want to disavow.

A number of us are well acquainted with what I would call this firmness in Irving's thought, but in these comments I want to draw attention to another aspect of his firmness, familiar to those of us who can add to knowledge of his work, knowledge of his working style. My own experience of working with Irving goes back almost as far as the *Enquiry* essay I have discussed. I did not know him when he wrote that but met him a few years later, when he joined the editorial staff of *Commentary*. I wrote for *Encounter* and the *Reporter* while he edited those, and we have collaborated in editing *The Public Interest* for more than twenty years. I have been struck over these years by a distinct quality of style or manner, and it can be summed up in a phrase that has leapt to my mind quite unbidden, "no footnotes." To one always worried about the right footnote, about locating the reference for a number or a quotation, about giving credit to those with whom one disagrees but from whom one might have borrowed something, this seems to me an enviable and indeed admirable quality. If the style is the man—who said that? (under the spell for the moment of Irving's "no footnotes" approach, I won't bother to check)—style does give us an insight into character and indeed can be seen as simply the other side, so to speak, of the content of the ideas. How ideas are expressed cannot be unrelated to what they are.

"No footnotes" evokes for me a number of different qualities. To begin with, it describes a style that is direct, firm, unqualified, very much—to use a rising phrase—"in your face," which is why Irving's columns in the *Wall Street Journal* regularly draw from its readers the most anguished and angry responses. How *can* he say that, they demand, or believe that? But I also have in mind the literal meaning of "no footnotes." Consider: here is a writer who keeps no bibliography of his writings. This is as if to say, there they are—look them up if you need to or want to, I won't bother. Neither will it be necessary for me (or, indeed, possible for me) to footnote a similar or related piece of writing in the past, unless I research the matter—not something a man without footnotes would do.

Further, there are literally almost no footnotes in Irving's writings. (One does find a rare footnote in his longer essays.) One, of course, wouldn't expect them in his *Wall Street Journal* columns. But there are many substantial essays, in journals and books, for which footnotes would be suitable. And, of course, footnotes would be quite in order in the books in which Irving's writings are collected. Looking over his three books, the most permanent and substantial form his writings take, one finds almost no footnotes. There are references to and quotations from Tocqueville or Adam Smith or Friedrich Hayek—but no page references. Occasionally Irving has to refer to statistics—these are not footnoted either. (In my experience they are almost always right.) I have heard this practice attacked, generally by sociologists and other academics. They consider it a sign of arrogance. It is as if Irving is saying, "You, reader, should know what Tocqueville, Smith, or Hayek wrote, and where they wrote it, if you are educated, and otherwise take my word for it."

Interestingly, the historian Gertrude Himmelfarb, Mrs. Kristol, is known as one of the great defenders of the footnote and its value. I do not mean to suggest by this apparent difference regarding footnotes that there is any disharmony in the Kristol household over footnotes. One could reconcile the two positions. Scholars, in particular historians, should footnote their facts, their conclusions from facts, should indicate their agreements and disagreements with other scholars. Columnists, of course, need not. But what of the longer essays, in which Irving Kristol argues for a significant position? Here there are a number of possible justifications for not using footnotes (not that a man who doesn't deign to use them would bother to make an explanation, but his epigones, followers, interpreters, and analysts might be so impelled).

One way of justifying the elimination of footnotes is the need for clarity and directness of argument. Irving Kristol is one of the great expositors of ideas today, and the presentation of the idea he may feel is hampered, obstructed, by too long quotation, too many footnotes in a smaller type size, too many numbers for page reference and date of publication and the like.

The policy of *The Public Interest,* since its founding, has also been one of no footnotes, which has led to much agony among many contributors, particularly since most of them are academics. I do not know whether this policy was argued for initially by Irving or by the cofounder of *The Public Interest,* Daniel Bell, himself a master of footnoting, or agreed on by both when determining the format and style of the new journal. *The Public Interest* at its founding had no existing models, and it could have gone either way. It did not take as its model somewhat similar journals (*Commentary, Atlantic, Harper's*). Nor did it take as its model scholarly social science journals, which are, of course, footnoted. Perhaps the point of the no-footnote policy was an assumed division of labor: there are those who are supposed to get the facts straight (footnotes essential) and those who make use of them in argument; then it's a question of only a general reference and the assumption on the part of the writer that the reader will have some degree of confidence that he got the quotation or the statistic right.

This is the point of view of *The Public Interest,* as well as of Irving Kristol when it comes to his own writing. That would explain the numbers without footnotes, but how about the references to the writing of major figures, also unfootnoted? There I suspect another explanation: there are only a few people whose writing one is expected to take seriously, and for them footnotes are neither necessary nor appropriate. One should have certain texts in mind, the way Plato and his partners in dialogue had Homer or Hesiod in mind (no page references were necessary, aside from the fact that, of course, there were no pages to refer to), the way the rabbis and Maimonides had the text of the Bible and chief commentaries in mind (no page references necessary there, either), the way those who talk seriously about the American commonwealth should have the writings of the Founding Fathers and the language of the founding documents in mind.

Irving Kristol at one point wrote that the two chief influences on his thinking were Lionel Trilling and Leo Strauss (writing about a man without footnotes, I take the license of his practice and will not bother to search for where he wrote this). When it comes to Leo Strauss (who himself used footnotes), the influence on footnoting is clear. From Leo Strauss we have the position that only some thinkers, some writings, matter. They should be kept in mind. The practice of Plato and Maimonides is thus suitable.

Lionel Trilling is a different kind of influence—nuanced, ambiguous, subtle. I don't know that he ever heard of Leo Strauss. Lionel Trilling reminds us of another origin for and rationale for no footnoting, and that is the *Partisan Review* essay. Lionel Trilling was not a typical practitioner of this style of essay—he was too elegant, too English, for the intensity, concentration, and flat assertiveness of the *Partisan Review* essay. For Trilling, I would guess, no footnoting suggested something quite different from what it meant for other *Partisan Review* writers. It suggested he was writing within and for the common society of educated people who don't have to go into detailed chapter and verse, page number and publisher, for each other. For some of the other *Partisan Review* writers, the no-footnote practice is the result of an assumption of authority. It says, we speak from the assuredness of knowing how the world works because of Marxism or because of psychoanalysis or because of both. We needn't go into picayune reference for support. The great expositor of this style of essay, which simply assumes overwhelming authority for its judgments, no matter how startling, was, of course, the art critic Clement Greenberg. (Clement Greenberg worked as an editor at *Commentary* when we were all there in the late 1940s.)

The phrase "of course" brings us closer to the heart of the no-footnote style. There are two uses of "of course." In one, nothing remarkable is being asserted, and the reader will nod with agreement: "Of course." In the other, one asserts something extraordinary, and the reader sits up and says, "*Why* 'of course'?" One might write, perhaps, "Of course, the only legitimate basis of culture is religion" or "Of course, there has been no significant contribution to the understanding of the crisis of modern society since Kierkegaard" (I am not suggesting that either of these phrases are quotations from Irving Kristol). This usage of the phrase "of course" is at the antipodes from the footnote, which attempts by reference to some authority to borrow support for something asserted that may not be obvious to or indeed may surprise the reader. Irving Kristol is a master of the second use of the "of course." When all his writings are put into a computer file, we will be able to study his use of the term and discover that perhaps I attribute to him greater use of the specific words "of course" to introduce some point that is not matter of course at all, than will be justified by computer search. But I am sure in one way or another the element of surprise in assertion carried by the second use of the words "of course" is central to his style.

In a recent column in the *Wall Street Journal* Irving writes:

> There is no reason to doubt that, in time, more progress would have been made [in race relations and the condition of blacks], if it had not been for the Supreme Court's role in school "integration" in the 1950's and the subsequent rise of "affirmative action" in that disastrous decade, the 1960's.

In that sentence, "there is no reason to doubt" serves as the functional equivalent of "of course." For we have here a rather surprising assertion that can be doubted. Indeed, it was doubted, strongly, in a letter to the *Wall Street Journal* shortly after this column appeared, as regularly happens after one of Irving's columns appears. No footnotes, of course: the necessity for any is dismissed by that "there is no reason to doubt." The assertion can be disputed, of course, but it gets one thinking. Would the condition of race relations have been better without the Supreme Court's attempt to move from nondiscrimination to integration, without affirmative action? The point can be debated, and the debate would be complicated.

"Of course," in the second usage I have described above, is a strong assertion. It concentrates the attention, it arouses controversy. It is the furthest possible from the pure academic style, which considers two or more sides of every issue. (That style is now in retreat—radical and unmodulated assertion now has a certain cachet in some academic fields, literary criticism primarily, but also anthropology, sociology, etc.) Also in radical opposition to academic caution are terms such as "everybody," "nobody," "completely," "absolutely." I think we would find a good sprinkling of such terms in the computer analysis of the style of Irving Kristol. In a recent letter to the *Wall Street Journal,* Irving takes issue with those humanists and philosophers and social scientists who try to apply discoveries in science (in this case, chaos theory) to their own fields. He writes: "Whatever the intellectual crises now being experienced in these sets of beliefs [such as the idea of progress and secular humanism] . . . they have *absolutely nothing* [my italics] to do with chaos theory." And in the next paragraph:

> Every time there is a major advance in physics or mathematics, some social scientists or humanists are quick to see in it a paradigm for their own modes of thought.... All such "trendy" efforts are soon revealed to be transient and foolish. The "balance of power" in international relations has *nothing* to do with Newtonian physics, and Einstein's theory of relativity has *absolutely nothing* [my italics] to do with relativity in philosophy and morals.

I agree with Irving. One reason I agree is that I saw something similar happen when terms and ideas developed in a technical field I knew something about, language, were applied wholesale in areas far distant from and much more disorderly than the narrow and precise field of linguistic studies. On the other hand, I doubt that all well-reputed philosophers, social scientists, and humanists would agree that it is "foolish" to apply the insights of mathematics and science to their own fields. They keep on doing so, in any case. I have just used the formulation "on the one hand" (I agree with Irving), "on the other" (I wouldn't put it so strongly). President Truman—reference not at hand—is reputed to have asked for a one-handed economist. He wanted no "on the one hand and on the other hand" from those who were supposed to give him advice. He would have liked Irving, who is quite willing to take a strong stand on economic issues, regardless of how divided econo-mists may be on them.

This is a style that has powerfully advanced certain ideas. More cautious and modulated statement would never have gotten so far. The ideas have, on the whole, been right and have contributed sig-nificantly to making the world of ideas in the 1990s radically differ-ent from that in the 1950s or 1960s. Irving's style is also a wonderfully effective approach if one is an editor, and he has been a powerful and effective editor of a number of influential journals. Years ago, when we were both at *Commentary,* an efficiency firm employed by our sponsor, the American Jewish Committee, went around asking us about our jobs. I recall vividly that one of the questions was, What is the hardest thing about your job? My immediate response was, Turning articles down. I had in mind articles by friends or that I had solicited or encouraged or didn't forcefully say no to when the idea for the article was proposed to me. When they didn't work out, I would go into long explanations and apologies. I don't know what Irving answered to this question. But I was present once when Irv-ing rejected an article. He said, "Why, you can't expect us to publish this. It's just not good enough!"

It was effective and saved a lot of time. Nor, as far as I know, did it affect friendships. It was so obviously the expression of an overriding concern for intellectual quality and appropriateness, expressed directly and without equivocation. Of course, one had to have a strong character to take it.

One can learn a great deal from working with Irving, and I have. One final example of the style of Irving Kristol. Over the years, a remarkable group of young people has come as interns and appren-tice editors to work in the office of *The Public Interest,* an office that Irving has always managed and in which he regularly works. (The coeditor, first Daniel Bell and then myself, has always operated from a distance, and, it has turned out, the same distance, Cambridge.) Visitors to the office of *The Public Interest* are often surprised by the layout: one big room, no separation between editor, secretary, managing and assistant editors, and interns. It's a rather old-fash-ioned arrangement and reminds one of the way lawyers used to work when they learned about law as apprentices in law offices, not in law schools. Originally this arrangement at *The Public Interest* emerged, I believe, because the space was made available as a matter of grace, first by Arthur Rosenthal, the publisher of Basic Books, where Irving was senior editor, and later by the publisher Harper and Row; it was an economical approach to the use of space.

This may be the way it started, and economy may be one reason it is still maintained. But it has always served an educational purpose. The young people hear Irving talking to contributors on the phone, hear him talking to visitors and interviewers. Irving says that is one way they learn. And they do learn, from his directness, clarity, and consistency in developing and presenting ideas. They learn too from the style, which exhibits the same characteristics of directness, clarity, and consistency. Irving is a defender of classic virtues and has had great influence in making the discussion of such virtues respectable. The examination of the way Irving thinks and writes and works tells us that his influence is based on more than the ability to present ideas. It is also based on a style fully matched to the ideas. And for style, one can read "character."

2

An Old Friend's Image

Earl Raab

A t one time, Irving Kristol might have been seen as a cross for me to bear. I was then part of the civil rights leadership in California, at the legislative stage. No small number of my colleagues were convinced that "conservatives," by nature and definition, were not only politically incorrect but also morally corrupt and constitutionally mean-spirited in all matters human.

Irving, friend of my youth, was then emerging as one of the foremost conservative thinkers in the nation, and our friendship was generally known in my circles. When I went across the country to meetings in New York, for example, my address would be that of Bea and Irving, whose warm hospitality made those trips worthwhile. My associates in the improvement of the world, especially my Jewish associates, found this continuing relationship either somewhat scandalous or wholly puzzling.

I didn't argue the point. There was no way for them to know how mistaken it was to cast Irving as mean-spirited. Of course, there was the time when a national leader of the Young Communist League threw a paper object in his face. Without losing his urbane manner, Irving pulled back his foot and sharply kicked his antagonist in the shin with his fashionably pointed shoe. That must have been painful, but it could not really be categorized as an uncompassionate act.

13

There was also the time when, during a Jingo Day protest at City College, an easily annoyed policeman threw our friend Hal Lubin to the ground and sat on him. Irving quietly jumped on the back of the beefy policeman, who in time noticed his presence.

Such a story of youthful passion directed against constituted authority would have led some of my liberal colleagues only to add another charge to Irving's list of villainies. He was prominent among those ex-radicals accused of being "scholars in retreat." But I don't believe he was ever in retreat—or ever much of a radical. From my vantage point, I see continuity; he has developed a great deal but changed not that much.

A couple of historians of life during those days in the steamy alcoves of City College have reported an anecdote about his and my official entry into the ranks of the Trotskyite party of the time. The party's leader had complained about the "periphery," those who hung around the edges but didn't join, which included the two of us. He pronounced it "perry-ferry." When we finally did join, we naturally took the party names of Perry, David, and Ferry, William.

But youthful folly aside, the reasons for Irving's involvement with the anti-Stalinist Left had little to do with Trotskyite ideology. It has even been said, absurd as it may sound, that being a Trotskyite at that time reflected an abhorrence of all-encompassing and utopian government. (Trotskyites, many with relief, knew well that Trotsky was not about to become a head of government.) In any case, such an abhorrence has remained at the core of much of Irving's mind-set.

But those early political associations also provided him a convenient way to express a temperamental rejection of mindless and despotic "political correctness," which in our milieu was Stalinoid in nature. Irving never retreated from that temperament, either, as he breasted wave after wave of political correctnesses in the years following.

Of course, the most direct motivation was probably that the most interesting fellows around at the time, the intellectual likes of Philip Selznick, were in the anti-Stalinist Left. And above all else, Irving was constitutionally an intellectual. He couldn't help himself any more than Joe DiMaggio could help being a baseball player. It was occasionally irksome for me to stand beside him in the library stacks, as I pored over some index and he digested book after book by riffling through most of them in a matter of minutes. I realized, though, that it was not trick virtuosity but simply a search, often futile, for new ideas worthy of attention and, perhaps, revision. He sometimes debated these ideas with himself, at the mumble, as he walked along the street.

But the trouble with being asked to recall memories about someone you admire is that the recital starts to sound like a funeral oration. I have developed some complaints about Irving over the years, beyond his unwillingness to recognize that I am the better ping-pong player. While I have agreed with most of what he has written, I have often been distressed over what he hasn't written. He can write an essay deriding equality of results, without mentioning that he is personally in favor of equal opportunity. Never rootless, Irving is a Jew with a Jewish memory, and he has never lacked concern for victims of oppression or disadvantage. Sometimes he throws in a line about the "scandal" of poverty and asserts the "unquestionable moral necessity to help the poor." But I guess he takes that imperative for granted, and he has always been less interested in saying that the poor must be assisted than in cautioning that this should be done only "in whatever way actually assists them." He does not feel obligated to parade his positive moral commitment to the involuntarily disadvantaged. Irving would have made a terrible politician. Of course, that isn't his business, and such protestations would probably not make most liberals think better of him. Still, the omissions have often offended my sense of community relations, which has been my business.

I have sometimes been disconcerted by Irving's reluctance to recognize the effect his thinking has had on "the folk," beyond inner political and intellectual circles. My particular reference is to the Jewish community, against whose liberalism he has often played. Loose cannons abound in the liberal Jewish political arena in particular, and national Jewish agencies have shifted positions on social policy slowly, as institutions do. But the attitudes of the general Jewish population have become more "conservative," in Irving's terms, on a number of items on the social agenda. The continuing addiction of Jewish voters to the Democratic Party is another matter and can be partly ascribed to the continuing inhospitability of the Republican Party.

The attitudes have shifted Irving-ward on such issues as law and order, government intervention, the realities of black-Jewish relations, and religion in public life. Irving has always been concerned with the cultural undergirding of political life, and his concern has grown with his perception of "the spiritually impoverished civilization that we have constructed on what once seemed to be sturdy bourgeois foundations." He has come to equate liberalism with that spiritual impoverishment and to define it as centrally antagonistic to the religious spirit.

Irving has complained that American Jews, in their liberalism, have abandoned the religious spirit. He has even admonished the Jewish community for its attacks on the fundamentalist Christians and some of their beliefs. Perhaps he has underestimated the uneasiness elicited by the call for a Christian "religious war" by some fundamentalist spokesmen. However few, they underestimated the extent to which many Jews—along with many other Americans—have come to a renewed understanding that, as he puts it, "men cannot for long tolerate a sense of spiritual meaninglessness in their individual lives."

Whether and how productively such an understanding will prevail is a separate issue. My travels around the country and in the trenches convince me that there has been a change in mood and that Irving has palpably contributed to that change. With inimitable wit and clarity, as a writer and as an editor, he has articulated ideas about values that have shaped and lent authority to more minds out there in the countryside than I think he knows. I am annoyed by the sense that Irving doesn't recognize that fact—although such recognition might serve him badly by blunting his indignation.

I must confess, however, that his intellectual efforts and their effects do not come first to mind when I contemplate Irving's seventy-fifth birthday (the mention of which I can add to my list of left-handed complaints). It's just easier to talk about less important—I guess I mean more impersonal—things, at least for those who normally specialize in leaving unsaid the unsaid.

When Irving jumped on top of that policeman some fifty years ago, it was not because of general outrage but because a friend was at the bottom of the pile. In that instinct as well as in his basic social values, Irving has not changed. As I among others can attest, but will not detail, he is a remarkable friend, quietly opening opportunities, prodding talents, and providing support and comfort.

There is merit in my apparent compulsion to merge the Irving I have known with the Irving I have read. There is an Irving "presence" in both. It was there long ago, when he played table hockey at uptown Broadway arcades of a Saturday night, at once fiercely competitive and lightly festive, or when he discussed whatever at downtown cafeterias or while drinking bad wine in Central Park, at once assertive and without vanity. It was there even when he imperturbably faced down wickedly horned Ayrshire cows in his working visits to the Maine farm that several of us owned. (Bea has her own inimitable presence, but it does not include facing down large cows or, for that matter, small dogs.) This amalgamation of the serious and the playful has continued through the years to mark his personal presence and, I would maintain, his public presence as well.

Michael Oakeshott has parodied on Plato's allegory of the cave with a tale about a theorist who has studied outside and returned to the cave with "a definitive understanding and language to supersede and to take the place of all other understandings and languages." When the theorist instructs the cave dwellers, out of his new store of knowledge, about the ways in which a horse is structurally like a zebra, they think him clever and applaud his performance.

> But if he were to tell them that, in virtue of his more profound understanding of the nature of horses, he is a more expert horseman, horse-chandler or stable boy than they...and when it becomes clear that his new learning has lost him the ability to tell one end of a horse from the other...the less patient would be disposed to run him out of town as an impudent mountebank. In short, what the cave-dwellers resent is not the theorist, the philosopher...but the "theoretician," the *philosophe*, the "intellectual"; and they resent him, not because they are corrupt or ignorant but because they know just enough to recognize an impostor when they see one.

Irving excommunicated such para-intellectuals a long time ago, and not just because he thought they constituted a new, power-hungry political class in America. He has been repelled by their tendency to have "definitive understandings...to take the place of all other understandings" in treating the problems of the world, and consequently to demand that government—under their control—apply their unending remedies for the good of all the ignorant cave dwellers.

Some would say that his arrogance matches theirs. And I can hear him reply that the difference is that he's right and they're wrong. But that would just be his pointed-shoe jab again. Their not knowing one end of the horse from the other is not a matter of their being wrong on this or that issue. Irving has been wrong on this or that issue. But he has never succumbed to the arrogant notion that he could solve the world's ills by some political or utopian set of ideas.

In short, it is the essence of Irving's presence, personal and professional, that he does not consider himself a savior. He's a nice Jewish boy who is repelled by ideas that fundamentally mistake the horse's anatomy, but despite occasional appearances to the contrary, he doesn't really want to cut anybody's heart out. Perhaps the key to understanding both his private qualities and his public proclamations is the genuine strength of his belief that "the satisfactions of private life are inherently superior to those provided by any political order."

Anyway, as one cave dweller, that's my image of Irving. Maybe I just like him, despite his faults, because we are two of the world's last principled smokers. Or because he sometimes gives me his old detective novels. But for all the reasons at my disposal, I'm glad we have coincided.

3

Irving Kristol's Moral Realism

Philip Selznick

I rving Kristol has been my friend, co-thinker, critic, and political "other" since 1940. At that time, we were members of
the Workers Party, a breakaway Trotskyist group led by Max
Shachtman. The Workers Party was formed after an intense fac-
tional struggle that led to rejection of Trotsky's leadership by
Shachtman and his colleagues. While offering a more profound criticism of the Soviet system, the Shachtmanites nevertheless retained
allegiance to Marxism and Leninism. For a number of us, however,
the conflict occasioned a deeper self-scrutiny. Some hard truths about
Leninism had been revealed, and this was an ideology we were ready
to reject.

Before the split, as we liked to call it, I had already distanced
myself from Marxism. For a time I entertained the rather odd but
not wholly original idea that revolutionary socialism and Leninist
strategy could be justified pragmatically, without accepting the philosophy and sociology of Marxism. (This was roughly the position
taken by Max Eastman in *Marx, Lenin, and the Science of Revolution,* 1926.) By 1940, having come to see that the evils of Leninism
could not be divorced from Marxist doctrine, and thinking to reform the Shachtman group, I proposed that Marxism should no
longer be taught as its official doctrine. This quixotic move was taken
quite seriously, and a formal debate was arranged between me and

Irving Howe, who was then a leader of the Shachtmanite youth. Each of us spoke for about an hour, followed by the customary discussion from the floor. Among the few who rose to support my view was a young comrade from Brooklyn. This was my first and very welcome sight of Irving Kristol.

A few months later, we and some others (the "Shermanites") left the organization. In those days, in that context, I was Philip Sherman and Irving was William Ferry. Irving and I collaborated on a letter of resignation, and most of our group joined the Socialist Party, then led by Norman Thomas. At the same time, while waiting to be drafted, we began publishing a little magazine, *Enquiry: A Journal of Independent Radical Thought,* which appeared intermittently from 1942 to 1945. In these pages we glimpse the future Irving. Here is the emerging writer, sensitive in language as well as thought; here some of his enduring preoccupations may be discerned. In one essay (on Lionel Trilling) we see him already intrigued by E. M. Forster's "two cheers for Democracy." He plays with the image, ringing its changes. The fascination will persist, as we know.

By the end of World War II, we had (quite independently) made a complete break with radical and even Socialist ideology. We firmly set aside the mistaken and dangerous views of our late teens and early twenties. Yet we could retain, even to this day, a certain nostalgia for the Trotskyist days—days of high political passion and, especially, of extraordinary intellectual stimulation. In retrospect, we could say we had had great fun; luckily, we were too insignificant to do much harm; and we learned much that stayed with us long after we in our turn had said "goodbye to all that."

As I reread Irving's essays, and think about his public life, I am struck by how many of his ideas I find wise and compelling— this despite the fact that since 1948 I have remained a Truman Democrat while he has taken a very different path. To be sure, my agreement is with broad perspectives rather than specific conclusions. There is no question of an iron logic, no question of supposing that "who says A must say B." Nevertheless, theory and philosophy are neither innocent nor impotent. They can deepen our differences or offer common ground and hope for reconciliation.

The most important perspective we share is the critique of utopian and rationalist thought. This owes much to our early history. As young Trotskyists in the late 1930s, we were fervent anti-

Stalinists; we despised the Soviet regime of terror and oppression; but we were not ready to generalize from that experience. Trotsky believed Stalinism was an aberration and the USSR was a "degenerated workers' state." Once we had rejected those views, we were in a position to draw far broader conclusions. We could examine, in a more basic way, the human cost of utopian ideals.

As we contemplated the moral ruin in the Soviet Union, and the responsibilities of Leninism, we felt seared by the breath of evil. In response, we earnestly sought a better understanding of human nature, leadership, organization, and mass politics. We turned to writers in theology and social theory—Reinhold Niebuhr and Robert Michels, among others—for help in articulating a deeper appreciation for the dilemmas and frustrations of social idealism. Those writers helped us understand the irrepressible role of power and domination in human affairs; the tyranny of means over ends; the subversion of good intentions by unintended effects; the recalcitrance and frailty of people and institutions; above all, the insidious collusion of good and evil.

To take evil seriously is to recognize that some amoral and immoral dispositions can be depended on to persist despite our best efforts to offset or restrain them.[1] Moreover, the most serious forms of evil are created by forces *within* the human psyche and *within* groups and communities. The most important evils are those we

---

1. As I have noted elsewhere:

Propositions about human nature usually purport to show that all people are alike in some relevant way. But that assumption may be too strong. The generalization may refer to attributes that are variable within a population. Not everyone has the same need for emotional support, the same capacity for self-transcendence, the same disposition to be greedy. To say with Lord Acton that "power tends to corrupt and absolute power corrupts absolutely" is not to say that everyone, or even almost everyone, will be corrupted by power. But the aphorism does say that the corrupting effect of power is sufficiently powerful and pervasive, as an attribute of *populations,* that every community should guard against it.

(*The Moral Commonwealth: Social Theory and the Promise of Community,* University of California Press, 1992, p. 120f.)

generate ourselves, from ourselves, rather than those that come from unforeseen misfortunes or from circumstances we did not create.

These conclusions were, of course, far from original. We were learning for ourselves, in our own way, what had long been understood by others. But for us these truths had a special salience. They formed our minds and thereby greatly influenced what we would find congenial in philosophy, social science, and politics.

A good example is the way we think about American democracy and the Constitution. Like our mutual, much-missed friend, Martin Diamond, Irving has emphasized the realistic premises and sober expectations of the American founders. He has stressed the need for a virtuous public, without which self-government becomes questionable and even a sham. Moreover, the Constitution is seen as a perfection or fulfillment of democracy, not as an assault on it.

I have long shared these views, which reflect a grave concern for democratic excess. As we have learned in many ways, and as has become ever more evident, widespread political participation carries great risks. To retain the integrity and moral worth of democratic government, participation must be channeled and tempered by institutional forms; democracy is distorted when it is detached from stable contexts of interest and association. A healthy democracy presumes people-in-community. Ordered liberty cannot be sustained by a mass of disaggregated, rootless, vulnerable individuals. As Irving puts it, more provocatively, the "mob" must become "a people."

Distrust of mass democracy underpins the need for constitutional constraints. Not only leaders but the people too must be, as Jefferson said, bound down "by the chains of the Constitution." We accept Diamond's idea that the founders created a "democratic republic," that is, a regime capable of "reconciling the advantages of democracy with the sobering qualities of republicanism." These qualities include the "republican virtue" of commitment to the common good, a virtue democracy *tout court* need not embrace.

This defense of constitutional constraint is something more than a familiar civics lesson. It looks to animating ideas as well as institutional forms; demands reaffirmation of fundamental principles; contests revisionist doctrines; and reflects a keen awareness of the damage done when constitutionalism is denigrated or taken for granted or dimly understood. That sensibility owes much to our youthful recoil from Lenin and Trotsky, who had only contempt for "bourgeois" institutions.

The wish to take evil seriously, and to cabin it as best we can, belongs to a general disposition we call moral realism. Moral realism tells us what we can *rely on* in human nature and social life and what we must *guard against*. Moral realists look mainly to the material foundations of morality, especially reliable incentives and controls, and to the corruptions and frustrations that undermine our hopes and plans. In addition, moral realism takes for granted that, in a humane and thriving community, indeed within the human personality itself, there is and must be a plurality of interests and values. This plurality makes trade-offs inevitable and compromise desirable.

For some, moral realism evokes a mood of tragic irony, a bleak vision of ideals relinquished, hopes forsworn. Indeed, we cannot escape hard choices among competing and intrinsically worthy goods. If my reading of Irving is correct, however, *irony* is appropriate but a sense of *tragedy* is not. Consider Irving's implicitly two-tiered approach to moral failing. On one hand are the truly great evils and their accompanying illusions. Communism, Nazism, and nihilism are the most important examples. These evils are special in part because they reject the world God made and found good. The consequences are devastating; they shake the foundations; they are not readily contained. In combat with them, no "tragic sense of life" should sap our confidence; nor should ironic distance stay our hands.

The other tier, though also marked by original sin, is in and of God's world. This is the realm of routine transgression, driven by ordinary impulses and shortcomings. Here is the main arena for moral realism, which seeks to limit and contain evil, not to eradicate it. We design institutions with sin or deviance in mind, without illusions, accepting them as belonging to a world we need not admire but in which we can feel at home.

Thus in creating constitutions, laws, and workable systems of management and accountability, we take delinquency and self-interest for granted. Moreover, we recognize that some deviations from official norms reflect genuinely competing values, such as the conflicting demands of love and work, and we know that self-interest, properly reworked and circumscribed, has moral worth as well as limits. Here irony is indeed appropriate. Here a loving casuistry is required, not prophetic or apocalyptic judgment.

The outcome is neither a dispassionate, impersonal morality nor one derived from abstract doctrine. It is Irving's fate to have labels pinned on him and to be in some sense ideologically committed, despite many qualms about ideological thinking. The more important truth is, however, that he has sought to anchor morality in the genuine needs, frailties, and potentialities—the strengths and virtues, as well as the defects—of ordinary people in ordinary circumstances. This respect for the ordinary shines a warming light on the cool logic of moral realism.

But is that enough? I think not. Although a strong dose of realism is surely necessary and healthy, it offers at best a partial view of the human condition. By itself, it cannot be a sound guide to personal life or to the design of institutions. Moral realism yields only a base-line morality preoccupied with the discipline of unruly passions. This cannot do justice to the human quest for a flourishing existence, which calls for a life guided by ideals of excellence and fulfillment.

Here is the taproot of our difference. In my view—the "communitarian liberal" view—realism and idealism must be combined, and they *can* be combined because ideals are latent in more rudimentary, less elaborated ways of thinking, acting, and relating. This way of thinking encourages a posture of criticism and reconstruction, especially self-criticism and self-reconstruction. It looks to the *promise* of our institutions as well as to their limiting premises, and it takes complacency to be a vice, not a virtue.

In interpreting the Constitution, for example, we should welcome the idea that its abstract clauses contain promises to be made good for new generations of Americans. These include, especially, promises of full citizenship and of legally protected moral equality. These promises should not be divorced from history, for it is from history, not abstract morality, that they must derive their main legitimacy. But history offers opportunities as well as perils. Discerning those opportunities, and responding to them, is a worthy engine of constitutional development.

It is wise to reject utopian ideas and projects insofar as they ignore or dismiss needed constraints and incentives. But we need not accept—we dare not accept—an enervating complacency. Human beings want to know what they can aspire to, as well as what they can rely on and guard against. To those questions the moral realist is likely to respond with embarrassed silence or with a gesture of irritation.

The alternative is to learn from Dewey as well as Niebuhr, from Aristotle as well as Hobbes. It is always important to secure a base-line morality and to face squarely the conditions that must be met if ideals are to be made good. Sometimes a base-line morality is as much as we can get; no doubt the corruption of ideals is easier than their fulfillment. Nevertheless, once a base-line morality is secure, we can respond to opportunities for moral growth and enrichment. We can bind self-interest to more comprehensive goals. We can extend the reach of justice.

4

Irving Kristol in London

Sir Peregrine Worsthorne

T he part of Irving Kristol's endearingly distinguished life that I have been asked to cover is the period—a mere five and a half years—he spent in London in the early 1950s as coeditor, with Stephen Spender, of the monthly political and cultural journal, *Encounter*, now sadly no more. Those cannot have been easy years for Irving (nor for me, as it happened). On this side of the Atlantic, he was a completely unknown American journalist thrown into the deep end of a London political and literary world still accustomed to American writers cast in the mold of Henry James or Henry Adams. Although, in succeeding years, New York Jewish intellectuals have become almost as valued a part of Britain's cultural life as of America's, they certainly were not then. Irving was the first such to arrive and caused quite a cultural shock. With the benefit of hindsight, one now realizes how much greater the cultural shock would have been had *Encounter*'s sponsors, the Congress of Cultural Freedom, appointed any other New York Jewish intellectual of that generation—Norman Podhoretz, for example. In their wisdom, however, they chose Irving, the most charming and Anglophile (at least at that time) of them all and therefore the least likely to stand out like a sore thumb. Nevertheless, he did stand out, all five feet six inches of him, and all the more so by contrast with the immensely tall and romantically handsome coeditor Stephen Spender. They made a remarkable pair, a bit like Don Quixote and Sancho Panza.

Much to everybody's surprise, however, the combination was not all that unbalanced. Irving more than held his end up, and right from *Encounter*'s first number succeeded in stamping his own personality on it. It was a remarkable achievement, considering Stephen's incomparably greater editorial clout, which enabled him to command contributions from all the greatest writers of the age— Moravia, Camus, Bertrand Russell, Koestler, Isaiah Berlin, to name only a few. But somehow, arising above that overwhelmingly powerful chorus, a Kristol descant rang out loud and clear, and even sometimes with striking discordance. One such an occasion, I recall, was an article in an early number by Leslie Fiedler—who is he? we all asked—coldly and unemotionally analyzing the execution in the electric chair of the American spies Ethel and Julius Rosenberg. Under no conceivable circumstances would any of Stephen's high-minded authors have ever composed such an uncompassionate piece. It was unmistakably Irving's idea. Not that he, the most subtle of writers and kindest of men, would have thought of writing such a piece himself. But in publishing Fiedler's, he was exerting his editorial independence with a bang. It was, if you like, a shock that echoed round the world. More than anything else, that article indicated that henceforth it was not only the statesmen and generals who were taking the cold war seriously—as a matter of life and death— but so also were at least some intellectuals.

Encounter's London office was bombarded with protests from the world's great and good who simply could not believe in the Rosenberg guilt, so reluctant were they to recognize the extent of Communist subversion in the United States. I remember visiting the *Encounter* office at this time. Stephen, much troubled, had taken time off, leaving Irving to hold the beleaguered fort. There this tiny figure sat behind a great mountain of letters and telegrams from indignant readers. Was he downhearted? Not a bit of it. "Oh shucks," he said, with a sheepish grin, "let's get out of here and have a drink."

That was my second meeting with Irving. The first, a few weeks before, had been at one of Margot Walmesley's parties. Margot—an inspired choice—had been taken on by Irving to run the office side of *Encounter* and having herself acquired this cozy billet on the

American gravy train was generously anxious to help her journalist friends, such as myself, to share in her good fortune. Being realistic as well as generous, she did not think that an unknown young right-wing journalist—I was then a junior leader writer on the *Daily Telegraph*—would have much chance of winning favor with the great Stephen Spender but just might with Irving, who, being new to London, had not yet had time to discover who was who, or rather, in my case, who was not who. How right she was. A rapport was instantly established. I think I can recall the subject of our first conversation. Irving, who had been in Britain for only a few months, had already been struck by the cohesiveness of the political and cultural elites, the extent to which everybody knew and was related to everybody else or at any rate had been at school with them. But instead of condemning this state of affairs as an unhealthy relic of feudalism and aristocracy, he rightly saw it as contributing a lot to the continuity, stability, and graciousness of English public life.

That was exactly my view, too. It was the cohesion of the British ruling class, I argued, that would prevent a demagogue like Senator Joe McCarthy (then at the height of his reign of terror in the United States) from ever running amok here. In any society, it was not enough for every new generation of meritocrats to rise to the top since such would be their mutual suspicions and the distance between them that they would never cohere into an authoritative establishment capable of upholding the proprieties. In this country, however, thanks to the hereditary class system, there was such an authoritative group and how lucky we were to have it. To my amazement, instead of responding contemptuously to such reactionary rant, Irving agreed. "It won't last long," he said. "Enjoy it while you can." This was in the early 1950s, mark you, when egalitarianism was the dominant intellectual creed quite as much in Britain as in America. To find an editor who was a kindred spirit was almost too good to be true. Thus it was that I found myself visiting the *Encounter* office, and being taken out by Irving to drinks and lunch.

For me, it was a momentous lunch since out of it came a commission to write for *Encounter*—my first breakthrough into the journalistic big league. It is difficult nowadays to explain why this was such a turn up for the book. Nowadays, young conservative writers take it for granted to be asked to write for all sorts of prestigious

magazines. But at that time in Britain, conservative ideas—or at
any rate High Tory ones—were much at a discount, unless aired by
someone of the literary stature of T. S. Eliot, whose name just about
carried them into print but not remotely into fashion. True, a Conservative government under Winston Churchill had recently returned to office but only on condition that it did nothing to reverse
the Socialist legislation of the previous six years. Like the Stuart
King Charles II after the Restoration, Churchill was determined
not to be sent on his travels again, and if pretending to believe in
the welfare state, social and racial equality, fair shares, social justice, and such like was the price the Conservative Party had to pay
for office, then pay it they would and did.

Such defeatism was not surprising. For just as Socialists generally were discredited by the defeat of communism—even the ones
with good cold war records—so were conservatives generally by the
defeat of Nazism, even the ones, like Churchill, who had taken the
lead in Germany's downfall. And none of conservatism's many strands
were more vulnerable in this regard than mine since some of its
favorite words—*authority, hierarchy, order, leadership*—unquestion-
ably did have offputtingly horrible echoes. So even the *Daily Telegraph*, than which there was no stauncher conservative newspaper,
felt compelled to pull its punches, taking it for granted that egalitarianism was the wave of the future which could be slowed down
but never reversed. There were plenty of closet conservatives, of
course, burrowing away underground to preserve what they could
of the old order, but the last thing they wanted was brash young
Tory journalists brazenly proclaiming the faith. "Bend with the wind"
was the Tory motto in those days. Scorned by the Left and looked on
askance by the powers that be on the Right, the lot of the Tory en-
thusiast was not a happy one—until, that is, Irving Kristol came to
the rescue.

I don't want to give the wrong impression here; Irving, at this
point, was not a conservative. His sympathies, I imagine, were with
the right wing of the Labour Party, whose intellectual luminaries
were then Hugh Gaitskell, Antony Crosland, and Roy Jenkins. But
I think he saw the point of High Toryism, at any rate so far as
Britain was concerned. It intrigued him. Of course, no country starting from scratch would be justified in creating a class system such
as Britain's, but having been saddled by history with this deeply

inegalitarian, snobbish monstrosity, then the only sensible course was to make the best of it. Perhaps this was not his view. But from the way he talked, and joked, it sounded as if it was. What struck him, I think, was the extraordinary pride of the English working class. Unlike their American counterparts, they did not, for the most part, want to better themselves by rising in the social scale. They liked it where they were and had no burning ambition to move into the suburbs and join the middle class. For the minority anxious for upward mobility, plenty of opportunities plainly existed. But for those who did not, there was no pressure—as there is in America—to make the effort. To rise was the mark of success. But not to rise was not a mark of failure. Those who wanted to rise could, but those who didn't feel the urge had no cause to feel ashamed of themselves for staying put. As I say, Irving did not necessarily approve of this state of affairs but neither did he disapprove. Since in any society there are always going to be top dogs and bottom dogs, he seemed prepared to give the British class system credit for evolving social attitudes which made the best of an inevitably bad job.

Irving's attitude to English top dogs was equally "nonjudgmental." Just as English history had produced a working class with a proud proletarian culture of its own, capable of inspiring great loyalty and cohesion, so had it produced a ruling class with a peculiarly gentlemanly culture of its own capable of doing the same. This, too, he saw as an asset rather than a liability. What would not most societies give to have such a relatively public-spirited, fair-minded, incorruptible, and experienced ruling class? Irving was interested in these English peculiarities rather in the manner of a good anthropologist, concerned less to condone and condemn than to understand and even, in his case, enjoy. It was an enormously refreshing approach. Everybody else at the time was taking it for granted that the class system was what was wrong with this country. Irving knew better. England without class, he once said, would be like *Hamlet* without the Prince of Denmark. And so it has proved to be.

But, of course, encouraging young High Tory writers just for the hell of it was not what the Congress of Cultural Freedom had sent him to London to do. What he had been sent to London to do was to rally Britain's intelligentsia behind America's leadership in the cold war by weaning them of their illusions about the virtues of Soviet communism and their scarcely less unhelpful illusions about the vices of American capitalism. In Stephen Spender's mind this primarily meant subjecting them to the same kind of political arguments which had converted him from communism to democratic socialism: and who better to do this than his fellow converts—Koestler, Silone, John Strachey, etc. Making the case for democratic socialism as against totalitarian communism: that was how Stephen saw *Encounter*'s function. For him the target readership was very much on the Left. For surely the Right were already anti-Communist and procapitalist enough and did not need any further encouragement in those directions.

Irving's aims, I think, were rather different. Here I am only guessing. But my hunch is that Irving never bothered too much about persuading the British Left to fight the cold war under American leadership: never doubted, indeed, that the converts from communism would turn out to be the fiercest pro-American cold war warriors of all, backing American military might to the hilt, as indeed many of their number—notably Robert Conquest and Kingsley Amis—were to do during the agony of Viet Nam. Nor was the hard center of British social and cultural anti-Americanism really on the Left since in many ways the openness, unstuffiness, and classlessness of American life were exactly the qualities which young Labour intellectuals like Tony Crosland and Roy Jenkins wished there were more of in Britain. Likewise, America's anticolonialism and antiimperialism—which were about to be demonstrated so brutally by Eisenhower during Britain's abortive military operation to reopen the Suez Canal in 1956—were profoundly sympathetic to the Left. No, where the deepest anti-Americanism in Britain lay was on the imperialist, inegalitarian, reactionary nationalist High Tory Right—among, that is, my kind of people. In other words, his encouragement of our lot—Henry Fairlie, Colin Welch, Peter Utley—was not so eccentric after all. There was method in his madness.

Not that the Right in those days wore its anti-Americanism on its sleeve, any more than it wore anything else it felt strongly about on its sleeve. Here again they resignedly took their lead from Churchill, who genuinely was pro-American. But in this, as in so much else, he was not at all in tune with his party or his class, the real views of which were far more truly embodied in the wartime monarch King George VI, who in 1940, presciently in my view, wrote as follows to the British foreign secretary, Lord Halifax: "I do hope that the Americans will not try to bleed us white over the dollar asset question. As it is they are collecting the remaining gold in the world, which is of no use to them, and they cannot wish to make us bankrupt. At least I hope they do not want to."[1] During and even after the war, Britain's dependence on the United States was so great that such sentiments were expressed only privately, but they were still there all right, as my letters and diaries of that date do not allow me to forget. Nowhere had *Encounter* a more difficult row to hoe than among the deeply rooted anti-American prejudices, not only of right-wing grandees but also of right-wing journalists, like George Gale, editor of the *Spectator*, and distinguished academics, like the historian Sir Herbert Butterfield and Maurice Cowling. Compared with the former Communists, who soon rolled over on their backs with pro-American sycophancy, these were the difficult nuts for *Encounter* to crack.

Not that all of them were cracked. But Irving's *Encounter* was certainly far more High Tory friendly than any other British publication of that period. They even allowed contributors to speak ill of democracy, which in those days really was to court trouble. Being the author of one such article myself, I remember Irving's editorial support with gratitude. My article addressed the question of what the North Atlantic Treaty Organization should do if Indochina or Italy, say, voted in a Communist government, which was then a real possibility. My answer was clear: NATO should feel free to intervene to overthrow it. Democracy, I argued, was sacrosanct only so long as it safeguarded its country's liberties, as it had in Britain. British liberties preceded democracy, not the other way round. Democracy was primarily about sharing power, not preserving liberty, and was acceptable only as long as that sharing of power led to the preservation of liberty. Once it ceased to do that—as it would in Italy, for example, if the voters chose communism—it was no longer worth preserving. NATO was an alliance of free peoples, first and foremost, and if democracy, in any member state, should prove a Trojan horse letting in Communist totalitarianism, then down with democracy.

Not only did Irving agree to print this piece, but in an editorial at the front of the issue carrying it he gave it a kind of blessing:

---

1. Andrew Roberts, *Eminent Churchillians* (London: George Weidenfeld and Nicolson, 1944).

It seems to us that events, once thought to be transparent in their significance, have become intractable to the understanding, and principles once regarded as for all practical purposes self-evident, have become tantalisingly obscure. We are moved to these reflections by Peregrine Worsthorne's essay on Democracy versus Liberalism. Mr. Worsthorne freely *confesses* [my italics] himself to be a young Conservative and since he is on the staff of the *Daily Telegraph* he can claim almost a professional standing. But what has struck us most forcefully about his article was not all its Conservative bias, but its freshness. There was a subject "free election" which has been much to the fore, and which has given rise to certain perplexities; and here was the first article we have seen which had made a serious effort to get to the root of these perplexities. We do not say we agree.

It was a surprising admission for those days. What it said, between the lines, was that in the postwar world where Russian communism had replaced German fascism as the principal threat, conservative thoughts about freedom were just as enlightening, if not more so, than democratic socialist ones. In subsequent numbers a long correspondence followed under the title "Democracy, Liberalism and Mr. Worsthorne." Even at this distance I remember the thrill of seeing those words. In no other profession is the transition from being a nobody to being a somebody more swift and sudden than in journalism. "Democracy, Liberalism and Mr. Worsthorne" indeed—a Walter Mitty dream come true.

Yes, I had much to be grateful for to Irving Kristol. And to his wife Bea too. I am sure it was Bea's understanding of English history and English conservatism which contributed so enormously to *Encounter*'s appeal in those early days, not just to progressive intellectuals—at which it was primarily aimed—but also to right-wing ones who sensed an affinity there which was certainly never openly avowed. Nor was that affinity felt only within the pages of *Encounter*. One also felt it when visiting Bea and Irving's many London homes. Often at dinner there, on their frequent visits to London, were Daniel Bell, Edward Shils, Nat Glazer, Irwin Ross, and many others, whose willingness to take High Tory ideas seriously was also in such marked contrast to the British intellectual fashion of that benighted era. Much more than Henry James and Henry Adams, who always retained their New England distrust of old England, these New York Jewish intellectuals were surprisingly at ease with its prejudices and peculiarities. Many bonds of friendship were formed. To what extent Irving's presence in London during that short period helped to diminish anti-Americanism on the Right generally, I do not care to hazard a guess. But certainly in my circle his impact was enormous and is still very keenly felt.

5

The Australian Connection

Owen Harries

T he connection between Irving Kristol and Australia is not obvious. Having politely but firmly rejected repeated invitations to do so, he has never visited the country. He has never written about it. Australia—along with a great deal of the rest of the Earth's surface, including all of Asia, Latin America, Africa, and Canada—does not claim his serious attention, which is reserved for what goes on in the United States, Europe, and Israel. I am the only Australian who has had a sustained working relationship with Irving, but he has shown a warmer interest in my original Welshness than in my acquired Australianness. (Not that Wales has a vital grip on his imagination either. True, he and Bea did visit the country once, when they were based in London in the 1950s. But when they got there, they managed to stay in the least Welsh place it was possible to find in the principality: the eccentric Italianate "village" created by Clough Williams-Ellis at Portmeirion, a location where one was more likely to meet Noël Coward than the Reverend Eli Jenkins.)

Still, a Kristol-Australian connection has existed for the past four decades, and it has had a significant effect on Australia's intellectual and cultural life. It should surprise no one that it has to do with magazines. Irving's working life has centered on magazines— creating them, publishing and raising money for them, editing them, and writing for them. A strong belief in their efficacy as instruments for furthering a cause and propagating a position is almost certainly the only belief that he has shared with the late Vladimir Ilyich Lenin. In Irving's own writing, the polemical magazine essay has been his weapon of choice, and he has become one of the acknowledged masters of the form in our time.

Except for a short break in the 1960s, he has been continuously involved with intellectual magazines from the time he became assistant editor of *Commentary* in 1947 until now, when he easily (and from my point of view, embarrassingly) combines being editor of *The Public Interest* and publisher of *The National Interest* with a variety of other activities. In between, Irving launched *Encounter,* in the opinion of many the single most important journal of ideas to appear during the cold war period; in his six years as its nominal coeditor but real editor (1953–1958) he gave the magazine its definitive character. (His partner, Stephen Spender, while distinguished and well-connected, was too impractical and vacillating to be effective. Not long after the Russian repression of the Hungarian Revolution, Spender was still feebly objecting to the term "Soviet empire" as unduly provocative.) Irving was also editor of Max Ascoli's lively magazine, the *Reporter,* for a short period in the late 1950s.

Like many others, I first got to know about—and, in a sense, to know—Irving by reading *Encounter.* That began in Sydney in 1955, shortly after I had arrived in Australia. I was a bit slow off the mark because I'd spent the previous two years doing my national service in the rural depths of Somerset, and new intellectual magazines were hard to come by in RAF messes. Then I got a job at Sydney University (advertised in the back of another magazine, the leftist *New Statesman and Nation,* which had a circulation of around 90,000 at that time and *was* to be found in the mess). Recently married, my wife and I made the long four-and-a-half-week journey from London in the P.& O. liner, the SS *Strathmore,* traveling the great British imperial route—Gibraltar, Port Said, Aden, Bombay, Colombo, Singapore, Perth—in its last days, just a year before the Suez crisis. (This may be as good a place as any to note that Irving is a great admirer of the British Empire. Kipling is one of his favorite poets, and *Zulu*—depicting the epic of Rorkes Drift, where a handful of redcoats fought off a Zulu army—his all-time favorite movie. One of his few disappointments with the United States, I suspect, is that it is constitutionally and temperamentally unsuited to sustaining the burdens of an imperial mission.)

Sydney was immediately and gloriously attractive, a marvelous technicolor relief after a gray postwar decade: flawless blue skies, palm and flame trees, yellow beaches, and, not least, plenty of red meat and fruit. But initially it was also lonely, isolated, and strange. We knew no one. The landscape was utterly different from anything we were accustomed to. There was not another country within twelve hundred miles, and not even another sizable city within six hundred. The politics were strange and harsh, involving Catholics and Communists as major actors in a way that was more European than British. (The Australian Labor Party had split along these lines the previous year, which was to keep it out of power for nearly two decades.) The newspapers were dull and parochial. Literary-political magazines were few and hardly readable. The most conspicuous of them was the antediluvian and xenophobic *Bulletin,* a survivor from the late nineteenth century that still carried the slogan "Australia for the White People" on its masthead.

Despite the *Bulletin* and the fact that Robert Menzies's Conservative Party was in office, the country's intellectual and cultural life was dominated by the pro-Communist Left, and a shallow, reflexive, progressive orthodoxy prevailed. A man widely regarded as Australia's leading historian—Manning Clark—went to the Soviet Union at this time and wrote a glowing book called *Meeting Soviet Man.* He singled out for special praise—a "very great man," one of "earthy images and folk wisdom"—none other than Alex Surkov, the thuggish secretary of the Soviet Writers' Union. The Fellowship of Australian Writers was so impressed that, shortly after the Hungarian Revolution, it invited that tormentor of Russian writers to Australia as its guest. And so it went.

Such behavior will not strike American intellectuals of a certain vintage as particularly unusual. There was a lot of it about in the 1950s in all parts of the West, and indeed to an extent Australian academics and intellectuals were only mimicking admired overseas models. But there was a difference. In a much smaller and more isolated cultural community—one characterized simultaneously by an aggressive commitment to an egalitarian ethos and by a desperate concern to distinguish itself from the surrounding philistinism—there was much less diversity and pluralism, less in

the way of countervailing challenges to this orthodoxy, than in either America or Europe. To the untutored eye, at least, the Australian cultural landscape seemed as flat and unvaried as an Australian
sheep station.

Although my own views at the time were leftish (I had, after
all, grown up in a South Wales mining valley), I found all this depressing. It was, for one thing, a coarse-grained radicalism, un-
adorned by any of the (in retrospect, perhaps spurious) sophistication
and glamour that the Bevans and the Crossmans brought to the
British version. For another, it was much more uncritically pro-
Soviet than I was used to—for, Kingsley Martin notwithstanding,
the British Left as a whole was not fellow traveling. But there was
another reason: once in Sydney, I began that important process of
self-education that is involved in preparing lectures, in my case
lectures on international affairs and on totalitarianism. Once engaged in a close study of these matters (something that I had managed to avoid at Oxford) and having to declare myself in public on
them, I quickly came to doubt and to move away from the prevailing
leftist interpretations.

In these circumstances, I discovered *Encounter,* and its effect
was exhilarating. I had never before heard the political and cultural case for the West argued with such assurance, style, and intellectual force. This was not surprising because for at least twenty
years no one else had heard it either—the initiative had been entirely with the Left. What celebration there had been of the West—
mostly during the war—had been left in the inadequate hands of
the likes of Sir Arthur Bryant. Otherwise, all had been denigration,
or at best gloom, of the sort expressed by Cyril Connolly in his noto-
rious sentence, declaring that it was "closing time in the gardens of
the West." Now Irving Kristol and *Encounter* appeared, combining
the panache and aggression that used to be the birthright of New
York intellectuals with the style and self-possession of the English
man of letters, to make an unapologetic case for the West. It was all
enormously liberating, as well as being a splendid read. (One remembers articles like Leslie Fiedler's "McCarthy and the Intellectuals," with its lines: "From one end of the country to another rings
the cry, 'I am cowed! I am afraid to speak out!' and the even louder
response, 'Look, he is cowed! He is afraid to speak out!'" And there
was Nancy Mitford's famous essay on U and Non-U.)

One of the interesting things about little magazines is that while they are produced in the great metropolitan centers with the readers of those cities principally in mind, they often have their greatest impact in the provinces and on the periphery. At the center, the magazine represents merely one form in a dense complex of activities (public meetings, debates, clubs, cafes, dinner and cocktail parties, many other readily available magazines and newspapers); on the periphery, a good magazine may be the only thing that effectively and regularly links someone to the larger issues and intellectual community, and it can assume an inordinate importance in a life. At least, that was substantially the case forty years ago, when communications were much more primitive—and Sydney was much on the periphery.

But it didn't take long to find out what should have been obvious from the start (I was very young at the time): there were others, native-born Australians, who were roughly in the same predicament and who had the same concerns, often in a much more developed form. They included some distinguished and interesting men: Sir John Latham (a former chief justice of the Australian High Court); John Kerr Q.C. (later to be the governor general who dismissed Prime Minister Gough Whitlam in controversial circumstances); James McAuley (one of Australia's best poets, and coperpetrator of the famous antimodernist Ern Malley hoax); Peter Coleman (writer and editor and politician-to-be, who would one day write the history of the Congress for Cultural Freedom); Donald Horne (author, later, of *The Lucky Country*).

And there was one other who was of outstanding importance: Richard Krygier, a Pole by origin, who in 1941 had, along with his wife, found his way to Australia via Lithuania, Siberia, Tokyo, and Shanghai. Arriving broke and with little English, he started by taking a job as a waiter in one of Sydney's nightclubs. By the 1950s, Krygier had a successful book-importing business. He was passionately, knowledgeably, uncompromisingly, and effectively anti-Communist. When the Congress for Cultural Freedom was formed, Krygier was determined that Australia should participate in it. Despite initial indifference in Paris, he succeeded: in 1954, a small Australian committee was formed.

How was that committee to be most effective in an environment made up in more or less equal parts of indifference and hostility? The answer was given to Richard Krygier by—Irving Kristol. And it was, in retrospect at least, a predictable answer, as well as being right on the mark. Peter Coleman has described the episode:

> Krygier's great achievement was the founding of *Quadrant*. Its conception was in 1955 in the Russian Tea Room on West 57th Street, Manhattan, where he met with Irving Kristol, the editor of *Encounter*, to discuss the Australian situation. You should start a magazine! Kristol said. Like *Encounter*! Krygier wrote to the Paris office of the Congress for Cultural Freedom and asked for a subsidy. Malcolm Muggeridge, who had returned from his first visit to Australia, supported Krygier and told the Congress executive that this was an idea whose time had come.[1]

Thus did Irving contribute to the founding of *Quadrant,* probably the most important and successful magazine of ideas in Australia's history. (Its only significant rival in recent decades has been the leftist *Meanjin,* but it has not been a serious one. The Australian writer Frank Moorhouse once explained that "meanjin" was an Aboriginal word meaning "rejected by the *New Yorker*.") Indeed, *Quadrant* was destined to outlast *Encounter;* forty years after that conversation in the Russian Tea Room—a long time for a little magazine—it is still a lively and substantial monthly, capable of starting a vigorous controversy and frequently quoted in the national media. It has even acquired a small but devoted following in the United States. William F. Buckley, Jr., was once generous enough to describe an issue of the magazine (a special one on China, put together by Simon Leyes) as "the single most liberating issue of any magazine I can remember." Its editors over the years have been James McAuley, Donald Horne, Peter Coleman, and now Robert Manne.

More generally, *Quadrant* became a rallying point for Australian intellectuals who rejected the prevailing leftism and the perverse but comfortable notion that principled liberalism required an anti-anti-Communist posture. Around it grew a pattern of activity involving seminars and lectures and dinners and committee meetings—as well as close friendships and intense rivalries. (When it

---

1. Peter Coleman, *Memoirs of a Slow Learner* (Sydney: Angus & Robertson, 1994), p. 134.

was eventually disclosed in the 1960s that the Paris congress, and through it the Australian association and *Quadrant,* had been funded secretly by the CIA, our general inclination was not to condemn but to congratulate the CIA for having been smart enough to give us the wherewithal to do what we wanted to do in any case—and then not to interfere or to impose conditions. The secrecy was regrettable, but we didn't live in a perfect world and it had been a condition for the thing being done at all.)

In due course, air travel became cheaper and quicker, and the tyranny of distance over Australian life slackened. In the 1960s, visits to the United States became less rare. When anyone from the *Quadrant* circle made it to New York, the preferred way of coping with the initial overwhelming impact of that city was to ring Irving Kristol. It must have become tiresome for him after a while, but he bore it with good grace, and many Australians enjoyed lunch in the agreeable setting of the Century Club as one of their first meals in the city. (When he lived in New York, Irving was a clubman; in Washington, he is not. I have forgotten to ask him why.)

My own first meeting with Irving was in 1968, when I spent part of a sabbatical in America. My initial impression, strengthened rather than changed over the years, was of how comfortably high intelligence and good nature—two qualities that are not habitually found together (or even separately) in intellectuals—were combined in him. The intelligence was evident in the way the conversation seemed to be happening in a higher gear than I was accustomed to: the sharpness of the wit, the speed in anticipating one's point, the shorthand in stating his own. (The latter easy to mistake initially for off-the-cuff dogmatism, until one probed and found that the arguments were all in place and that it was just a case of dispensing with the recitative. When, say, Irving pronounced flatly that NATO should be abolished, it was after he had thought hard and carefully worked out his position on the issue.) At the same time, there seemed to be none of the insecurity or vanity that is commonly part of the makeup of intellectuals, no urge simply to score points or put down or claim credit. The wit was funny—very funny—but not vicious, and the gossip was affectionate and tolerant. Irving was, and remains, a kind man: what he does not like he usually prefers to dismiss rather than attack. As it happened, when we met we had both just had articles published in *Foreign Affairs,* and Irving helped put me at ease by adopting the flattering fiction that the two articles were equally vital contributions to the intellectual life of Manhattan. Shortly after, he invited me to a dinner party at his home at Riverside Drive, and I met Bea. Before the evening was over, an enduring and, to me, greatly valued friendship had begun.

In the mid-1970s, I left academic life—left with no regrets whatsoever, for the foolishness and cowardice of the American university scene had been faithfully copied in Australia. For the next seven and a half years, I worked for the Australian government. As part of my job was to help interpret the political culture of the United States, and as the tide of neoconservatism was running strong in those years, Irving Kristol continued to figure prominently in my thought and work. As a self-conscious position, neoconservatism was to all intents and purposes his creation, and in explaining the phenomenon to my political masters, I drew heavily on his ideas. (Our professional diplomats, like their counterparts elsewhere, spoke mainly to other professional diplomats and officials and were slow to recognize and to appreciate the significance of intellectual innovations; I recall having great difficulty explaining to the man in charge of the American desk at the Department of Foreign Affairs the difference between "neoconservatism" and "the New Right.") In explaining the significance of the sudden appearance of numerous conservative think tanks—a startling and unsettling new form of institution for many Australians, who had been schooled to believe that conservatives didn't think—one also had to talk about Irving. His belief in the importance of the struggle of ideas in determining who would own the future meant that his ramifying practical activities—particularly in encouraging young talent—were shaped by a determination that it would be right-thinking conservatives who would do so.

When I had to write a major speech outlining Prime Minister Malcolm Fraser's political philosophy—not the easiest of tasks, given that Fraser, though gifted with a strong intelligence, was not comfortable expressing himself in terms of abstract ideas and principles—I did so with Irving's *Two Cheers for Capitalism* open at my elbow. The speech was later published as a definitive statement of Fraser's beliefs, and I wish I had a copy on hand to find out how much I had plagiarized.

Fraser's period in office came to an end when he lost an election to Bob Hawke in the spring of 1983. This also brought to an end my spell in Paris as ambassador to UNESCO (a personal highlight of which had been a dinner I hosted at which a group of Parisian intellectuals led by Raymond Aron—ailing, but still with a hearty appetite for both conversation and food—met a group of New York intellectuals led by Irving). I retired to Washington and spent a productive year at the Heritage Foundation, writing and helping to get the United States and Britain to leave UNESCO.

But what to do next? Irving Kristol had the answer ready, and it had a familiar ring: Why not start a magazine! Like *Encounter,* but mostly about foreign policy! Irving's friend, Michael Joyce, was thinking along the same lines and was in a position to help make it happen. So *The National Interest* was conceived, and so exactly thirty years after first reading Irving Kristol, I began to work with him.

Irving was to be the publisher, and Robert Tucker, of Johns Hopkins, and I the coeditors. Bob and I had never met, but any worries we might have had about each other were overshadowed by our shared uncertainty about how Irving might interpret his role as publisher. He was, after all, one of the great editors of his day and a man of forceful opinions. Would he not want to have his say, and would not a triumvirate of editors, each with firm views, be disastrous? Our concern was strengthened by Irving's opinion, freely offered, that one didn't actually need to *know* anything to write about foreign policy, it was only a matter of applying common sense. This was a view of things that left me uneasy, but Tucker, who had devoted his whole working life to an exhaustive study of the subject and was one of the country's leading scholars of foreign policy, found it positively alarming. As an amiable and relaxed Irving cheerfully held forth on the virtues of common sense, Bob would tense. A softly muttered "man, oh man" would come from his direction. Things didn't look altogether promising.

In the event, all our worries were misplaced. Bob and I got on famously, and Irving, perhaps remembering the trouble that he himself had experienced with interference from the Paris office of the Congress for Cultural Freedom during his *Encounter* editorship, performed immaculately as publisher: always interested and supportive, always respectful of editorial autonomy, ready with praise and tactful with advice and criticism, taking on himself the onerous but crucial responsibility of looking after the funding. On one thing Irving was firm: *The National Interest* would not be a "journal," it would be a magazine. It would be concerned about reaching the educated general reader, not the specialist; it would give attention to ideas and arguments and policy, rather than emphasize scholarship; it would put a premium on decent writing.

After a quiet start, *The National Interest* steadily gained prestige and influence. Oddly, though we could be fairly characterized as a "cold war magazine" when we began (in our first issue, we asserted quite firmly that "the Soviet Union constitutes the greatest single threat to America's interests, and will continue to do so for the foreseeable future"), we performed rather better after the collapse of communism and the Soviet Union. We took up the questions of the nature of the post–cold war era, and of the appropriate American foreign policy for it, more quickly and in more lively fashion than most others. Francis Fukuyama's "The End of History?" (1989) gave us a flying start, and we have continued to be pacesetters in the discussion of the character of the new era.

While the magazine has always welcomed a variety of conservative and centrist views, the prevailing editorial position—or disposition—has been one of realism. Initially, this was something that Irving—a New York intellectual accustomed to focusing on the role of ideas—did not altogether share. In the lead piece that he contributed to our first issue—"Foreign Policy in an Age of Ideology"—he declared the traditional conception of national interest to be "dead beyond resurrection"—thereby directly challenging the validity of the new magazine's name! But over time *The National Interest* has succeeded in converting its publisher, and he has now sometimes taken to describing himself as a neoconservative neorealist when the subject of foreign policy comes up.

One of the great pleasures of going to work as editor of *The National Interest* is that one gets to meet Irving—sitting just across the room as editor of *The Public Interest*—on a daily basis. As befits a New York intellectual, he is rarely to be caught without firm—or at least definite—opinions on both current issues and editorial matters, and listening to them is a stimulating way of starting the day. (On the editorial questions, he is tough-minded and he quotes with relish Cyril Connolly's response to an author complaining about the nonappearance of his article: "Well, it was good enough to accept, and it was good enough to set in type, but it wasn't good enough to publish.") As is much rarer in the case of intellectuals, Irving is also an exceptionally good and responsive listener.

Another major advantage of working with him is that one gets to meet a lot of bright and nice young people. Irving is a great believer in and practitioner of the intern system; there has been a flow of such young talent through both our offices during the ten years that I have been there. More often than not, he and I have been the only people over thirty on the premises.

This commitment to the young is a matter of affinity as well as policy: he *likes* the company of young people. When I was beginning to write this piece in the fall of last year, Irving and Bea gave a party for those who had worked on the two magazines as interns over the past twenty-five years. Nearly fifty men and women turned up, a fair sample of Irving's young people over three decades and with an age range from the early twenties to the early fifties. They included many who now hold prominent positions in government, universities, think tanks, newspapers, foundations—as well as some editors of magazines. These are all people who, at a crucial stage of their lives, benefited greatly from exposure to Irving: from his instruction, his advice, his encouragement and care and friendship— and most of all from his example of how to live honestly and creatively on that uncertain ground where the worlds of ideas and of public policy meet. At that party, affection for him radiated through the company. Brilliant writer though he is, and enormously influential though he has been, I suspect that Irving might regard the people in that room as his most satisfying achievement.

6

A Letter from Paris

H. J. Kaplan

I had intended, still do, to begin this letter with an account of the Fiftieth Anniversary of the Liberation of Paris, this being the morning after—August 23, 1994. But it turns out that I have a couple of other anniversaries on my mind, together with some strictures by my old friend Irving Kristol, entitled "All That Jazz." This would appear at first sight to make a bit of a jumble. But *tout se tient,* as the French say—everything holds together—to which one sometimes feels like replying, in the spirit of Samuel Johnson, that it damned well better. Anyway, patience; we'll start with the facts.

Last night's fête at the city hall ended with fireworks and dancing on the Place de la Concorde; to American music, I presume, although I wasn't there. People dance mostly to American music in Europe nowadays, just as they watch American television and pay their pounds, francs, and deutsche marks to see American films. No need to belabor the point—it keeps coming up in the GATT negotiations, and in the groans one has been hearing over here about cultural imperialism, so-called, for just about as long as I can remember.

Now it so happens that I was in the American hospital in Neuilly last week—another anniversary, since I celebrated Victory in Europe Day on a rooftop of that establishment in the spring of 1945—and there I caught up on some reading, including a recent issue of the French quarterly *Commentaire*, where I found Irving's grim and gritty piece on American popular culture, "All That Jazz." Oddly, I did not at first realize that I had already read the piece in English, indeed that it was simply a translation of an article that had already appeared in our own foreign policy magazine, *The National Interest*, causing shockwaves, no doubt, at a time when my seismograph was down. In French, for various more or less obvious reasons, "All That Jazz" came out sounding at once angrier and sadder than I remembered it, more sunk in decline-of-the-West pessimism, and—perhaps because I am culpably soft on popular music myself—more impatient with our common humanity than any conservative, let alone this one, had any right to be. So I decided, as I have many times done over the years, to remonstrate with my dear old friend.

* * *

The plot thickens, however, now that I'm back in Paris, sleeves rolled up, the stereo playing Duke Ellington in the background. For one thing, I've witnessed the reenactment of the liberation in living color. For another, I've reread "All That Jazz" in English, and Kristol's argument is growing on me, as it always does. And finally, I've read some mail and found a message from faraway Washington, D.C., to the effect that a stele is to be raised in honor of Irving K., precisely on the occasion of his seventy-fifth birthday. It is vexing, on top of everything else, to be reminded that practically everyone living, *et tu* Kristol, is younger than I am. Nevertheless, there will be a volume of essays in Irving's honor. So I sit down to write, what else?— a Paris Letter, the sort of thing I was doing for the *Partisan Review* when the Kristols came to see my wife and me in Montparnasse, shortly after the war.

* * *

How shortly? I can't remember. Anesthesia affects the memory, but that should pass. The real problem is that I have no papers covering the postwar period, everything having burned up in a warehouse in Créteil early in 1972. Not that there would have been much in the way of a paper trail in this case, but I used to keep those little Hermès agendas. The Kristols were in town for a few days, knew people we knew in New York, had read my Paris Letters in the *Partisan Review*, etc., and, of course, we should get together over a drink, dinner, whatever. And so we did. In those days, it seems to me now, this was standard operating procedure, because we came from the same place, as it were. If I had occasion to go to Berlin, I would have rung up Mel Lasky, although I had never met him; in Rome, Leslie Fiedler; in Tokyo, Herb Passin. Anyone who wrote for or simply read *P.R.* or *Commentary* or one or two other more or less obscure periodicals was *ipso facto* a countryman, a *Landsmann*, although this fellowship or family feeling hardly precluded disagreement and disaffection, alas, as people went their several ways.

Of that first encounter with Irving Kristol I remember almost nothing but can speak with a modicum of assurance, my chief informant being a trained and distinguished historian, Gertrude Himmelfarb, a k a Bea Kristol, who accompanied Irving to my place. They were a warm and friendly couple, but reserved, almost diffident, as if they had already been touched by the manners of the British politicos, journalists, and academics among whom they would settle when Kristol launched *Encounter*. Kristol was a slender, tweedy young man who already had, it seems to me now, the same serene and blue-eyed look, slightly quizzical and humorous and misted by cigarette smoke, that he would have forever after—in my own mind's eye, at least, like Mallarmé's faun:

Tel qu'en lui-même enfin l'éternité le change.[1]

My place was perched high on the Boulevard du Montparnasse, and since they arrived before nightfall, we must, at the very least, have taken them out on our balcony to look down on all the rooftops and north to the Sacré Coeur, east to Notre Dame, and west to the Eiffel Tower—the standard tour, gossiping all the while. About what? About mutual friends probably: for example, Saul Bellow, probably living on the Rue Marbeuf and writing *The Adventures of Augie March*; Meyer Schapiro, at work at the Bibliothèque Nationale; Lionel Trilling and Uncle Clem Greensberg and all. And surely there was some moaning and groaning, especially on the distaff side, methinks, about the sinister drift of things in the beleaguered free world: the inadequacy of our leadership, the absence of *virtù*, the misery of philosophy.

---

1. "Such as into himself at last Eternity has changed him." Stéphane Mallarmé, "*Le Tombeau d'Edgar Poe,*" in *Poésies*.

In short, we were on Hayek's road to serfdom, unmistakably—although I cannot resist remarking (as the closet optimist of that day) that this has turned out to be a very long road, with the traffic running in both directions. But the outlook was certainly bleak, and nothing I could tell my new friends about the local scene was likely to cheer them up. A translation of *The Road to Serfdom* was actually brought out here in 1946, as I discovered later, but I can't recall that it was much noticed. A quarter to a third of the population was voting Communist at the time, and the reigning literary intellectual, Jean-Paul Sartre, was a man who believed that in political economy, if not in philosophy, Marxism was *indépassable*, meaning the final word.

How much moaning and groaning we accomplished that day I cannot remember, but I do know that this dolorism stayed with us, became something we had in common. We were the unhappy few. The daily newspapers, the television, the literary-and-political magazines—everything became grist for our mill, although the time would come all too soon when a new generation, in the person of Elizabeth Kristol, for example, not to speak of my own children—*O, sharper than a serpent's tooth*—would find these litanies absurd.

They were not entirely absurd. The indignities, turpitudes, and horrors were all too real. But I should concede that Liz Kristol's father was probably less subject than the rest of us to these deplorations, in part because he had less time for them (since he was by way of becoming the brilliant social philosopher Irving Kristol) but also because he was an activist and he needed to believe that something could be done. Hence *The Public Interest,* the foundations, *The National Interest,* but this is a twice-told tale. The fact remains that we understood when we first met in Montparnasse that it would comfort us somehow to suffer and deplore things together. And forty years later, when we were living within a few blocks of each other in Manhattan, my wife—if Bea Kristol called to ask about her health—would tell her not that her own life was ebbing away, which it was, but that the world was going to the dogs.

* * *

It still is, to be sure, and this is the gravamen of "All That Jazz." But now, having fought my way out of Neuilly and joined the throngs of returning Parisians and vacationing foreigners, I am reminded that the worst is not always inevitable. Things in the real world, if not among the intellectuals, do sometimes go right, and this is why the Kristols were able to visit us when they did, instead of months or years later, and why the city we were able to look down upon from my balcony was quite intact. Seedy, yes, and hungry, dirty, and disgruntled that it was taking too long to resupply the urban centers in France and get the economy working again. But the old stones were still standing. This is the miracle the French have been celebrating this week.

Just half a century ago, plus one day, General Philippe Leclerc's lead tanks came through the Porte d'Orléans, fanned out northward to the Seine and across the mined but undamaged bridges to the Préfecture, the central police headquarters, and the city hall, which were already occupied by French gendarmes and armed civilians. It took most of August 25 to round up General Dietrich von Choltitz and his top commanders and get them to the Montparnasse railway station, where Leclerc and Colonel Henri Rol-Tanguy, the Communist chief of the main Resistance groups, accepted their formal surrender.

Paris, by then, was already encircled by George Patton's tanks, and the Germans were in full retreat toward the Rhine. We now know that von Choltitz was not inclined to blow up those bridges, although he had orders from Hitler to burn the city to the ground. Eisenhower's decision to let Leclerc peel off and drive in may have helped the Prussian commander to make up his mind. The upshot, in any event, was to legitimize General de Gaulle's Fighting French, once and for all. The *Capital* had "liberated itself," as the general put it when he arrived with miraculous celerity, like a reincarnation of Joan of Arc, at the Mairie (city hall) and proclaimed that the Republic was back. Then he walked up the Champs-Elysées through a sea of celebrating people—Gaullists, every last one of them—to lay a wreath on the tomb of the Unknown Soldier, who also became an instant Gaullist, presumably, since we were living through one of those rare and mystical moments of national unity when France rises to the greatness that is her essence, as the general explains in his memoirs.

All this, of course, wiped out Roosevelt's idea that we should institute a military government and let the French decide about their political future after the dust had settled. How seriously

Eisenhower ever took this notion I don't know; he had to handle the boss with care. But no one could doubt that when he told Patton to send in his crack French division, he was settling the political question, for the moment at least. And since then I've often wondered what would have happened if Mr. Win-the-War, as Roosevelt liked to call himself, had had the time and the stomach to revert to the OMGUS (Office of the Military Government, United States) plan, as it was called, before we got to Paris. I was a long way off to the south at the time, in Algiers, about to take off for Marseille. I belonged to an outfit called P.W.B. (Psychological Warfare Branch), which would have had to broach the matter to our French colleagues, practically all of whom were partisans of General de Gaulle's provisional government of the French Republic.

I also, as it happened, belonged to a "band of brothers," an utterly imaginary and nonexistent outfit of deep thinkers, mostly ex-radicals of both sexes, who could have explained to Roosevelt quite cogently why his scheme to set up a military government hadn't a chance. We were young and without rank but very hip about ideological politics, having been radicalized by the depression, read ourselves into and out of Marxism, for the most part, and then been prematurely "mugged by reality," as one of us put it later. The same man—Irving Kristol, of course, *toujours lui!*—defined us as "public affairs intellectuals"; he had a flair for inventing such phrases. But it was not yet clear whether being a public affairs intellectual was a métier or only an avocation or both. In the great expansion of American services after the war, we would become journalists, academics, foreign service people, editors, and, in a few cases, elected officials. Scattered by the war around the world, we did not all know each other at that point, but we had a good deal in common: we were writers and talkers, had European parents and ravenous intellectual appetites. We read a lot and knew a lot, including many things that were not true—but this is taking me too far afield.

* * *

The French, few of whom have ever heard of the OMGUS plan, fortunately, and none of whom have ever heard of my band of brothers, have been celebrating the Fiftieth Anniversary since August 19, on the grounds that the liberation actually began on that day when the gendarmes went on strike and barricaded themselves in the Préfecture. These *flics*, as the French call them, had a rotten reputation, since they had done a lot of the Nazis' dirty work, including rounding up Jews for deportation. But now they were heroes, and indeed several hundred of them were killed in the fighting that went on around town during the following days. It was thanks to them and the Resistance people that there was an honest-to-God uprising, and this was heavily stressed at the climactic spectacle that was staged last night at the city hall. There were speeches by Mayor Chirac and President Mitterrand, followed by a pageant and fireworks and a midnight ball on the Place de la Concorde, the magnificent square where so many victims of the revolutionary Terror were guillotined, two hundred years ago: an unmistakably *real* event. The pageant we saw on television was a *pseudo-event*; a reconstitution of Leclerc's drive from the Porte d'Orléans to the Mairie, with professional actors in costume driving the tanks and half-tracks, or accompanying them on foot, or cheering them on, so that it was sometimes difficult to distinguish the professionals from the thousands of Parisians and tourists who came out to watch and be watched.

* * *

Perhaps because I am confined to quarters at the moment, the fact that these ceremonies were cooked up and *catered*, as it were, struck me rather more forcibly than heretofore. Even Messrs. Mitterrand, Chirac, and Balladur looked as if they had been hired for the occasion, as in a sense they had been ... And this aspect was also present, if less blatantly so, at the ceremonies that were organized in Normandy early in June to mark the Allied landings, the airborne assaults farther inland, and the true beginning of the end of the war.

The commemoration of Overlord, the speeches of our leaders, the laying of wreaths, the trooping of colors, interspersed with grainy old black-and-white film clips of the fighting—all this was deeply moving, to me, surely, and to all those who have some memory of what happened fifty years ago. The stakes were so immense, the task so daunting, the courage of our men so great. We all lost friends on those beaches, and indeed, as we watched in pity and terror, every young man lost there became our friend. So it made our hearts ache, literally, to go back to all that. And whenever the material we were shown on the screen or heard in a reenactment or a commentary seemed perfunctory or wrong or in doubtful taste, we felt that we, and the men we had wept for, had been betrayed.

* * *

What transpires on the public square at moments like these is important, or should be. It affects the morale of the community, and it provides us with a sense of who we are and have been, and with an occasion to pledge ourselves solemnly to a shared view of the future. There was a time when in our primary schools we learned by heart the words spoken on such an occasion. Perhaps our children still do, here and there. But words, even Lincoln's words, no longer resound in our lives as they used to do—not without the help of the electronic media, in any event, the images, sound effects, and other claptrap that tend to overlay and alter the verbal dimension, but rarely, if ever, to enhance it. Chirac's and Mitterrand's words last night, for example, were well written and well spoken. These men are rooted in a living—and still lively—rhetorical tradition. But one cannot imagine that they were better heard or understood for being part of a sound-and-light show: the Fiftieth Anniversary of the Liberation of Paris.

* * *

The modern sound-and-light show dates back at least to the 1930s, that "low dishonest decade," and not only in France, as Leni Riefenstahl still lives to remind us. It seems to me that the advent of television, and later of the theme park, has had the paradoxical effect of democratizing and banalizing public ceremony and history— of making these public goods more readily available, even as the costs and technologies involved in producing these spectacles remove them from any semblance of popular control—except of course the negative constraints of the market.

Not that we have any reason to believe that such control, assuming we knew how to exert it, would improve matters, rather than make them worse. The people, sir, remain a great beast—indeed the beastliness seems to increase with prosperity, leisure, and individual freedom: all those good things that a successful market economy is supposed to provide, and does, to ever larger numbers. Which reminds me of the rather somber and comminatory conclusion I retain from Irving Kristol's brilliant study of Adam Smith, a book from which I cannot quote, unfortunately, since my copy is packed away in Plainville, Massachusetts, but which I believe can be fairly summarized as follows: affluence breeds hedonism, a demand for instant gratification, impatience with the old disciplines of orderly living and work. In the absence of commonly accepted moral standards and the institutions (for example, family and religion) that inculcate and transmit them, liberating people from penury may simply expose them to social pathologies. And this is bound to degrade the civil society and the polity—not to mention what we have come to call the "culture," including what transpires on the public square.

* * *

The weather over here has turned autumnal, after an unusually hot summer, so that I am encouraged to set up my typewriter table and my battered old Olivetti outside, on the white-tiled terrace that abuts our little garden on the edge of the Parc Monceau. If this were a proper Paris Letter, I would take a moment perhaps to report on the present state of this charming little park, with its statues of romantic poets and their winsome muses, but I shall soon be running out of moments and I still have my old friend Kristol on my mind. In a few days the *rentrée* begins, the Parisians flowing back from countryside and beach, bronzed and disgruntled. The economy is looking a little better, according to the prime minister, although unemployment still hovers around 12 percent, a figure that would have been politically unacceptable in the old days. But now there is no one around to exploit it, the "Socialo-Communists" having been so thoroughly discredited and their old leader, Mitterrand, mortally ill and on his way out. The Fiftieth Anniversary is behind us, or will be this afternoon when 6,000 children parade up the Champs-Elysées waving multicolored banners and forming *une grande vague déferlante*,[2] as the announcer said this morning on the radio. Well, long may they wave—I don't plan to be there. As Duke Ellington used to growl in that song of his, I don't get around much any more.

The children are professionals presumably, recruited for this occasion, like everyone else these days. Will they be paid in candy bars, I wonder? Or will they be given free condoms out of the ma-

---

2. A great, breaking wave. Ed.

chines installed in the secondary schools by Jack Lang, Mitterrand's culture minister, before the new Conservative government was voted in? Unlike the popular M. Lang, the Culture Ministry in Mr. Balladur's government has sent no commission to the United States to study rap and other advanced forms of music. But whether those condom machines have been removed I cannot say, since there's been nothing in the press. Anyway, this is what the French call a *grave* or a *vaste* question, meaning one that they would rather not be bothered with. I'd willingly pass it up myself, were it not for the fact that it leads me back, as everything seems to do this morning, to Irving Kristol's "All That Jazz."

The title, by the way, for those who have not read this piece or seen Bob Fosse's autobiographical movie, refers not simply to jazz as such but to the common colloquialism meaning "the whole damned mess," thus conflating certain forms of music and American popular culture in general with the social pathologies so often associated with them—for example, sex, violence, drugs, and heedless instinctual or hedonistic behavior.

Kristol loathes this stuff, to put it mildly. He sees it—rock music, especially—as a corrosive element, a sort of poison, eating away at the norms of civilized behavior and hence at the health and future of our society. Nor is it anything new in America, he suggests, but rather the outcome of a long and devastating rebellion against the inherited standards and "elitism" of the founders. By now, having absorbed or displaced high culture at home, American pop music, films, fashions, and *all that jazz* have moved out to conquer the world. And this they are doing with enormous success, to the growing chagrin of our neighbors and trading partners, friends and foes, whose old elite cultures are being subverted and destroyed.

Kristol shares their chagrin. He concedes that the most democratic country on earth is naturally good at this sort of thing, and even that it occasionally turns out some fine entertainment; but the total effect of our popular culture is disastrous, a threat to civilized society, and he deplores that we should produce such stuff ourselves, let alone inflict it on others.

Now all this strikes me as a bit much, but the glow of the liberation lingers, hope springs eternal, and I'm just not up to an argument with Irving this morning. The jazz I love is rooted in a sort of classical antiquity, the golden ages of New Orleans, Kansas City, and Chicago—and yes, to lump this music together with the latest heavy metal horror, this is much too much. And how can one include the art of the film in "All That Jazz," without making the faintest distinction between Charlie Chaplin, say, and Mel Brooks? But never mind the more obvious cavils. What about the questions of causality? And what is to be done?

Ah, well, from long experience I've learned at least this: the muchness of Irving Kristol tends to fade into the background as the central point he is making sinks in. Meanwhile, the master has touched a nerve and brought us to attention. We are wondering about *all that jazz,* concerned with it, as if we had never noticed it before. Needless to say, we had, in one way or another, noticed it before. But it took a truly seminal thinker, the best of my band of brothers, to frame the question and to point us toward the answers and the new questions to which they give rise inevitably. And this is not the least of what Irving Kristol has been doing for us with his brilliance, his erudition, and sometimes, yes, with his muchness, all these years.

7

Following Irving

Norman Podhoretz

I rving Kristol is ten years older than I, and we do not, so far as I am able to tell, look alike: he even has hair whereas I, alas, am bald. Yet I have by now lost count of the number of times people have greeted me with a "Hello, Irving" or taken their leave of me by asking to be remembered to Bea or congratulated me on the growing fame of my son Bill.

Irving has even received fan mail about a book of mine. Think of it: a reader of *Why We Were in Vietnam*, which has a dust jacket and a title page prominently featuring my name as the author, addressed a letter to Irving Kristol thanking him for having written that book. Evidently not even the sight of my name in print, which bears even less resemblance to Irving's than my face does, can overcome the idea that I am he. The whole bizarre business also extends to the magazines we have edited: I have more than once been identified as the editor of *Encounter*.

Irving—who has also been taken for me, though much less frequently—has a characteristically no-nonsense explanation: all neoconservative Jews from New York look alike. It is a plausible theory, and it may in fact apply in the case of strangers or casual acquaintances. But how can it account for the people who know us both well? Once, for example, I was called Irving by a man who had been his neighbor and friend for more than twenty years and with whom I had had a long conversation only a few days earlier, during which he gave no indication of having forgotten that my name was Norman; not only that, but this man was himself a neoconservative Jew from New York. And—in the most bizarre manifestation of all— Bill Buckley (an old friend to both of us) concluded a half-hour conversation with me on his TV program *Firing Line* by thanking "Irving Podhoretz" for having been with him.

Another problem with Irving's theory is that, while we are indeed both neoconservative Jews from New York, by no means do we always agree on everything. In the past few years alone, we have been on different sides of a number of important issues, including American policy toward Russia and the question of intervention in Bosnia. To be sure, not everyone is aware of these disagreements or even notices them when made aware, as I discovered when, in the course of a debate with a noted British conservative (it was Peregrine Worsthorne), I was attacked for positions held by Irving that I had only moments earlier loudly and explicitly repudiated.

In short, I am no more politically than physically identical to or interchangeable with Irving. What then can account for so widespread an impression that I am he?

Up until now, I have been unable to answer that question to my own satisfaction. But in thinking about it again while reviewing my relations with Irving over the past forty and more years, I have begun to suspect that there may be good reason for the confusion.

Of course, it was not always thus. I first met Irving in London in 1954. He was there to launch *Encounter*, and I was there on a short furlough from the army base in Germany where I was then stationed. In those days, we were both what would later become known as cold war liberals, and we got along fine. I looked up to him for the essays he had written, mainly for *Commentary* (where he had worked for a spell as a member of the editorial staff), and he thought of me, on the basis of the few pieces I had by then published, also mainly in *Commentary*, as a promising young literary critic. A few years later, when he left *Encounter* to edit the *Reporter*, he recruited me as one of his regular reviewers.

By then, however, we were beginning to part ways politically. He was still a cold war liberal, though a sharp and prescient eye might already have detected signs of a shift to the Right, while I was moving, as it took no special powers of perception to notice, in a decidedly leftward direction. This naturally caused a certain strain between us that sometimes erupted into unpleasant confrontations.

The first of these, if I remember rightly, broke out when we were having lunch together shortly after the appearance in *Commentary* of an article by Michael Harrington, "Our Fifty Million Poor" (the germ of the book *The Other America*, which would later be credited with launching the "war on poverty"). I had not yet become the editor of *Commentary*, and I had played no part in the publication of the piece, but I had been sufficiently impressed by it to be shocked by Irving's cavalier dismissal of both the assumptions and the statistics on which it was based. I thought he was being complacent (a word, incidentally, that was often used by leftist critics of cold war liberals); he thought I was being ignorant and sentimental. Neither of us became openly hostile, but there was a nasty undercurrent to the argument.

As well there might have been, since this argument foreshadowed the rift between us that was soon to open. When I became the editor of *Commentary* in 1960—a job I took against Irving's advice, which in my observation is usually as poor on practical, personal matters as it is brilliant on questions of public policy—I began by making a real effort to hold onto the cold war liberals even as I very visibly steered the magazine to the Left. Thus, while featuring radical social critics like Paul Goodman and cold war revisionists like Staughton Lynd, I also published pieces by Irving himself as well as by Lionel Trilling, Sidney Hook, and Daniel Bell. But the disagreements between the two camps—about the nature of American society and about the causes and conduct of the cold war—were too fundamental to be bridged, and (since I was with the radicals) Irving and the others began feeling less than comfortable with me and I with them.

Whether it is a mark of the commendable seriousness with which they take ideas or a deplorable sign of uncivilized behavior or both, the fact is that intellectuals are notoriously unable to keep political or ideological differences from spilling over into their personal relations. And so it was with us. As the 1960s wore on, Irving and I had less and less to do with each other either professionally or personally, and we were more and more dismissive of each other's ideas. In 1965, together with Daniel Bell, he founded *The Public Interest*. I had unkind thoughts about it, some of which I expressed in public. He for his part had unkind thoughts about *Commentary*, all of which he expressed only in private.

But a funny thing happened to me on the way out of radicalism, and Irving had more to do with it than he ever knew (perhaps to this day).

Having supported and helped to spread the new radicalism of the 1960s, I found myself growing increasingly unhappy with the vicious hatred of America that had by the end of that decade come to pervade both the New Left and the counterculture (or the Movement, as they were collectively called). I was, however, still committed in some sense to the Left at this point in my own political evolution, and so in my attack on the Movement I made common cause with the "other Irving"—Howe—and his fellow social democrats, who were similarly disenchanted with the turn that leftist radicalism had taken.

At the same time, with the Movement now as the main target, it became possible to effect a rapprochement with Irving Kristol and his fellow neoconservatives (as they were just beginning to be known). Irving himself soon appeared in *Commentary* again, as did a number of his colleagues on *The Public Interest*.

Yet long before I invited him to return to the pages of *Commentary*, I had been reading Irving's pieces here and there and taking what I can only describe as a guilty pleasure in them. In retrospect, I can see that his influence over me was much greater than I realized at the time and was limited only by the resistance arising from my residual loyalty to the idea of the Left. As the 1970s wore on, that resistance weakened, and as it did, Irving's influence became commensurately stronger. First I followed him into neoconservatism while recalcitrantly rejecting the label, and then I followed him in proudly embracing it.

An epiphenomenal case, also involving labels, was the dispute (friendly this time) we had over the term *capitalism*. Having been converted to the belief that capitalism was a good thing, I still thought that the word had been so besmirched that Irving was mistaken in his insistence on using it. Why not resort to a euphemism like "the free market" or "free enterprise"? But he was persuaded that this would be an overly defensive tactic and that the fight to rehabilitate the reputation of the system would be incomplete unless its name were rescued from discredit as well. Eventually I came around, even

to the point of writing an article of my own entitled "The New Defenders of Capitalism."

This process set a pattern that has continued to mark the intellectual relation between us: I am influenced by Irving, I resist
that influence, and then I am finally forced to admit that he is right.

Happily for my self-esteem, the traffic has not all gone in one
direction. During the Nixon administration, Irving was a great defender of *Realpolitik*, applauding the "Europeanization" of our foreign policy under Kissinger. I believe it was I who eventually
persuaded him that ideology was and should be a central element
in America's relations with other countries. (On this point he may
have done a bit of backsliding by now.)

I could cite other such cases: for instance, I suspect I had something to do with his thinking about Israel. And there are also issues
on which I still believe he was dead wrong (his support of "no first
use" of nuclear weapons was one, and his opposition to independence for the Baltic states was another).

Nevertheless, it has mostly gone the other way. Indeed, so often have I come around to Irving's position on questions both large
and small that a careful observer might be forgiven for thinking
that any disagreement I have with him is bound to be only tempo-
rary. And a less careful observer might be forgiven for detecting so
little difference between me and him as to take me for him.

It happened again only the other night, when at a dinner party
a woman with whom we are both acquainted and who lives in Washington informed me that she had just taken up residence in my
building. "Really?" I said. "I'm amazed to hear that you've left Washington." Looking a little bewildered, she replied, "No, no, I mean
the Watergate. Don't you live in the Watergate?" Smiling the special smile that, after much practice, I have developed for this special experience, I said, "I'm Norman. It's Irving Kristol who lives in
the Watergate. But don't worry, people often mix us up."

Now, living in Washington is one of the things about which I
have strongly disagreed with Irving, and in public. After the Kristols
moved there from New York, Irving wrote an article explaining why,
and I then did a piece taking issue with him. It began as follows:

> Ever since my old friend Irving Kristol, who is univer-
> sally regarded as the quintessential New York intellec-

tual, wrote an article explaining why he recently moved to Washington, . . . people keep asking me if I think he is right about the decline of New York as an intellectual center. The answer is yes.

But when they then go on to ask whether I also agree that Washington is replacing New York as the nation's intellectual center, the answer is no. And when, finally, they ask whether I intend to leave New York and move down there myself, the answer is again no and a thousand times no.

Here I am, then, disagreeing with Irving about as emphatically as it is possible to do. And yet today, only about six years later, I find myself contemplating a move to Washington sometime in the near future. So just as, after adamantly resisting it for a long time, I ended by following Irving into neoconservativism, it is possible that I will one day be following him (despite my "no and a thousand times no") to Washington.

Nonetheless, I certainly have no intention of following him into the Watergate. Or so I say now. But what if, in placing me there, Irving's new neighbor was experiencing the same kind of prevision that has been vouchsafed to so many others who have seen me heading toward him intellectually long before I myself did?

It is a scary thought. But then again, I ask myself, what would be so bad about living in the Watergate and in such close proximity to a man to whom I owe more than I have ever, until this moment, fully recognized or properly acknowledged?

8

The Common Man's Uncommon Intellectual

Michael S. Joyce

> *The great men of culture are those who have had a passion for diffusing, for making prevail, the best ideas of their time; who have laboured to divest knowledge of all that was harsh, uncouth, difficult, abstract, professional, exclusive; to humanise it, to make it efficient outside the clique of the cultivated and learned, yet still remaining the* best *knowledge and thought of the time, and a true source, therefore, of sweetness and light.*
>
> MATTHEW ARNOLD
> Culture and Anarchy

I t sometimes seems there are two Irving Kristols: one, the affable and witty conversationalist, chatting freely with unlearned yet spirited youths; the other, the intellectual giant who, if there were a Mount Rushmore for wise men of letters, would be the model for one of its faces. But there are not two Irving Kristols.

The Irving Kristol who argued politics in alcove 1 of the City College of New York cafeteria and joined the Young People's Socialist League of Trotskyists is the very same Irving Kristol who challenged prevailing intellectual political conventions and fashions in *The Public Interest* and joined the *Wall Street Journal*'s board of contributors. There is only one Irving Kristol.

He tells us that, as an adolescent in the 1930s, he experienced a vivid "flash of insight" that attracted him to socialism. In New York City, he saw around him unemployed men eager to work, factories standing idle, abundant resources lying fallow, and a population sorely in need of all the goods these components stood ready to provide. He remembers thinking: "Why in hell can't someone put all this together? This situation is not only tragic, it is stupid."[1]

Epiphanies are so rare, it may seem a shame for Irving to have squandered a perfectly good one in being converted to what he himself has called "a political fantasy incarnated into a reign of terror."[2] But Irving's flash of insight wasn't specific about the need for central planning and four-hour speeches advocating the transmogrification of human nature. Its main theme was, "Why in hell can't someone put all this together?"

The intellectual odyssey begun with this objective—which is not by any means concluded—has been traced by writers wise enough to know that along its path lie the keys to the deliverance of the twentieth century, or perhaps the twenty-first. It is a course of thinking that is fascinating for where it began, where it went, and where it leads and for its outstanding integrity. It is this integrity, this wholeness, that so distinctly marks the thought of Irving Kristol and everywhere illuminates his pages.

An astounding number of intellectuals, when their beloved abstractions conflict with reality, dismiss reality as flawed. Their betters, including some of the great thinkers of the West, prefer equivocation to absurdity and simply speak with two contrasting voices. This was the case with John Stuart Mill, in whose works the brilliant historian Gertrude Himmelfarb (known, of course, to their many friends as Bea Kristol, Irving's wife of more than half a century) has found "the two Mills," *here* advocating "one very simple principle" of absolute liberty and *there* championing the limits of "custom and prescription."[3] Like Mill, Irving Kristol has held disparate positions; unlike Mill, he has resolved them. If ever two precepts clashed in his thinking, one of them had to go.

---

1. Irving Kristol, "The Cultural Revolution and the Capitalist Future," *The American Enterprise,* vol. 4, no. 2 (March/April 1992), p. 45.

2. Ibid., p. 44.

3. Gertrude Himmelfarb, "Liberty: 'One Very Simple Principle'?" *American Scholar,* vol. 62, no. 4 (Autumn 1993), pp. 532–47.

Gracefully, deliberately, actively, he thought through the consequences of ideas and provided us with a model of how to learn. When a policy he had supported showed evil consequences, most often unanticipated consequences, he did not become its apologist—he became its adversary. The Marxist anti-Stalinist became a liberal anti-Communist, but it was not enough for Irving to be antisomething. He recognized Cardinal Newman's principle that an erroneous idea can be expunged from the mind only by the active presence of a better idea. And rarely in this world have ideas so fully achieved the status of being an "active presence" as they have in the mind and words of Irving Kristol. He has written:

> It is ideas that establish and define in men's minds the categories of the politically possible and the politically impossible, the desirable and the undesirable, the tolerable and the intolerable.[4]

Ideas matter to Irving Kristol. And vice versa. For none of his insights, important as they certainly have been, would have mattered much had Irving Kristol not always been so manifestly unignorable. Through his magazines and essays, his status among intellectuals, his personal magnetism, his integrity, and no doubt through Divine Providence, he is an unforgettably influential man.

The intelligentsia, when Irving came aboard, was wholly in the grasp of a "gnostic movement...hostile to all existing laws and to all existing institutions."[5] It will be difficult, I pray, to convince our children that once there was a time when among established intellectuals in a free country it was controversial to be "anti-Communist." The Socialist project, in mockery of its own proletarian rhetoric, was uniquely attractive to intellectuals, who would head its committees, receive its titles and entitlements, and—at least in the West—chatter endlessly about the truth and purity of theory. And to such people Irving Kristol—originally one of their own—uttered the word "capitalism" and spoke respectfully of "bourgeois" values. He led as many as would hear him out of the radical wilderness, but he also realized that ideas deserved an audience wider and more

---

4. Irving Kristol, *Reflections of a Neoconservative: Looking Back, Looking Ahead* (New York: Basic Books, 1983), p. 106.

5. Ibid., p. 317.

universal than a small set of intellectuals. Economic theory should be heard in corporate boardrooms; politicians should know something of the ideas their country was founded on; reporters should have many learned people to interview, so that the people they inform will be exposed to criticism and policy recommendations supported by sound thinking.

In the 1960s, as he witnessed the capitulation of culture to counterculture and the leftward turn of liberalism, his personal journey, like that of Ulysses, was expedited by circumstances. In order to become a neoconservative, he remarked, "All you had to do was stand in place." Irving's temperament and political instinct took him in new directions. Wisely, he took full advantage of the platform this new term "neoconservative" provided him to become a more active critic of modern liberal policy. To his writing, publishing, and teaching efforts, he added an organizing role that has had a profound and lasting effect on the political landscape of America. He persuaded corporations and foundations to support intellectual journals and think tanks so that universities, so thoroughly corrupted by the end of the 1960s, would not be the only source of policy or of employment for thinkers.

Irving spoke from many pulpits—to large audiences, to groups of four at lunch, and to hotel clerks and cabdrivers. Never in the style of Jeremiah or of John the Baptist, he spoke of ominous evils and possessed a vision for the future, but his powerful message was moderate, constrained by a realistic assessment of the human condition. For Irving, it was always: Here's the problem, here's what we might do about it.

Let us understand the bases on which our country was founded and their meaning for us today, Irving warned, because "to the extent to which our idea of democracy is vague or unrealistic, we shall be less able to resolve the issues that divide us."[6] We must be citizens, not mere subjects or inhabitants or consumers. "The purpose of democracy cannot possibly be the endless functioning of its own political machinery"; and "if you want self-government, you are only entitled to it if that 'self' is worthy of governing."[7] Democracy works wonderfully for a people who possess the "'republican virtues' of self-control, self-determination and a disinterested concern for the

---

6. Irving Kristol, *On the Democratic Idea in America* (New York: Harper and Row, 1972), p. 1.

7. Kristol, *Reflections of a Neoconservative*, pp. 50-51.

public good."[8] But can it endure a descent into nihilism by its immoderate extension to every aspect of our moral, social, and cultural lives?

Irving has taught us that capitalism, like democracy, is an engine of good that can be turned to evil ends if driven by debased motives. It may promote the very hedonism that would destroy it, but there are compelling reasons to hope that hedonism is not the inevitable destiny of man.

Religious faith, he has said, is essential, but its more prophetic visions can cause believers to strive to transform human nature rather than to sanctify it. Churches ought not be "surrendering to the spirit of modernity at the very moment when modernity itself is undergoing a kind of spiritual collapse."[9]

In his *Wall Street Journal* columns, Irving took on the issues of the day, more often than not providing his readers what they would describe as a mind-opening experience. As he has said, "When we lack the will to see things as they really are, there is nothing so mystifying as the obvious."[10] The greatest impact of these essays, and of much of Irving's writing, was to establish a language in which "the obvious" can be acknowledged. Plain speaking is characteristic of Irving's writings, as it was of all the classic authors of Greece and Rome, whose writings he admires and has mastered. With the literary equivalent of a shrug, he would demolish complex schools of thought, expose beguiling social theses to ridicule, or correct the suddenly glaring errors of popular political rhetoric. The air would clear. The obvious would be demystified. Citizens would shake their heads and say, "Well, of course, Irving Kristol is right," and wonder how they had been tricked into thinking otherwise. Rarely has a modern author read human nature with a keener eye or weighed the character and merit of ideas with finer scales.

To all his audiences, Irving in one way or another has pointed out that "human nature and reality are never transformed."[11] It is a lesson taught by socialism. If man cannot be refashioned to comport with political and economic theory, then perhaps he ought to accept

---

8. Ibid., p. 81.

9. Ibid., p. 326.

10. Irving Kristol, "'When Virtue Loses All Her Loveliness'—Some Reflections on Capitalism and 'the Free Society,'" *Capitalism Today,* Daniel Bell and Irving Kristol, eds. (New York: Basic Books, 1971), p. 3.

11. Kristol, *Reflections of a Neoconservative,* p. 318.

human nature and make the best of it. For this task, religion and culture are necessary. Even the wisest of political and economic systems, including those that are not necessarily incompatible with human nature, are formulas whose outcomes depend on the values put into them.

Although Irving Kristol has been a major influence in the epic and victorious struggle against communism, and although Irving Kristol has—it seems almost single-handedly—terminated the intellectual hegemony of liberalism in America, merely to look back at his accomplishments is to look in the wrong direction. Certainly, he has had a big hand in the history of our time. But that is not enough. In a dynamic world, he reminds us, politics "must be committed to shaping the future with at least as much energy as [is given] to preserving a traditional attachment to the past."[12]

So he shaped the future. He guided the development of organizations to nuture, employ, and sustain the bright minds whose serious discussions of political thought would cut through the fog of postmodern nonsense. Because of Irving Kristol, rational institutions, however fragile, are in place; ideas and their consequences are active presences in discriminating minds; absurdities of modern thought are being challenged with voices that will not be ignored. Often he has been called the godfather of neoconservatism, and Irving Kristol's growing brood of "godchildren" is steadfastly committed to shaping the future. The model for this task is clear enough: Ask not, *what* utopian vision *is next*; ask, "Why in hell can't someone put all this together?"

* * *

In my own modest efforts to put all this together, no element of Irving's work has been more enlightening or instructive than his subtle, nuanced teaching about the virtues and vices of the everyday bourgeois citizen.

On the one hand, as is clear from what I've noted above, there is no disputing that Irving displays in all his writings as well as personal dealings a "genuine affection for the common man."[13] Indeed, his chief quarrel with the "feverish mélange of gnostic hu-

---

12. Ibid., p. x.
13. Ibid., p. 107.

mors" and other political and social theories that have gripped our intellectual elites in the course of this century often seems to be precisely their complete lack of congruity with or sympathy for the way the common man—the average citizen of bourgeois liberal democracy—typically behaves in the real world.

Sometimes, those theories have erred in the direction of presuming or demanding *too much* of our average citizen, as when they call for the complete denial of that self-interested pursuit of wealth characteristic of bourgeois liberalism, in the name of one or another form of utopian or "scientific" egalitarian community. Sometimes, those theories have erred in the direction of expecting *too little* of our average citizen, as in the case of those contemporary economic theories that reduce citizens to bits of self-absorbed matter mindlessly pursuing gratification, thereby ignoring the oft-displayed capacity of the average citizen to make genuine sacrifices in the name of family, faith, or (nonutopian) community. In all such collisions between abstract or utopian theory and mundane bourgeois practice, Irving invariably chooses bourgeois practice, knowing full well that it alone accords with the modest but real possibilities for improvement in the human condition latent in human nature.

On the other hand, Irving cannot be said to subscribe to the "transcendental faith in the common man"[14] espoused at least publicly by so many academics and politicians today. As he learned from sustained attention to the writings and actions of the Founding Fathers, decent, stable, moderate popular government is so vanishingly rare in human experience that the founders themselves undertook the American experiment in democracy only with sustained critical introspection and the utmost caution.

At the core of their enduringly wise caution is the realization that human nature is full of potential for evil as well as for good. Insofar as democracy traditionally, almost by definition, had meant the indiscriminate unleashing of all human passions, evil as well as good, small wonder that the founders were careful and self-critical. (Today's wildly utopian and unreal faith in the common man, by contrast, calls for just such an indiscriminate unleashing as part of its program of untrammeled "self-expression" and cultivation of "self-esteem." The results are vividly displayed in America's television studios, public schools, and inner cities.)

14. Ibid., p. 101.

Irving's "genuine affection" for, in contrast to a "transcendental faith in," the common man is rooted in an understanding drawn from the Founding Fathers. The bourgeois citizen, they taught, is capable of working responsibly and diligently to improve his material condition; of sacrificing or modifying self-interest on occasion in the name of some higher cause; and of sustaining the first stable democracy in the history of the world—*if* he is first shaped, molded, educated, and modestly elevated by the humble, homely institutions of bourgeois civil society. Among those institutions are strong families, vibrant neighborhoods, "local school boards, religious congregations, professional organizations, trade unions, trade associations, organized charities, organized enthusiasm for almost any imaginable activity."[15]

These local, small civic institutions, the founders understood, tamed unruly passions and supplied a necessary counterweight to capitalism's self-interested pursuit of wealth by engendering "civic virtue"—one of Irving's perennial concerns. Like so many other of his concerns, civic virtue has suddenly been elevated from "quaint" and "idiosyncratic" to the covers of the national newsweeklies. The American Revolution, Irving maintains, was able to establish "mild government"—that is, a free, limited government—precisely by anchoring our national political life in the "solid bedrock of local self-government." There, "through the shaping influence of religion, education, and their own daily experience"[16] as embodied in bourgeois civic institutions, people could acquire the degree of civic virtue essential to the first large-scale and workable democracy.

Along with a balanced, realistic assessment of the bourgeois citizen's virtues and vices, Irving has constructed an equally balanced and realistic assessment of the prospects for that citizen's survival in today's intellectual and cultural climate. On the one hand, it is beyond dispute that the constant hammering administered by hostile intellectual doctrines (which, beneath their bewildering variety, all seem to share as their starting point a profound contempt for bourgeois civilization) has taken its toll. As Irving suggests, the bourgeois citizen—in his well-intentioned quest for that form of self-transcendence of which he is capable and desirous, despite theories to the contrary—all too often flirts with cultural beliefs and doctrines ultimately subversive of his very existence.

15. Ibid., p. xiv.
16. Ibid., p. 90.

But, fortunately, Irving insists, "bourgeois, property-owning democracy tends to breed its own antibodies," which "immunize it . . . against the lunacies of its intellectuals and artists."[17] The average citizen, if on occasion temporarily intoxicated by gnostic humors, is quickly sobered up by the lessons in economics taught by mortgages, in politics taught by school board meetings, and in governmental "social engineering" taught by "trying to raise their children to be decent human beings"—all lessons best taught within the virtue-generating institutions of civil society.[18]

Some of us, alarmed by the threats to bourgeois society noted by Irving but emboldened by his unfailingly cheerful conviction that all is by no means lost, have set about to do what we can to strengthen the antibody-producing institutions of the American republic. Whenever I am permitted, I talk about the need to cultivate a "new citizenship" among Americans today, which would draw them out of their present state of understandable alienation from public affairs and reengage them precisely with the virtue-generating institutions of civil society—family, neighborhood, church, voluntary association, and local government. On that basis, and only on that basis, as the founders noted, it then becomes possible to make the larger case for a return to limited, "mild" government.

I am prudent enough not to claim that this would amount to a "second American Revolution," because I am certain Irving could write a sparkling, splendidly instructive essay on just how many second American revolutions have been proudly proclaimed by academics and public figures since the first, and just what this tells us about the subtle, wildly infectious diseases of modernity that claim even the wariest of us.

Nonetheless, I hope it is not immodest to suggest that the new citizenship does, indeed, proceed in the wake of Irving's monumental intellectual project. Just as he set about "to infuse American bourgeois orthodoxy with a new self-conscious intellectual vigor," so a new citizenship would infuse bourgeois orthodoxy with a new cultural and political vigor. Just as he fought to dispel modernity's "feverish mélange of gnostic humors," so the new citizenship proposes to do battle with the "coercive bureaucracies" that once expressed and enforced those humors, but that now have been stripped of any claim to legitimacy by Irving's antignostic campaign. Just as

17. Kristol, "The Cultural Revolution and the Capitalist Future," p. 51.
18. Ibid., p. 51.

he aimed to "explain to the American people why they are right, and to the intellectuals why they are wrong," so a new citizenship labors for that moment when a reassured and reinvigorated American people will take back management of their daily affairs from the discredited intellectuals.

Clearly, what remains to be done is a massive undertaking. But none of it would have been possible, or even thinkable, without Irving's uncommon affection for the common man.

9

Twice Chosen: Irving Kristol as American

Michael Novak

I really cannot believe that Americans are a historically unique and chosen people. I am myself a Jew and an American, and with all due respect to the Deity, I think the odds are prohibitive that He would have gone out of His way to choose me twice over.

When he wrote these words, Irving Kristol was modest to a fault. He had been, in fact, twice blessed: first blessed by being born Jewish, twice blessed by being born American. Not that, from a Catholic point of view, these two blessings are on the same level. Those of us who are Catholic (including Tocqueville and the Third Plenary Council of Baltimore) do see the founding of the democratic experiment in America as an act of Providence. But the first blessing appertains to the City of God; the latter, only to the City of Man.

One of Irving Kristol's quiet contributions is to have restored to many on the American Left a profound—almost a biblical—understanding of the American idea, which most of us had left behind in moving leftward. The comprehension of the American idea most common among journalists, intellectuals, and public officials, he prodded us, is quite unworthy of the sober political philosophy worked out by this nation's founding generation, and embodied in its institutions.

The Years of National Turbulence

Two or three times, when I was young, I wrote a note of appreciation to a writer who had done something really good. I remember writing such a letter to Irving Kristol in about 1972 on reading his little book—I still think it is his best—*On the Democratic Idea in America* (Harper & Row, 1972). Like his other books, this was a collection of essays, the first of which had been published in 1967. Those were the years, 1967 to 1972, of student riots, antiwar protests, the assassinations of Robert F. Kennedy and Martin Luther King, Jr., and Watergate. A new utopianism was bursting out everywhere, paired (of course) with a rapidly spreading cynicism. Some intellectuals were beginning to lose faith in socialism, and even in European social democracy. I was one such.

The questions we were asking ourselves had this central core: if I am not a Socialist, or a Social Democrat, what am I? In the dark clouds and electrical energy that were gathering in my mind at that time, Kristol's reflections on America broke like a long and brilliant lightning flash. Once you reject socialism, his book suggested to me, one place to look is the American experience—the most neglected experience of political economy in modern intellectual life.

The Attraction of the Complementary

Since my own interests and biases are religious, I was most interested at that time in writers who, while not necessarily hostile to religion, wrote from a point of view that could be read without discomfort by agnostics or atheists. I liked, as it were, the abstinence and self-denial implicit in Kristol's prose. In his essays of that period, he for the most part kept his serious religious inquiries to himself; for all I knew, he could have been an agnostic. When he happened to corroborate my views, therefore, his was an especially valuable corroboration. When he contradicted them, he raised an especially demanding challenge.

I also liked Kristol's dry sense of irony and tragedy. This is what had attracted me to Reinhold Niebuhr during the preceding decade. Moreover, Kristol wrote with the sort of skeptical attitude that especially pleased me, in part because it ran against my own tendencies. I tend to look for the good sides of things. Irving is always looking for the things to be questioned, the things that are suspect, the things that might go wrong. For me, this was a wonderful balancing mechanism. I resolved to read everything of Irving Kristol's I could lay my hands on (a pledge that some twenty years later I am happy to have kept).

There is another aspect of Irving Kristol's thinking that greatly attracted me. One always feels in reading him that he has kept his worldly eyes open. He listens to what people say, reads carefully what they write, and watches for those small, significant events that shed light on whether words have purchase on reality—or not. He is an empiricist, not in the sense that he counts up numbers, but rather in the sense that he watches for those concrete occurrences that jut out where they're not supposed to; he has a sharp eye for events that falsify grand theories. He practices the falsifiability principle, a favorite of Karl Popper's. This habit somehow seems very American. To me it represents, as well, a habit of rabbinic Judaism, the habit of looking for sharp counterexamples, based on a highly refined version of common sense. Instead of keeping one's eyes on the heaven of theory, in other words, one makes better progress by carefully watching the ground of empiricism.

Let me just run through the titles of the eight chapters of *On the Democratic Idea in America*. Even the titles convey an impression of the mental landscape I am trying to describe. Savor them: "Urban Civilization and Its Discontents"; "The Shaking of the Foundations"; "Pornography, Obscenity, and the Case for Censorship"; "American Historians and the Democratic Idea"; "American Intellectuals and Foreign Policy"; "'When Virtue Loses All Her Loveliness'—Some Reflections on Capitalism and 'The Free Society'"; "Toward a Restructuring of the University"; "Utopianism and American Politics." There is a mixture of both hope and realistic expectations in these titles. They aim at a better future. But a large part of what we may expect to be better, they suggest, is that we will have abandoned illusory expectations. A sane, hopeful realism will have replaced the cynicism that follows from extravagant utopian hopes.

In some respects, Kristol's point of view reminded me of G. K. Chesterton's, especially the latter's *Outline of Sanity*. Kristol is far less the fantasist, of course, far less the romantic, and he is hardly tempted to be so playful with words. (He does share Chesterton's love for mystery stories—as a reader who devours hundreds of them, though, rather than as an author.) The Chesterton-Kristol commitment to common sense, their war against the intellectual illusions of the age, and their love for the literary essay bear a curious resemblance.

The Difficulty for Democracy

In order to remind myself why Irving's essays had such a big effect on me, I recently returned to *On the Democratic Idea in America*, and especially to its fourth chapter, "American Historians and the Democratic Idea." Irving says that he had intended to write a book on this subject. But of course he did not. The irony his mind is suited to works best in shorter essays. While his method needs the grist of concrete persons and concrete events, his mind is not really a historian's mind, committed to patient searches through historical detail. It is, rather, the mind of the social philosopher. It is not so much that Irving concentrates on big ideas; about these he is properly skeptical. But he does like to examine those ideas that shape the mind, those that operate perhaps as frameworks, or, in that contemporary term, as paradigms. There are certain ideas that structure the imagination, and it is these that fascinate Kristol. They are always the subject of his best essays.

The first thing that Irving Kristol observes in the chapter in question, based on an address to the Organization of American Historians at Philadelphia in April 1969, is that the democratic idea in America, remarkably clear in the minds of the founders of this nation, became quite confused within a generation. The second thing he observes is that American historians have themselves been thoroughly confused about the idea of democracy. Kristol cites an example: almost invariably, American historians regard the increasing frequency of the popular referendum as a progressive step forward, for both democracy and liberal purposes. But is it really? For one thing, the popular referendum is often used by a conservative population in rebellion against a liberal legislature. For another, it is an expression of the direct popular will, which the framers of the Constitution feared as a type of majoritarian tyranny. Historians don't seem troubled by such facts. For them, democracy is always progressive, no matter what.

In this fashion, historians have developed a way of thinking that has become, by now, "an ideology so powerful as to represent a kind of religious faith." This "democratic faith" places much more emphasis on men's good intentions than on the way their actions actually work out. Many historians tend to believe such propositions as Al Smith's, "the cure for democracy is more democracy." Thus, they displace evil from inside the democratic faith to outside it: if there is evil, it must come from a conspiracy of wicked vested interests or from ideals alien to the democratic faith. By contrast, Kristol points out, the founders of this nation had a clearheaded political philosophy, not a quasi-religious faith:

> The difference between a democratic faith and a democratic political philosophy is basically this: whereas a faith may be attentive to the *problems* of democracy, it has great difficulty perceiving or thinking about the *problematics* of democracy. By "problematics" I mean those kinds of problems that flow from, that are inherent in, that are generated by democracy itself.... It really is quite extraordinary how the majority of American historians have, until quite recently, determinedly refused to pay attention to any thinker, or any book, that treated democracy as problematic.

As of 1969, no American historian, Kristol noted, had yet written a book on *The Federalist*. Among prominent historians were plenty of Turnerites and Beardites and even Marxists, portraying a course of unproblematic, irresistible progress—but few Madisonians or Hamiltonians. None were disciples of the greatest historian of democracy, Henry Adams, whose vision of democracy was dark and complex. Although many historians quoted from Tocqueville, one could find among them no Tocquevillians.

By contrast with most historians, the founders of this country held that democracy is quite capable of bringing evil into the world. With considerable forethought, they designed a system to frustrate its evil tendencies and provided it with spurs toward self-correction. The American founders thought hard about the systemic remedies that might correct deficiencies inherent in democracy.

> In short, the founding fathers sought to establish a "popular government" that could be stable, just, free; where there was security of person and property; and whose public leaders would claim legitimacy not only because they were elected officials but also because their character and behavior approximated some accepted models of excellence.

Kristol was always sensitive to the moral dimension of the good society. Whether men judge their society to be moral, just, and even noble is important to them—not least when they are asked (as Kristol's generation was) to lay down their lives for it. It is important, Kristol believed, for a democratic society to work hard to establish high moral standards for its citizens to aspire to—critically important, since democracies do not tend naturally to do this on their own. The framers "thought that political institutions had something to do with the shaping of common men, and they took the question, *'What kind of common man does our popular government produce?'* to be as crucial a consideration as any other."

Kristol quotes Matthew Arnold's warning: "The difficulty for democracy is, how to find and keep high ideals." In aristocracies, this function was supplied by aristocrats. What can a society without aristocrats do? He quotes Arnold again:

> Nations are not truly great ... solely because the individuals composing them are numerous, free, and active; but they are great when these numbers, this freedom, and this activity are employed in the service of an ideal higher than that of an ordinary man, taken by himself.

In this respect, democracies depend on moral ideas even more than nondemocratic societies do, because they depend on the free choices of their citizens. For their very survival, they must shape ordinary people into an extraordinary moral force. If they depend on a democratic faith that supposes that within democracy there

are no evils to be combated, they err disastrously. They require a
realistic philosophy, alert to the systemic weaknesses of democratic
institutions, as well as to the fallibility and evil in the human heart.

"Not Jacksonian Democrats"

Kristol then turns to the nation's first major historian, George
Bancroft. Barely fifty years after the Constitutional Convention,
Bancroft was already ignoring *The Federalist* and claiming that
the men who framed the Constitution "followed the lead of no theoretical writer of their own or preceding times." Bancroft replaced
the authority of the founders with an exaltation of the common man,
as if the common man were a supreme arbiter of the beautiful and
the ugly, good and evil, progress and decline. From within a religion of the common man, Bancroft treated the founders as if they
had been aristocratic interlopers, temporarily standing in the common man's way.

Three generations later, such supremely influential historians as Frederick Turner and Charles A. Beard were explicitly repu-
diating the political philosophy of the Founding Fathers. Whereas
the framers had taken care to supply remedies for the dangerous
tendencies of democracy, the historians now meant by "democracy"
a Jacksonian-egalitarian-populist faith in the common man. Further, they held that this new faith "was something different from,
and antithetical to, the kind of democratic political philosophy that
the founding fathers believed in." They were ready to supplant the
nation's original founders.

In his reading of the historians, Kristol had come upon an essay by E. L. Godkin entitled "Aristocratic Opinions of Democracy,"
published in 1865 but hardly ever read or cited by other historians.
Unlike Bancroft, Turner, and Beard, Godkin held that egalitarianism is a problem for democracy. He was dismayed by "the aggressive, self-seeking individualism, the public disorderliness, the
philistine materialism of the American frontier that prevented
American democracy from achieving a more splendid destiny."
Godkin believed that certain high republican ideals, once protected
by the American aristocracy, remain crucial to the high degree of
civilization aimed at by American democracy but are often thwarted
by its vulgarity, under the malign influence of egalitarianism. That

is to say, Godkin identified another difficult *problematic* in the American democratic idea.

By contrast, Charles A. Beard "ended up with the aggressive assertion that the founding fathers were not Jacksonian democrats." To which Kristol comments: "He was right, of course. The really interesting question is *why* they were not." Perhaps they had good reason for being, as Beard called them, "men of only partial democratic faith." Maybe they had thought more deeply about evils that lie in the heart of common men than Beard had.

Kristol recognizes that later "revisionists" have exposed the shallowness of the progressives' accounts of reality. But even among the historians who thrived after World War II, he finds an unwillingness to come to grips with a serious political philosophy. Take Louis Hartz. Hartz, in particular, interprets the American idea as "compounded of a few Lockean dogmas." These he describes as involving certain mechanisms of self-interest, such as "group coercion, crowd psychology, and economic power," out of whose push and pull there emerges a kind of gross public interest. Hartz himself points out that there is no mind in this mechanism, only blind political forces, locked in checks and balances, pulleys and gears. Here is Kristol's succinct comment: "Only in America ... could a historian of ideas...end up with the assertion that political mind has no dominion over political matter."

Reflecting on how badly American historians have understood the realistic political philosophy of the founding generation, Kristol is struck by the fact "that America has been a very lucky country." But luck does not prove that America has a *good* form of government. Kristol finds it impossible to believe that Hartz—or any of his predecessors—actually lived by the shallow idea that the mind has no dominion over political matter.

> I honestly don't see how any intelligent man with even the slightest bit of worldly experience could entertain this belief. The political ideas that men have *always* [have] helped to shape the political reality they live in—and this is so whether these be habitual opinions, passive convictions, or explicit ideologies. It is ideas that establish and define in men's minds the categories of the politically possible and the politically impossible, the desirable and the

undesirable, the tolerable and the intolerable. And what is more ultimately real, politically, than the structure of man's political imagination?

The Stagnation of Political Philosophy on "Automatic Pilot"

There we have it. *"What is more ultimately real, politically, than the structure of man's political imagination?"* Irving Kristol is, pre-eminently, a social philosopher of the political imagination, especially the American political imagination. The ideas that most interest him are those that intersect with the imagination of active human beings. What such human beings will find tolerable and intolerable varies enormously across history. It depends very much on the ideas they carry in their heads, and the shape of the drama in which they see themselves playing a part.

It is the impoverishment of the American political imagination, the failure of later generations to come up to the measure of the political philosophy of the founding generation, that is our gravest national danger. "Is it not possible that many of the ills of our democracy can be traced to this democracy itself," he asks, "or, more exactly, to this democracy's conception of itself?"

All those historians who attempt to glorify the common man seem to have forgotten the dangers inherent in "the tyranny of the majority," that tyranny which the founders so much feared. Whether it appeared as an essentially mindless, self-seeking majority or simply a rancorous, divisive coalition, they feared it. And they took practical steps to block its unchecked action.

Democracy as a form of progress on automatic pilot, a sort of mindless movement forward of the common man in history, does not seem to Kristol an especially attractive religious faith. "I do not see that the condition of American democracy is such as automatically to call forth my love and honor."

Kristol has a number of important questions to raise, which have scarcely even today been addressed:

To begin with, one would like to know *why* the political philosophy of the founding fathers was so ruthlessly unmanned by American history. Was it the result of inher-

ent flaws in that political philosophy itself? Was it a failure of statesmanship? Was it a consequence of external
developments that were unpredictable and uncontrollable?
These questions have hardly been asked, let alone answered.

The Right Questions

Not many years ago, the fifth-grade daughter of a philosopher friend
at the university where I taught took an exam in a history class.
The question read "Socrates was—" and she filled in the blank space
with "the philosopher who taught by asking questions." The exam-
iner marked her wrong. The correct answer, he said, should have
been "a Greek philosopher." When this was reported to him, my
philosopher friend was ready to tear out his hair, except that he was
already bald.

Like that earlier Greek philosopher, Irving Kristol's way of
teaching is often by asking questions—questions that we have all
been avoiding. He does not do this out of laziness. It takes quite a
lot of effort to fight one's way through many mazes and false turns,
only then to discern what the truly useful questions are. Irving
Kristol seems to have unerring instinct in his pursuit of such questions. Why did the political philosophy of the Founding Fathers meet
such an early and unmourned death? And why have so many im-
postors been allowed to speak in their name?

Twenty-five years after he raised such questions in his essay,
they still remain urgent questions for this Republic. They may even
be more important. More than two-thirds of the public in recent
polls believe that the nation has "gone off the track." Irving Kristol
suggests some of the basic reasons why that might have happened,
and his essay still urges us to get the conversation going that will
put us back on track. That will require a more realistic brand of
thinking than we typically encounter in current discourse. It has
been Irving Kristol's vocation to call us back to such discourse and
to deepen and enrich our public life.

10

A Tribute to Irving Kristol

William E. Simon

T he last decade of the twentieth century began with freedom's historic and thrilling victory over communism in the Soviet Union and Eastern Europe. In five years, we will reach the twenty-first century, when another great and potentially decisive battle for moral, spiritual, political, and economic liberation looms here in America—on one side, those who champion greater individual freedom and self-reliance; on the other, the die-hard apologists for the paternalistic policies and increasingly heavy hand of big government liberalism.

We stand at a crossroads. What we must do to achieve victory is to build a conservative movement that is energized, engaged, and totally committed to dominate the debate and put freedom on the offense in every area of our country and around the globe—not only in politics and the economy but also, and most important, in the academic world, as well.

I know one American who will continue to throw down the gauntlet and join this battle with the power of his ideas and ideals. And that is Irving Kristol, a man of courage and principle in the world of politics, the economy, and our society. He is the brilliant author and official godfather of the neoconservative movement, who, for years, has lent his intellect, dignity, and authenticity to enhance conservative ideas.

Indeed, Irving has not only enhanced the credibility *of* conservatism, but he has confidently and continually reclaimed the future *for* conservatism, as he cheerfully fires volley after volley into the soft underbelly of liberalism. Now, that may sound a bit inflated in describing this self-professed ex-liberal, who once said the definition of a neoconservative is a liberal who has been mugged by reality.

And, indeed, to be called a neoconservative in America today is to invite criticism from those who may view with smug suspicion any parishioner who was not an original member of their church. I've always believed the door should be wide open for all believers. But I can also attest that Irving is no Johnny-come-lately to conservatism. His visionary writings launched the competitive, intellectual challenge to liberalism, and the sheer power of his pen has lured countless newcomers to our movement, as well.

More than four decades ago, in 1952, when I had just graduated from Lafayette College, Irving was already swimming in deep, controversial waters. In essays such as "Memoirs of a Cold-Warrior," he did not hesitate to tweak the nose of the political establishment by defending Senator Joseph McCarthy, a political pariah in the eyes of those fashionable thinkers who always know better than we do what we should read and hear and think.

"There is one thing," wrote Irving, "that the American people know about Senator McCarthy: He, like them, is unequivocally anti-Communist. However, they feel they know no such thing about the spokesmen for American liberalism."

By 1970, he was on record, far earlier and more forcefully than most, against the growing contamination of higher education by the politically correct on campuses nationwide. In a *New York Times Magazine* article, he cast a critical eye on the academic community and blasted the hypocrisy and double standards that others were refusing to see. "On practically every campus of this country," Irving observed,

> learned professors are vociferously demanding the prohibition of cyclamates or DDT or whatever—while in the same breath arguing for the legalization of marijuana or hashish or whatever.
>
> Similarly, most professors and college administrators have concluded they have neither the obligation nor the

capacity to supervise the sexual habits or elevate the moral characters of their students—but they appear to have concluded that they do have the obligation and capacity to solve our urban problems, conduct American foreign policy, reshape the American economy and perfect the American national character.

They will abolish violence from American life—but they will stoically tolerate it on the campus rather than take "repressive" action. They will protect their students from air pollution—but not from venereal disease, drug addiction, pregnancy or psychedelic psychosis.

In 1983, a full decade before Dan Quayle decried Murphy Brown's parading of single motherhood, Irving Kristol was expressing alarm at the soaring illegitimacy rate for black teenage girls. "The greatest single cause, by far, of black poverty," he wrote, "is the increasing number of female-headed households in the ghettos."

In 1978, the very year Jimmy Carter's leftward lurch was decimating economic stability and prosperity at home, and an emboldened Soviet Union was on the march in the world, Irving Kristol wrote his most controversial article yet. In "Socialism, an Obituary for an Idea," he wrote,

> The most important political event of the 20th Century is not the crisis of capitalism, but the death of socialism. . . .
>
> In the case of contemporary socialism, the ideal itself has ceased to be of any interest to anyone—it has not been adapted to reality, but contemptuously repudiated by it.

And finally, in 1993, surveying the wreckage of modern liberalism, he offered this characteristically blunt assessment: "Liberals were wrong, liberals are wrong, because they are liberals. What is wrong with liberals is liberalism—a metaphysics and a mythology that is woefully blind to human and political reality."

Perhaps the only thing that rivals the lucidity and power of Irving Kristol's ideas is his fearless courage and audacity in stating them. His throwing down the gauntlet has thrown liberals off balance for years. In fact, Irving's idea of the breakfast of champions isn't cereal, it's the opposition!

My association with Irving began in the late 1970s, when we collaborated to found the Institute for Educational Affairs. I had been a friend of Irving for many years and an admirer of his prolific writing. And one of his recent articles, "Two Cheers for Capitalism," had made the compelling case that, despite its many flaws, free market capitalism remains the best political and economic system for bringing freedom, prosperity, and happiness to the most people.

We decided to form a partnership that would bring together businessmen and right-thinking intellectuals in common cause, that is, intellectuals open-minded and sensible enough to understand that business should be managed by hard-nosed professionals, rather than by, as Irving put it, the editors of *The New Left Review*. We wanted these leaders to appreciate the importance of free market principles, beginning with the central truth that our personal, political, and economic freedoms are inextricably linked and that we permit government to undermine one at the expense of all.

At the same time, we wanted to persuade businessmen to make the commitment to compete and win on the battlefield of ideas, as well as to support their friends rather than foes in this battle. I regret to say that results of this particular enterprise have been mixed, at best. While efforts continue and some progress is being made, mostly by mobilizing small and medium-sized enterprises fiercely determined to guard their independence, it is difficult not to feel discouraged.

At a time when the movement toward free ideas, free markets, and more limited government is the most powerful force on the planet and when the popular revolt against big government and the vigor and vitality of conservatism have never been more evident in America, two underlying problems have not changed.

First, too many leaders of our largest corporations continue to undermine freedom. Second, the academic community probably remains the last, great bastion and fertile ground for Marxist thought and teaching in America today. It is a community where the hammer and sickle remains a fact, not an artifact, and where the students who are discriminated against are those who show any tendency toward conservative thought and writing.

Those who today would dare to challenge the liberal dogmas of tenured faculties and who would insist that the imbalance in many universities be corrected had better brace themselves for a storm of abuse. Louis Farrakhan's disgusting antisemitism and Catholic bashing are routinely condoned, even welcomed, in the name of free speech and protecting the First Amendment by passive university presidents. Communist Party partisan Angela Davis was named woman of the year and boisterously cheered by the faculty at Dartmouth College, while Jane Fonda was invited to a lecture series at Lafayette.

But invite a genuine intellectual and true conservative such as Jeane Kirkpatrick to speak, someone who doesn't reserve all her indignation for America, and university presidents such as Lafayette's will jump like trained seals when faculties demand that they spike the invitation.

And how could it be that Bill Bennett, who is not only a former secretary of education but also the author of a runaway bestseller, *The Book of Virtues,* did not receive a single invitation to deliver a graduation speech to a major American university? What does that tell us about the closing of the American mind? If Mr. Bennett desires such an invitation, he'd better follow up with *The Book of Vices*!

Martin Anderson, a brilliant scholar who has spent much of his adult life in academia and government and who is a distinguished fellow at Stanford University and at the Hoover Institution, where I also serve on the board, has cataloged the dark realities of academic intolerance in his superb book, *Imposters in the Temple.* While professing great admiration for the men and women who love their craft and retain a passion for genuine freedom of thought and expression, he presents a telling indictment against those who have betrayed their profession, shown scorn for their students, represented research and writing as important and relevant when it is not, and demonstrated an attachment to radical politics that brings them into direct conflict with the truth.

Second, while popular wisdom has Lenin predicting that "the Capitalists will sell us the rope with which we will hang them," I doubt that even Lenin himself dared to dream the remarkable phenomenon we've witnessed in modern-day America. And that is the seemingly relentless determination of America's largest corporations to set aside a portion of their earnings for the benefit of their enemies. Incredibly, America's largest corporations are using the largesse of the free enterprise system to finance their own destruction.

With some notable exceptions, American corporations have largely gone AWOL in the struggle to defend freedom where it is under siege every day, not just in Congress, but in the academic institutions of our country. Egged on by a philanthropic elite claiming to act in their name, the leaders of our free enterprise system are living proof of what Milton Friedman has called the suicidal impulse. A review of recent grants made by our largest corporations revealed that left-of-center recipients consistently received more than twice as much financial support as their counterparts on the Right.

And the great irony is that the simplest measure of progress is the achievement of positive results, and the policies pursued by so many of those receiving most of the funds fail even this test. Instead of encouraging individual creativity and equal opportunity, they proliferate and perpetuate government programs that spawn a corrosive psychology of dependency. They pursue an agenda that, no matter how superficial its rhetoric, boils down to one simple proposition: trust the state, not the individual.

Why does corporate America not only countenance this charade, but too often subsidize it? There are a myriad of reasons. One is simply a lack of awareness. Corporate heads are too busy running their own businesses to pay attention to what is going on in the intellectual and political world around them, unless their companies themselves are being attacked. Such ignorance can be economically fatal.

Others, while aware of the drumbeat of attacks on capitalism from the Left, simply lack the logic and rhetorical skills to articulate convincingly their own position. Still others shun all political involvement. They blindly assume that, somehow, this system of which they are a part, and on which they depend, will survive the attacks of its enemies without their participation. They behave like ostriches in a country symbolized by the eagle. When the attack hits home, some of them may wake up, but by then, it may also be too late. As Edmund Burke warned prophetically: "The only thing necessary for the triumph of evil is for good men to do nothing."

And the worst are those who yield even before the assaults of their enemies begin. They long to be viewed as progressive and socially responsible, no matter what the cost or to what asinine end their behavior leads them.

Fortunately, there is much that a determined and aroused business community can do. Witness the leadership by those who answered Hillary Clinton's attacks with the highly effective Harry and Louise ads, which pointed out in plain English the Clintons' disastrous plans to socialize the American health delivery system.

There can be no substitute for corporate resolve. Irving Kristol warned more than two decades ago that corporations were under tremendous attack and criticism but they had not yet learned to think and act politically. The mission of corporations is to produce goods and services and to earn profits to reinvest for the good of employees and shareholders, not to try to buy friendship, respect, and popularity from their enemies.

Corporations cannot buy friendship and respect. They should spend every dollar of every contribution with the same care they devote to decisions about corporate strategy and capital investment, employee compensation, and new equipment. Companies should give as though their futures depended on it, for in a very real sense, they do.

Some specific suggestions. First, business leaders can direct corporate giving along constructive lines by playing an active role on the boards of foundations that enterprises like theirs have made possible. They've been all too ready to cede operational control of their giving to a philanthropic class that sets their giving priorities for them.

Second, I have always believed, and never more than today, that we in the American business community have a duty to insist that the great values of Western civilization receive a full and fair hearing on American campuses and that we must steer our gifts to institutions committed to maintaining freedom.

And here again, no one has done more to lead by example than Irving Kristol. As president of the John M. Olin Foundation, I've had the opportunity to observe Irving when he was a John M. Olin Scholar and subsequently as a John M. Olin Distinguished Fellow at the American Enterprise Institute, as well as in his position as publisher of *The Public Interest*. In each capacity, he has been a champion for free market principles while encouraging and nurturing aspiring conservative writers, lending his support to conservative newspapers and publications on campuses, and keeping in close contact with conservative academics.

Nevertheless, neither Irving nor I would ever suggest that business people, any more than government or anyone else, have a right to dictate what our universities teach. But we most certainly do have a right and a responsibility to demand balance and to defend freedom when the Left, under the sheltering arm of tenure, is so clearly tilting many schools toward statism, even as the despots of the world like Fidel Castro are retreating in intellectual, political, and economic disarray.

No other society in the world has given greater liberty to those who are so contemptuous of that liberty as has America. Nor has any other society reached such heights of prosperity for its citizens and yet raised an entire new class of people who are hostile to the institutions that made that progress possible.

For too long, too many alumni have avoided facing these unpleasant facts. But the situation will not improve until more of us shed our ambivalence, renounce any posture of passivity, and wade in, as Irving Kristol has done all of his life, as aggressive participants in the great battle for the ideas that will shape our future.

Alumni can work positively and constructively for their ideas and ideals. We can take time to identify and to reach out to support scholars and intellectuals who are committed to freedom, men and women who understand the nexus between economic freedom and political freedom, the link between capitalism and democracy, and who also know the intellectual jobs that need to be done.

Today, publications like the *Dartmouth Review* dot dozens of campuses. One gift of $100,000 would more than triple most of their budgets. Rather than blindly tossing $1 million into a general fund, concerned alumni can work to create a nesting place in their schools for brilliant scholars whose writings, research, and testing would otherwise be rejected by the academic chic—scholars like Irving Kristol, proven visionary and freedom fighter for the American spirit, whose brilliant insight continues to expose the failures and follies of Big Brother liberalism.

The conservative movement could no more do without him than D-Day could have done without Dwight Eisenhower or Desert Storm could have done without Norman Schwartzkopf. May Irving remain a conservative burr under the liberal saddle until liberalism's ride finally comes to an end. Yes, we are profoundly indebted to you, Irving, for all you have done, and continue to do, as a great writer and citizen of America, in our noble struggle to defend and advance the cause of freedom for all.

11

A Third Cheer for Capitalism

Irwin Stelzer

To the convinced free market economist, Irving Kristol is a gale of creative destruction. One's clear understanding of the ingredients of sound economics becomes confused (he would say nuanced); a sure sense of how to enable people to attain the good life gives way to uncertainty as to what the good life is all about. In short, to read Kristol is to replace certainty with doubt.

Economists who believe that unfettered market capitalism is a system that maximizes human welfare know a thing or two—or even three. We know that higher prices call forth greater supplies of goods and services, while constricting the demand for them, producing an equilibrium in which demand and supply are in balance. We know that those goods and services will be distributed in proportion to the incomes and preference of individuals and that those whose marginal product is greatest (and we take marginal product to be a reasonable measure of each person's contribution to society) will claim more goods and services than those whose output has a lesser value.

We know, too, that attempts by governments to interfere with the operations of markets reduce well-being and freedom. Price con-

---

The footnotes in this chapter, included lest the author be accused of "moral lapses," are dedicated to Gertrude Himmelfarb. See her "Where Have All the Footnotes Gone," in *On Looking into the Abyss: Untimely Thoughts on Culture and Society* (New York: Alfred A. Knopf, 1994), pp. 122–30.

trols, for example, eventually—and, most often, sooner rather than later—reduce the supply of goods to a point where demand remains unfulfilled, requiring government to decide who gets how much of the artificially limited supply. And outright restriction of the production and use of a good produces even greater problems: witness Americans reduced to relying on gangsters for liquor when Prohibition was in force; President William Clinton reduced to sneaking cigars in the White House when a no-smoking ban is introduced by an authority considerably more effective in enforcing her ukase than Elliott Ness was in enforcing Congress's; and a booming business in Britain in pirated videotapes banned by the government as too sexy or too violent or containing too much material now called by the single word "sexandviolence."

All these things we economists know. Or thought we did until Irving Kristol decided that free market capitalism is worth a mere two cheers rather than a rousing three.[1] Kristol's decision to withhold that third cheer—a decision as yet unchanged by the success of the Reaganism for which he might, were he not so modest, claim paternity or by the collapse of planned economies in countries as diverse as democratic Britain and the totalitarian Soviet Union—is a serious matter for free market economists, as serious for them as Thomas More's decision to withhold his endorsement of the divorce of Henry VIII from Catherine of Aragon was to the Crown. In both cases, the silence was shattering. This essay aims to elicit from Kristol that crucial third cheer for market capitalism and thereby gain release from the anxiety that he has caused among economists who overflow with admiration for his contributions to political economy, in the old-fashioned sense of the term.

It is important, at the outset, to understand Kristol's reasons for denying us his third cheer. The first appears in his preface to *Two Cheers for Capitalism* and is, on its own terms, unanswerable: "A capitalist society does not want more than two cheers for itself."[2] For to aspire to unambiguous acclaim is arrogant: capitalism provides bread in abundance, but man does not live by bread alone. Moreover, it is to claim to have met "some utopian standard" rather

---

1. *Two Cheers for Capitalism* (New York: Basic Books, 1978). This volume is a handy compendium of essays written by Kristol in the 1970s.

2. "Preface," in *Two Cheers for Capitalism,* p. ix.

than the more realistic one of superiority to other available forms of economic organization.

There can, of course, be no arguing with the notion that capitalism can never meet utopian standards of perfection. But surely Kristol will concede, with the inevitable mellowing that must have come with the passage of almost two decades since he contented himself with two cheers (a mellowing discernible more to his dinner companions than to his millions of *Wall Street Journal* readers), that an imperfect system, but one that is "more efficient and humane" than any other,[3] that is "organically linked" to American democracy,[4] and that "is peculiarly congenial to a large measure of personal liberty"[5] deserves another cheer.

Indeed, Kristol himself dismisses as "utopian fantasy" efforts "to eliminate all of these [capitalism's] costs while preserving all its benefits."[6] He cites with approval the willingness of "the ordinary man . . . [to] settle for a 'merely satisfactory' set of social arrangements," as opposed to utopian ones.[7] Is not the unrestrained cheer the characteristic expression of the sports event celebrated by Kristol as the quintessence of the American spirit (in contrast to the genteel harrumph of the academic seminar or the organized chant of the political rally)? And is it not therefore the appropriate acknowledgment of the ordinary bourgeois virtues of capitalism?

Assuming, then, that Kristol will, at some point, follow his pragmatist's instincts and grant the approbation of a third cheer to a nonutopian capitalism, we can proceed to his reservations about the way in which free markets produce and distribute goods. These can, for convenience and without doing excessive violence to a body of writing that defies easy classification, be grouped under the following headings: (1) we don't understand business cycles; (2) the

3. Ibid., p. xiv.
4. "Corporate Capitalism in America," *Two Cheers for Capitalism*, p. 4. See also Kristol's "Adam Smith and the Spirit of Capitalism," in *The Great Ideas Today, 1976* (Chicago: Encyclopaedia Britannica, 1976), p. 299: "Though, in the abstract, capitalism may be regarded as one thing and democracy as another, *modern* democracy . . . is incomprehensible without its capitalist underpinnings." Hereinafter, *Great Ideas*.
5. "Preface," in *Two Cheers for Capitalism*, p. xi.
6. *Great Ideas*, p. 299.
7. "About Equality," in *Two Cheers for Capitalism*, p. 186.

large corporation—the bearer of capitalism's standard—is often managed by executives who ignore shareholders' interests and fail to comprehend that their "job assignment" has changed;[8] and (3) unconstrained markets may produce results that undermine the "traditional institutions . . . which conservatives wish to preserve"[9] and which are essential to a capitalist system. To put this last point differently, Kristol prefers that Adam Smith's *Wealth of Nations* be read only in tandem with *The Theory of Moral Sentiments* and fears that Milton Friedman's reluctance "to impose any prohibition or inhibition on the libertine tendencies of modern bourgeois society" may produce a society "that despises liberal capitalism, and uses its liberty to subvert and abolish a free society."[10]

Let us consider these objections in turn in the hope of persuading Kristol that, valid though his reservations about capitalism may once have been, they need no longer concern him, either because the economy has developed in ways that should reduce his concerns (I almost said "anxiety," but that is not an emotion readily associated with Kristol) or because we economists are now so aware of them, so sensitized to these problems, that an enthusiastic third cheer will not turn our heads and produce an arrogant disregard for the noneconomic consequences of unfettered free markets.

We Don't Understand Business Cycles

In his 1991 Francis Boyer Lecture, Kristol noted that "the sad truth is that we have no theory of what we call the business cycle" and went on to say:

> I myself will always retain a gnawing uncertainty about the future of our market economy until our economists can reassure me that at least they have got the theory of it [the business cycle] right, so that if politics and politicians then proceed to mess things up, I'll know whom, in good conscience, I can blame.[11]

---

8. "The Corporation and the Dinosaur," in *Two Cheers for Capitalism*, p. 75.

9. "On Conservatism and Capitalism," in *Two Cheers for Capitalism*, p. 136.

10. "Capitalism, Socialism, and Nihilism," in *Two Cheers for Capitalism*, pp. 67 and 68.

11. "The Capitalist Future," Francis Boyer Lecture, December 4, 1991, mimeograph, p. 5.

Note a typical Kristol demand: give me a proper theoretical basis for the practical steps I must take—theory not for theory's sake but for action's sake.

Alas, we cannot satisfy Kristol completely. For he has put his finger on something economists have tried to avoid revealing for generations: the macroeconomist truly has no clothes. There is no satisfactory theory of the business cycle. The monetarists claim that we could understand and, perhaps, control the business cycle if only we would concentrate on the money supply; the Keynesians tell us that the answer lies in manipulating aggregate demand; the Kempians tell us not to bother with all those things: watch gold instead; and the Greenspanians enjoin us to look at everything—inventories, prices, levels of employment and capacity utilization, changes in the banking system, and a host of other variables—and then apply judgment (or just trust Alan's).

What Kristol has divined is that monetarists cannot define "money," much less control its volume or the velocity with which it circulates; the Keynesians don't know how to manipulate aggregate demand without creating unforeseen consequences in financial markets and adversely affecting business confidence; the gold bugs are engaged in a quest for an indicator of inflationary expectations, and instead have found one that tells them how much jewelry Asians are stacking away against the day when some lunatic despot will decide he has had enough of economic reform.

In short, there is no credible theoretical explanation of the performance of the macroeconomy. That is one reason why, as R. H. Coase has observed, economists lurch from prophet to prophet in their search for an explanation of the business cycle. After Friedrich Hayek gave his famous lectures at the London School of Economics in 1931, recalls Coase, "We knew why there was a depression." And he adds, "What now strikes me as odd is the ease with which Hayek conquered LSE."[12] Keynes's subsequent displacement of Hayek was as quick and easy as Hayek's earlier triumph, and the success of Keynes's theory "was such that by the outbreak of war in 1939, it could be said to be the orthodox approach among British economists."[13]

---

12. R. H. Coase, "How Should Economists Choose?" in *Essays on Economics and Economists* (Chicago: University of Chicago Press, 1994), p. 19. Hereinafter, *Essays.*

13. Ibid., p. 21.

The story of eventual disillusion with Keynesianism does not require repeating here. Nor need we recite the fall of the monetarists, who displaced the Keynesians next to the seats of power in the 1980s, only to prove unable to provide us with a clear understanding of what Kristol calls the "relatively rare but so very traumatic and memorable . . . malfunctioning of the system."[14] So we are left with the Greenspanians, the one faction honest enough to concede Kristol's "sad truth"—that we have "no theory of what we call the business cycle, no theory worthy of the name."[15]

But is it not possible to persuade Kristol that the discovery that there is, indeed, no theory of the business cycle is a good thing, rather than one of the "major weaknesses in a market economy"?[16] As Coase points out, "In public discussion, in the press, and in politics, theories and findings are adopted not to facilitate the search for truth but because they lead to certain policy conclusions. Theories and findings become weapons in a propaganda battle."[17]

Thus, one of the attractions of Keynes's system was that it "offered a cure for unemployment without requiring any sacrifices,"[18] perhaps one reason why Kristol says that "economics ceased being a 'dismal science' with the rise of Keynesian theories."[19] Part of gold's luster, in the eyes of gold bugs, is that it relegates government to the role of observer, rather than of macroeconomic manipulator; part of the attraction of monetarism to its adherents is that it confers power on austere, responsible central bankers rather than on democratically elected politicians.

In another connection, Kristol cheered George Gilder for freeing "the idea of a free-market economy . . . from the dialectical prison of orthodox economic theory."[20] Surely, freeing the idea of a free market economy from the fruitless hunt for a nonexistent theory of macroeconomic behavior is as worthy of his approbation. For a frank

---

14. Boyer Lecture, p. 2.

15. Ibid., p. 5.

16. Ibid., p. 2.

17. Coase, *Essays,* p. 30.

18. Ibid., p. 21.

19. "Inflation and the 'Dismal Science,'" in *Two Cheers for Capitalism,* p. 104.

20. "A New Look at Capitalism," *National Review,* April 17, 1981, p. 414.

confession of failure purges economics of a succession of theories designed to support preselected policies. We can now admit that business cycles will always be with us: overoptimistic businessmen will, at times, accumulate excessive inventories in the expectation that this year's Christmas demand for Hula-Hoops will equal last year's; labor unions will at times overreach and establish wage levels that make some industries unable to compete in world markets without paring their work forces; property developers will never abandon the lemminglike behavior that causes booms to alternate with real estate busts; consumers' moods will swing from excessive exuberance, for example, when house prices and stock markets are rising, to excessive pessimism when television anchors persuade them that the economic sky is falling; greedy or ignorant politicians will always be tempted to control prices or fix exchange rates or fine-tune the economy to bring it to a peak in November of every even-numbered year; and mad Arabs will always be tempted to unsheathe the "oil weapon," causing severe dislocations that, among other things, drive down the value of their own investments in oil-consuming countries. Policy makers, devoid of a guide through the maze of the myriad cause-and-effect relationships in a market economy, can—if wise—mitigate the effects of these cyclical and random phenomena, but they cannot eliminate them.

And, freed of the search for the compelling theory that Kristol (like the rest of us) would find comforting, policy makers can retreat to Greenspanism. Not much of a retreat really, for they have been expending an enormous amount of time—human and computer—on money and graduate student dissertations, not in the difficult search for a black cat in a dark room, but in groping around an empty, dark room.

We are left with a situation not uncommon in the field of economics. We have masses of data, all containing relevant information: the flow of credit, inventory changes, consumer purchasing patterns, housing starts and sales, rail shipments, prices, and thousands of other bits, not to mention anecdotal evidence that often has the virtue of being available before official statistics are compiled and released. All these data tell us something. But all are flawed in two ways. For one thing, they are subject to revision, often massive revision, leaving analysts unclear as to where they have been and now are. Second, at best such data provide a clear view through the rearview mirror but not through the windshield to the road ahead.

But these flaws in our data, this inability to develop what Kristol would call a "theory worthy of the name," need not, as Kristol seems to think, result in that "gnawing uncertainty about the future of our market economy" that afflicts him. "Art, instinct, intuition, hunch and pattern recognition," Professor Charles P. Kindleberger tells us, "may be among the missing ingredients of the economic tyro and the unrecognized asset of the magisterial one."[21] Not all of our Fed Reserve and Council of Economic Advisers chairpersons have been magisterial. Nor will all future appointees. But most seem, in the end, capable of applying informed judgment— informed by training, information, and sheer intelligence—to economic policy making with sufficient skill to avoid crash landings. True, we would prefer instruments precise enough to permit soft landings. But consider this. When the stock market dropped some 500 points in October 1987, Greenspan's Fed knew how to pump enough liquidity into the economy to prevent a major crisis. When America's bankers seemed intent on self-immolation on a pyre of unwise loans to sovereign nations, to wildcatters hunting for $100-per-barrel oil, and to real estate developers intent on building office buildings and shopping malls with neither equity investments of their own nor tenants, Greenspan did manipulate the spread between long- and short-term interest rates with sufficient dexterity to permit the banking system to survive and the bankers to live to err another day. And when the debt crisis of the less-developed countries threatened both borrowers and lenders with ruin, policy makers, applying a trial-and-error method that maintained global financial stability and avoided a "1930s-style collapse,"[22] gave "an uneven performance that is turning out well;"[23] the banks didn't collapse and Latin America "didn't throw itself into the arms of

---

21. Charles P. Kindleberger, *Historical Economics: Art or Science?* (New York: Harvester Wheatsheaf, 1990), p. 350.

22. Paul Krugman, "LDC Debt Policy," in Martin Feldstein, ed., *American Economic Policy in the 1980s* (Chicago: University of Chicago Press, 1994), p. 719.

23. Thomas O. Enders, "LDC Debt Policy," in Feldstein, *American Economic Policy*, p. 723.

dictators of the Left or the Right but made breathtaking steps toward democracy."[24]

And when policy makers mess things up, as Kristol and the rest of us know they will, our system proves either remarkably immune to their errors or amazingly resilient or both.[25] Even Jimmy Carter, perhaps the economic mismanager par excellence of our time, was unable to kill market capitalism. The system proved too tough and too capable of producing antitoxins—Volcker and Reagan—for him to damage it either seriously or permanently. This is partly because our decentralized system shields it from the big error that can make a shambles of centrally directed economies. The follies that governments commit (and those follies are now limited by knowledge hard won in the Great Depression) immediately produce correctives: millions of entrepreneurs scheme and plot to keep their businesses going; millions of families adjust by sheltering incomes from rapacious tax collectors or by sending more members to work or to school, as circumstances warrant; and hundreds of politicians rush forward to offer alternatives to the erroneous policies of their adversaries. No all-inclusive theory of the business cycle needed, thank you.

Corprocrats Are Irresponsible

Another problem Kristol has with market capitalism relates to the role of the large corporation. He does not join John Kenneth Galbraith in believing that such corporations have sufficient power to avoid responding to market forces. But he does worry that "every day, in every way, the large corporations look more and more like a species of dinosaur on its lumbering way to extinction."[26] This is for reasons small and large. Among the large: corporate executives' insistence on "entrepreneurial rewards instead of merely managerial ones," even though "corporate executives are *not* entrepreneurs; they do not take the risks of entrepreneurs and are not entitled to the rewards," rewards that are seen by the public as "indecently high." And with reason—above what is necessary to attract the requi-

24. Ibid.

25. In this connection, see Herbert Stein, "A Soothing Economics Lesson," *Wall Street Journal,* July 19, 1994.

26. "The Corporation and the Dinosaur," in *Two Cheers for Capitalism,* p. 73.

site talent, and unrelated to performance, these rewards are set by "directors," that is, other executives: "a very cozy arrangement."[27] Besides, the managers of modern corporations can and do ignore shareholders' interests and act "under the illusion that they *are* the corporation."[28]

That corprocrats are, at times, arrogant[29] and, at times, overpaid there can be no doubt. But the general structural problem—executives beyond the reach of shareholder-owners—whatever its validity at one time, no longer provides a good reason for withholding a third cheer for capitalism. For Michael Milken has bested Adolf Berle and Gardner Means.[30]

More than sixty years ago, Berle and Means developed the thesis that widely dispersed shareholders were in no position to control the actions of the corporate executives, who were, theoretically, merely managers employed at the pleasure of the shareholder-owners of the corporations. Instead, these executives had become the "anonymous oligarchy" to which Kristol referred more than forty years later.[31] This is the root of the other problems: excessive executive compensation, overmanning, and other indicia of a stockholder-bedamned attitude.

True—once, but no longer. A funny thing happened on the way to complete control of the American corporation by its managers: the hostile takeover. The overpaid, overperked corprocrat, "committed to no line of business,"[32] found that shareholders had an alternative to selling their shares—the only means they had of expressing

---

27. "The Credibility of Corporations," in *Two Cheers for Capitalism*, pp. 116–17. See also Kristol's scathing criticism of executives who borrow money from their companies and who reduce options prices when share prices fall, in "Ethics and the Corporation," in *Two Cheers for Capitalism*, pp. 80–82.

28. "Ethics and the Corporation," in *Two Cheers for Capitalism*, p. 79.

29. In this connection, see, for example, Kristol's discussion of oil company responses to the opportunities for price increases created by the cartel of the Organization of Petroleum Exporting Countries (OPEC), in "The Corporation as a Citizen" and "The Corporation and the Dinosaur," both in *Two Cheers for Capitalism*, pp. 93–94 and 76–77, respectively.

30. Adolf A. Berle and Gardner C. Means, *The Modern Corporation and Private Property* (New York: Macmillan, 1932).

31. "Corporate Capitalism in America," in *Two Cheers for Capitalism*, p. 5.

32. Ibid.

unhappiness until then. Instead of dumping their shares, they could now dump their managers, for Michael Milken ended the monopoly of top corporations on access to credit. Until Milken put in place the mighty Drexel Burnham "junk bond" machine, only 5 percent of all companies were deemed sufficiently creditworthy to earn the investment-grade rating that made their bonds acceptable to institutional buyers. Other companies had to rely on more costly bank credit—when they could get it.

By putting his academic research to practical use, Milken showed investors that a portfolio of bonds with lower than perfect credit ratings yielded returns so much higher than those of the rated, low-risk bonds of old-line companies that the added default risk was well worth bearing. This opened the credit markets to what frightened corprocrats called predators—the smooth Sir James Goldsmith and the not-so-smooth entrepreneurs previously relegated to the corporate world's second tier, called on by corporate blue bloods only when crucial to the success of the charity balls they chaired and to which they donated their shareholders' money. Thus, for example, when Ronald Perelman, "an Orthodox Jew from Philadelphia," wrested control of Revlon from suave Michel Bergerac, one commentator noted:

> The struggle for possession of Revlon was more than just another fierce takeover battle. It pitted the corporate and Wall Street mainstream against an outsider whose arriviste status was further underlined by the fact that he was financed by Mike Milken's controversial junk bonds.[33]

Another was more graphic: "Bergerac with his Chateau Lafite, and Ronnie with his Diet Coke," a match not made in heaven. "In the old days, people to whom the banks would not lend went to pawnbrokers .... Now Drexel has inserted itself between the pawnbrokers and the banks," complained Bergerac.[34] More precisely, money was suddenly available to potential owner-managers to en-

33. Judith Ramsey Ehrlich and Barry J. Rehfeld, *The New Crowd: The Changing of the Jewish Guard on Wall Street* (Boston: Little, Brown, 1989), p. 303.
34. Connie Bruck, *The Predator's Ball* (New York: Penguin Books, 1988), pp. 193–97.

able them to unseat entrenched managements, to replace those managers' efforts at perk maximization with the old-fashioned profit maximation that had been the driving force when owner and manager were one and the same.

The rest is history: shareholders saw that the values of their investments would increase if their businesses were run by the predators—a tough breed of men willing to shed unprofitable divisions, sell corporate jets, and make their own fortunes contingent on the performance of the companies they were taking over. This latter feature, accentuated by the need to maximize earnings to pay off the mountain of debt that Milken created for this new breed to scale, combined with the substantial stake the predators had in the target companies, did something Berle and Means could not dream of—it relinked management and ownership. The interests of the owners of the corporations and its managers again became coincident. Not everywhere and always, of course: Oliver Williamson still contends that "lacking control over the board, equity holders are vulnerable to expropriation."[35] But, as Tim Opler reports after an extensive study of leveraged buyouts (LBOs), although other factors might account for his results, "improvements in cash flow following LBOs suggest that these transactions mitigate management-shareholder agency conflict and force disgorgement of free cash flow."[36]

Not all companies went through the wringer of a hostile takeover. But managers of those that weren't actually threatened, or at least many of them, could see the handwriting on the wall and began to behave differently. There is a new emphasis on core businesses, rather than mere size, with divestitures—either to correct past errors or cash in on past sound investments—now a prominent part of corporate strategies to increase shareholder values. The return from such policies "constitute[s] reliable evidence" that at least some firms are following "their perceived comparative advantages,"[37] surely an indication that corprocrats no longer dare accumulate and retain assets that aggrandize them but are of no value to shareholders.

---

35. Oliver E. Williamson, *The Economic Institutions of Capitalism* (New York: Free Press, 1985), p. 323.

36. Tim Opler, "Operating Performance in Leveraged Buyouts: Evidence from 1985–1989," in Patrick Gaughan, ed., *Readings in Mergers and Acquisitions* (Oxford: Basil Blackwell, 1994), p. 84.

37. J. Fred Weston, "Divestitures: Mistakes or Learning?" in Gaughan, ed., *Readings in Mergers and Acquisitions,* p. 281.

Witness, too, downsizing, a painful process that managers often avoided in the days when shareholders could not bring pressure on executives in underperforming companies. Finally, note the growth of corporate "investor relations" departments, easy to sneer at but important factors in improving the flow of information to "the Street" and in meeting Kristol's demand that shareholders be "candidly and fully informed of how the company is doing, what the company is doing, and why"[38] by a managerial bureaucracy that he once fairly characterized as preferring "to have as little to do with them [shareholders] as possible."[39] "It really is extraordinary," wrote Kristol, "how little attention management now pays to its shareholders."[40]

But that was twenty-five years ago. The hostile takeover movement sounded an alarm bell that still, in this post-Milken era, echoes in executive suites—perhaps not as loudly as Kristol would like, but certainly loudly enough to arouse all but the stone deaf. And its echoes did not die out when Mike Milken departed the scene. Hostile takeovers, out of style in the late 1980s and early 1990s, have come back into vogue, representing nearly 8 percent of the near-record volume of takeovers in 1994.

And if the sound of that bell becomes muted, there is always another development to keep managers alert. The modern pension funds, no longer automatic and passive supporters of whatever men and women sit in executive swivels, have let it be known that they will no longer content themselves with unloading their stock if they think managers are subordinating the interests of shareholder-owners to those of executive employees. Instead, they will, if necessary, vote their substantial holdings to turn control of the offending corporation's board over to directors more sympathetic to the wishes of the company's owners. Indeed, they have little choice. As one economist-investment banker points out, the very size of an institution's holdings often makes it difficult for the institution to sell without depressing share prices.[41] Unable to cut and run, the institutions stay and vote.

38. "The Shareholder Constituency," in *Two Cheers for Capitalism*, p. 149.
39. "Corporate Capitalism in America," in *Two Cheers for Capitalism*, p. 20.
40. "The Shareholder Constituency," in *Two Cheers for Capitalism*, p. 149.
41. Elaine Sternberg, *Just Business: Business Ethics in Action* (London: Little, Brown, 1994), p. 208.

So even if we do not soon again get to dance at a latter-day predator's ball, neither should we have to call on a latter-day pair to repeat Berle and Means's warnings of the 1930s or again on Irving Kristol, whose talents are more usefully devoted to solving problems more pressing than the partially solved one created by the separation of ownership and management in the modern corporation.

Markets Don't Always Do What Is Good for Us

The last barrier to Kristol's final cheer is the most formidable. Capitalism produces material goods in abundance; over the long term, "everyone does benefit, visibly and substantially"[42] from this abundance; markets are demonstrably more efficient than central planning; alternatives to capitalism "range from the hideous to merely squalid."[43] And yet . . . and yet . . . .

In the end, Kristol stops short of unequivocal praise for market capitalism for what appear to be two profound reasons. First, capitalism assumes that the individual can "cope with the eternal dilemmas of the human condition." But he can't: he needs "the moral authority of tradition." How that idea "can be assimilated into a liberal-capitalist society is perhaps the major intellectual question of our age."[44] A question of such importance and difficulty can properly and with great relief be left by economists to philosophers. Indeed, we economists are virtually commanded by Kristol to keep our hands off of subjects such as these. Economists, he says, are nice to have on your side. But they can only make "economic sense" of an issue, "and the world does not move by economic sense alone."[45] A good thing, too, he adds:

> One would have to be some kind of self-denying fanatic, a monster of dispassion, always to be on the side of the economists, and most of us are just too human to manage it. On the whole, being a humanist rather than an economist, I think this is a good thing.[46]

---

42. "Preface," in *Two Cheers for Capitalism,* p. x.
43. Ibid., p. xiii.
44. Ibid., p. xi.
45. "The Corporation as a Citizen," in *Two Cheers for Capitalism,* p. 90.
46. Ibid., p. 91.

When provided with such an exit from an intellectual difficulty, an economist with any sense takes it—but not without three
shots in parting. First, Kristol's preference for his trade, humanism, over mine, economics, relies on a fundamental economic idea:
that the division of labor is efficient. Economic analysis, it seems,
can be useful to a humanist. Second, *no* economic system can supply the "moral authority of tradition" since such intergenerational
transmission of a body of beliefs inevitably relies on history, culture, and social structures. Third, economic systems that have tried
to provide an answer to the "eternal dilemmas of the human condition" have produced uniformly monstrous results.

Turn now to the second problem raised by Kristol. He is not
certain that the free expression of choice by consumers, facing sellers in a free marketplace, produces results that are in some broader-
than-economic sense acceptable—except to libertarians, a group with
which Kristol has little patience. This brings us to pornography.
Some things, Kristol contends in another connection, "are quite obvious and easily comprehensible—only they are terribly difficult to
explain to economists.[47] Count this poor soul among those who have
difficulty understanding why a free exchange of money for goods by
two informed adults should be prevented—and by government, yet—
as Kristol argues it should.[48] True, Kristol makes the standard externalities argument—that the transaction imposes costs on those
not party to it. He cites some evidence to support the proposition
that television or, at times, "our popular culture" stimulates aggressive criminal behavior in youths and is somehow causally connected
to "the plagues of sexual promiscuity among teenagers, teenage illegitimacy, and, yes, the increasing number of rapes committed by
teenagers."[49] Conclusion: "The government, at various levels, will
have to step in to help the parents."[50]

This is not the place to argue the validity of the evidence linking antisocial behavior to television. Suffice it to say that it is at

47. "Capitalism, Socialism, and Nihilism," in *Two Cheers for Capitalism*, p. 57.
48. "Sex, Violence and Videotape," *Wall Street Journal*, May 31,
1994.
49. Ibid.
50. Ibid.

best equivocal, with some respectable observers arguing that television programmers take their cues from society, rather than the other way around,[51] and some contending that the causal link between real-world and television violence runs from the former to the latter: violent people watch violent programs. Kristol recognizes that "clear-cut, causal relations are beyond the reach of social science" but finds the "circumstantial evidence so strong as to raise no reasonable doubt in the minds of ordinary people"[52]—a standard of proof that is arguably excessively relaxed, given that it is used to support a verdict of more government intervention.

In short, Kristol finds the uncertain evidence sufficiently persuasive to justify government intervention in the market for pornographic, violent, and other objectionable programs and films. These audiovisual products would, somehow, be banned or their circulation restricted.

Leave aside the question of whether such rationing—for that's what it is—can work. In Britain, which Kristol cites approvingly for having barred youngsters from buying or renting what are there called video nasties, pirates are already doing a multimillion-pound business in producing and selling now-illegal videotapes. Leave aside, too, questions of constitutionality: if society has the will, it will find an acceptable way to censor these materials. Finally, leave aside a danger that Kristol cites in other contexts: "It is so easy to move from the moral to the moralistic" to allow "moralistic enthusiasm to overwhelm all prudential judgment."[53]

But consider Kristol's willingness to accept the evidence concerning the externalities associated with violent videos—to allow the slight evidence to carry the burden of a significant expansion of intrusive government—with his views on government regulation of the environment. This is not a totally inapt comparison. Much of the political impulse behind environmentalism is purely aesthetic; witness green opposition to unsightly oil rigs off the beautiful coast of Santa Barbara, as great an offense to the aesthetic sensibilities of some as nude women on the cover of *Hustler* is to others.[54]

---

51. See, for example, George Vradenburg, remarks at National Review Institute Conservative Summit, Los Angeles, October 8, 1994. Hereinafter, Remarks. Vradenburg is executive vice president of Fox, Inc.

52. "Sex, Violence and Videotape," *Wall Street Journal*, May 31, 1994.

53. "The Environmentalist Crusade," *Two Cheers for Capitalism*, pp. 44–45.

54. I am indebted to Christopher DeMuth for this comparison.

Kristol begins by being consistent with his stand on pornography: government intervention in environmental matters is acceptable where externalities cannot be controlled by any single enterprise. But when it comes, for example, to restrictions on drilling for oil offshore, Kristol puts a far heavier burden on those environmentalists who support government intervention to prevent this assault on their sensibilities than he puts on those who would empower censors to ban television programs that offend their sensibilities. Evidence that the cost of marine life destroyed might exceed the value of oil found is not considered: it "verges on madness" to think that the benefits of drilling restrictions exceed the costs of such rules. So, too, with such pollution-control regulations as the Environmental Protection Agency's insistence on reviewing the effects of further concentrations of automobiles and trucks in urban areas and its only "grudging" approval and frequent "peremptory" disapproval of shopping centers, housing projects, and the like are "really bizarre."[55]

This presumption against allowing government to determine how our oceans and land should be used is perfectly and neoconservatively appropriate. After all, private parties are best able to decide—through bidding in the case of ocean drilling rights and through purchase and sale in the case of land—the highest and best use of these resources. If there are externalities, create property rights in the threatened resource and step aside, as is being done with pollution permits. To do otherwise is to give the EPA "far greater direct control over our individual lives than Congress, or the Executive, or state and local government. . . . Clean air is a good thing—but so is liberty, and so is democracy, and so are many other things."[56]

Do not restrictions on pornography create similar problems? Is it not likely that, like environmentalism, censorship will become "an exercise in ideological fanaticism"?[57] Are the censors not likely to follow the road traveled by the EPA and make "an utterly irresponsible use of such power"?[58] Should we not weigh the problem of market failure against the possibility of political failure in *all* cases?

---

55. "The Environmentalist Crusade," in *Two Cheers for Capitalism*, p. 47–48.
56. Ibid, p. 47.
57. Ibid., p. 46.
58. Ibid., p. 47.

More important, why is Kristol willing to run these risks to ban pornography but not to ban pollution? After all, the causal link between offshore drilling and "the risk of increasing the mortality rate among the fish of the Atlantic Ocean,"[59] as Kristol puts it, is more firmly established than is the link between on-screen and real-life violence.

Part of the answer lies in Kristol's confidence in his own brand of rough-cut cost-benefit analysis. Without going through the elaborate computations to which economists are prone, he feels safe in concluding that offshore oil is worth more to society than the forgone catch is to fishermen and seafood lovers and that reduced crime and promiscuity are worth more to society than the forgone videos are to television producers and porn lovers. Probably right. And that the risks created by an overweening environmental police force are greater than those created by a potentially overweening corps of culture cops. Probably wrong. Jesse Helms as an out-of-power art critic is amusing and at times useful; Jesse Helms in control of television fare is terrifying.

But a rough-and-ready cost-benefit calculus is only one reason for Kristol's willingness to expand government, to allow it to cancel buy-sell arrangements between private parties. Another and more important one is his firm belief that the need to preserve certain institutions, most notably the family and organized religion, overrides the need to preserve free markets or, more precisely, that the preservation of certain institutions is essential to the survival of capitalism. Kristol's economics are, in the end, results-oriented. Just as capitalism can be defended by pointing out that it delivers the goods—widely shared prosperity—so free markets should be circumscribed when they deliver the wrong goods. Note his relatively mild objection to Prohibition: a commendable "reform movement" aimed at ameliorating the ravages of working-class alcoholism is condemned only when it "degenerated into . . . [a] crusade [that] ended up by alienating public opinion."[60]

Is this conception of free markets—allow them to function but only so long as they produce acceptable goods—good policy? Those who argue that it is point out that free market capitalism operates in a larger framework, one established by the good sense and judg-

---

59. Ibid., p. 49.
60. Ibid., p. 45.

ment of the ordinary folk who compose the body politic. This good sense will, in the end, enable society to draw the line between an ordinary thriller and an invitation to violence, between a movie that is merely sexy and one that incites to promiscuity and rape. And such lines must be drawn if society is to preserve the institutions that underpin capitalism and the "solid bourgeois virtues"[61] of diligence, trustworthiness, prudence, hard work, and the willingness to defer gratification, without which it would be impossible to accumulate the capital needed to make capitalism productive.

In the face of such arguments, a mere economist, even one who has no quarrel with Kristol's view that "the world does not move by economic sense alone,"[62] must content himself with a warning. Interference in trade between willing buyers and sellers inevitably produces its own decline in public morality—a willingness by ordinarily law-abiding citizens to deal with gangsters, as during Prohibition, or to pay illegal prices, as when governments ration goods or fix their prices. Just as the criminalization of drugs turns law-abiding "high" seekers into criminals, criminalization of pornography will turn law-abiding thrill seekers into criminal thrill seekers—despite the huge new bureaucracy that will inevitably be erected to enforce the censors' rules.

So why not, instead, rely on markets to solve the problem? The organized opposition of consumer groups has already forced advertisers to withhold support from the seediest programs. The availability of technology that extends the effectiveness of parental control will soon permit parents to block reception of any programs they deem unsuitable for their children to watch. Audience reaction is already causing a shift in program and filmmaking from violent and sexually explicit programs and films to family entertainment. As George Vradenburg recently told a Hollywood audience, "To attract mass audiences, we [studios] must seek out what is universal, not what is deviant, and what is shared, not what is offensive or divisive."[63] Society's preferences, reflected in market choices, may work their way through the system more slowly than

61. "A New Look at Capitalism," *National Review*, April 17, 1981, p. 414.

62. "The Corporation as a Citizen," in *Two Cheers for Capitalism*, p. 90.

63. Vradenburg, Remarks, p. 3.

government edicts, but they are, in the end, less dangerous to those noneconomic values Kristol cherishes—liberty and democracy.

All of this said, this economist cannot rid himself of the doubts Kristol has aroused in him. I have been assured that a personal note is not out of place in this volume. At Irving's urging, I departed my beloved but at that time increasingly unlovely New York for Washington and the American Enterprise Institute, confident that I was entering a milieu in which no one, least of all Irving, had any doubt that welfare is maximized when consumers are left free to make choices among the goods available to them, after earning wages in jobs in which they maximize their productivity. To be sure: not all markets are perfect. But by and large, confine public policy to eliminating imperfections such as lack of knowledge, monopoly power, and unnecessary government regulation, and all will be well.

How naive. The man I took as a principal opponent of limitations on economic freedom and government intervention in markets—*Two Cheers* was, I thought, a title designed merely for its catchiness—proved to have grander goals than maximizing efficiency and the gross national product. Corporations should, he said, no longer seek solely to maximize profits but should instead, in the interest of their survival, recognize their political and social obligations; consumers should not be allowed to spend their honestly earned incomes buying pornography; Milton Friedman and Friedrich von Hayek are not always right; economics is only one of the social sciences, and probably not the most important one. Hence, market capitalism, although the best system on offer, is sufficiently limited in what it can add to human well-being and happiness and sufficiently flawed even when viewed more narrowly as a method of organizing productive activity to deserve only two cheers, which is all it should aspire to.

I have tried to extract a third—and am willing to cut a deal. The terms: Irving Kristol is to lower his standard for a full three cheers to one that concedes that free markets are the best available means of achieving material well-being (a concession he has already made); that developments in the 1980s have made corporate capitalism sufficiently responsive to owners rather than to managers to allay his fears about self-perpetuating corprocrats; that we have learned so much about how to moderate business cycles that we can live comfortably without a compelling theory of macroeconomics;

and that markets might solve some of the problems he has with "the culture," more permanently and with fewer impositions on individual freedom, if more slowly, than government regulation. If he will, with characteristic graciousness, make these few concessions, I will concede that the market system we both admire cannot, without some other food for our "spiritually impoverished civilization,"[64] produce a degree of contentment sufficient to sustain market capitalism; that such a soul-sustaining dish is beyond the ability of mere economists to confect; and that we need humanists as chefs for such nourishment.

A third cheer? Please.

<hr>

64. "'When Virtue Loses All Her Loveliness'—Some Reflections on Capitalism and 'the Free Society,'" in *Two Cheers for Capitalism,* p. 270.

12

The Need for Piety and Law: A Kristol-Clear Case

Leon R. Kass

O nce one gets right down to it, the difference between liberals and conservatives traces home to a disagreement about the basic source of human troubles. Liberals are inclined to blame external causes—for example, poverty, prejudice, poor rearing, or just plain misfortune—against which they take up arms in order progressively to enable man's natural goodness and felicity to emerge out from under; for liberals, it is the scientists, inventors, and caregivers who are the truest benefactors of the race, helping to overcome necessity and to extend human dominion over an inhospitable world. Conservatives are inclined to blame human misery rather on causes lurking naturally within the souls of men—for example, pride, vanity, jealousy, greed, and insatiable or unruly desires. Accordingly, conservatives are skeptical about human perfectibility and suspicious of utopian projects, not least because they would have to be conducted by imperfect fellow human beings, always dangerously unfit to remake the world; for conservatives, it is the priests, prophets, and lawgivers who are the truest benefactors of the race, helping to restrain vice and to encourage human self-command in the ceaseless struggle raging in the human soul between our better and worse natures.

Irving Kristol's intellectual and political odyssey has led him through all sides of this controversy, from the high-minded Trotskyism of his youth to the still more high-minded but also tough-headed conservativism of his full maturity. In recent years he has written frequently in support of biblical religion. Without religion, he insists (shall I say prophetically?), our public and private morality are doomed, and with them, so also our (until recently) flourishing liberal democratic society.

But biblical religion—especially as interpreted today—does not speak with one voice. Curiously, liberals and conservatives both find intellectual and moral support in the same traditional sources. For example, the prophetic and messianic strands of biblical religion inspire many a liberal activist to build a world in which men will turn swords into plowshares; and the early intellectual founders of modernity—like Bacon and Locke—took God's primary exhortation in Genesis, "to have dominion," as a religious warrant for the technological project to master nature. Yet neighboring passages of Genesis are said by conservatives to show man's radical sinfulness, and the weight of scripture is usually regarded as falling on the side of lawgivers and priests, not scientists and inventors. The truth that the Bible says shall make us free is surely not the knowledge of the laws of Newton.

In his writings on religion, Irving Kristol looks to the law (his expressed preference), not to the prophets; his eye sees not some far-off utopian future but today's moral and spiritual decay. This essay shares his concerns and his outlook, and it follows his implicit advice: it looks to the Bible as the source of moral wisdom and instruction. I trust that Irving won't mind if I find there a Kristol-clear case of the need for piety and law.

The Twisted Roots of Civilization

What does the Bible actually teach about the source of human troubles? What is its author's view of civilization and the arts, or of the prospects for overcoming hostility and misery among men? Though the Bible's first word cannot be its last word, one would do well to begin near the beginning, in the book of Genesis. The first exploration of this subject comes with the story of Cain and Abel.

The story of Cain and Abel (Genesis 4) is, in fact, not a separate tale but, rather, a continuation and conclusion of the story of the Garden of Eden. It completes the story of Adam and Eve (begun in Genesis 2.4), of whom we shall not hear again. More important, by presenting an account of primordial life outside the Garden— the life of human beings born of woman, living without imposed law but (instead) under the newly obtained "natural" knowledge of good and bad—it shows us what natural or unregulated human life might be like.

This final episode of the primordial story features fundamental elements of human existence, psychic and social: (a) the first household and family, that is, the first human *institution*, and therewith the first element of society; (b) the first attempts, through sacrifices, at a relationship between man and God; (c) distinctive human passions, preeminently wounded pride, anger, jealousy, and fear; (d) violent death, crime and punishment, and the rudiments of (natural) justice; and (e) the emergence of agriculture and settlements, the arts and the city. As a result, this tale manages to introduce, in a mere twenty-six verses, many of the essential elements of a "natural" anthropology, showing us to ourselves in a mirror and making vivid how humankind would live on its own without moral instruction. More anthropological than historical—these are *paradigmatic* more than they are "real" people—the story helps us see clearly some of the reasons why the "natural" or uninstructed way does not work, and, therefore, why the giving of God's law might be both necessary and welcome.

Everyone knows that Cain committed fratricide. But few people remember that he is also the first farmer, the initiator of sacrifices, and the founder of the first city, as well as the progenitor of a line of men that invented the arts—including music and metallurgy. Why does the first family issue in fratricide? And what has fratricide to do with the city or with all these other—and usually celebrated— features of civilized life? Is there, perhaps, something questionable, even destructive, at the heart of civilization? The text that prompts these questions does not simply answer them. To pursue them we must submit to the careful work of exegesis and interpretation— setting aside, as much as we are able, our preexisting prejudices.

The Birth of the Brothers

And the man knew Eve his wife, and she conceived and bore Cain, saying, "I have gotten [or "created"; *kanithi*] a

man [*ish*] with the Lord." And she again bore his brother
Abel. (Genesis 4.1–2)

The first word about life outside the Garden is not as harsh as we
had been led to believe. On the contrary, it celebrates the birth of a
son, without report of (the predicted) pain or trouble to the woman,
received joyously by his mother. Adam, having known his wife, re-
cedes into the background; Eve, in her generational fullness, occu-
pies center stage, to her great delight. Boasting of her own creative
powers, Eve compares herself as creator to God: though the conventional translation of *kanithi ish eth adonai*, "I have gotten a man
with the help of the Lord," makes Eve seem grateful and even pious,
"with the help of" is an interpretive interpolation. In my view, the
context clearly favors "I have gotten [or "created"] a man [*equally*]
with God"—or, in plain speech, "God created a man, and now so
have I."

Who could blame Eve for such an attitude? Absent some divine
revelation about God's role in generation, all the evidence naturally
supports Eve's view: she conceived, she labored, and she bore; and
the child grew and emerged out of her own substance. Having been
named Eve (*Chavah*) by her husband because she was to be the
mother of all living (*chai*), she now exults in her special creative
powers. She takes special delight in her firstborn.

Cain, the pride of his mother's bearing, bears the name of his
mother's pride: Cain (*Kayin*), related to *kanithi*, from a root *kanah*,
meaning to possess; also perhaps related to *koneh*, meaning to form
or shape or make or create. Cain, a formed being, a being created
and possessed by his mother, will become a proud farmer, the sort of
man who lays possessive claim to the earth and who is proud of his
ability to bring forth—to create—fruit from the ground. Cain, the
firstborn,[1] is sitting pretty.

In contrast, the birth of Abel, the younger, is uncelebrated by
his mother. Though no explanation is given for his name (unlike for
Cain's), he is, prophetically, given a name that means "breath-that-
vanishes." Abel, introduced only as "his brother Abel," seems to be

---

1. Cain is firstborn not only in his family. He is the first human being to
be born of woman, that is, to be *born* at all. His father was made from the
dust; his mother from the father's rib. Thus Cain, rather than his parents,
is truly the human prototype, his pride included.

an afterthought. There is no described relation to his mother; instead he is important only or mainly as Cain's brother.

Were we to know nothing more of the two brothers, we would still have enough with which to think about their relationship. Even apart from differences in inborn nature or those resulting from parental favoritism or neglect, birth order alone sets the stage. Younger siblings face difficulties because they come on the scene with their older brothers (or sisters) firmly established—in size, in ability, and in their parents' affections. The younger, regarded as underdog, elicits our sympathy. But the eldest, too, faces serious and more subtle difficulties. The object of parental pride, he feels that more is expected of him—and, more often than not, it is. More than his younger siblings, he bears the burden of a need to please; his failures he knows will disappoint.

Moreover, the birth of his siblings makes a radical change in the world as he has known it. Previously the sole apple of each parent's eye, now he has competition—especially for his mother's attention. Why, he must silently ask himself, did they have another one, unless there were something wrong with me, something they are keeping hidden? Because anger at his parents for his displacement is dangerous and counterproductive, the firstborn lodges all his resentment with the innocent newcomer. (As one firstborn nakedly put it when baby sibling was but a few days old: "Mom, why don't we flush her down the toilet before she gets too big?") The more beloved and favored and happy the firstborn, the more difficult it may be for him to accept the second, and the more important it will be for him to prove himself superior. These rivalries can be further accentuated by differences in habits and ways of life, as, indeed, they are in our present story.

Occupational Difference and More

Now Abel was a keeper of sheep and Cain was a tiller of the ground. (Genesis 4.2)

The two occupations of the brothers echo two earlier remarks about the human work. Herding sheep reminds us of having dominion—ruling—over the animals, the work announced in Genesis 1.26, 28, the majestic story in which man is godlike, the world harmonious,

and all is seen to be very good. Tilling the earth is the way anticipated and forecast in the so-called second creation story (Genesis
2.5, 3.23), the story that shows how badness and hardship enter
and complicate human existence. Cain, the new man and heir of the
second account, appears to be following the life God foretold for man
outside the Garden (like many a firstborn, he takes over "the family
business"); in this sense, one might think Cain "obedient." But, as
Robert Sacks observes,

> The only disturbing thing is his name. It implies that,
> for Cain, to be a farmer means to put up fences and to
> establish a private tract of land which one can call one's
> own, rather than fulfilling one's duty to the fruitful-
> ness of the earth. Abel's way of life leaves the world
> open. Shepherds need no fences and roam through the whole.[2]

Yet the difference is greater still.

Farming requires intellectual sophistication and psychic discipline: wit is necessary to foresee the possibility of bread from grain,
to develop tools, to protect crops; self-control—indeed, a massive
change in the psychodynamics of need and satisfaction—is needed
before anyone will work today so that he might eat months later.
Agriculture goes with possession of land and settled habitation; it
represents a giant step toward human self-sufficiency, yet it is also
precarious and very dependent on rain (Genesis 2.5). Because he
mixes his labor with the earth, the farmer claims possession not
only of the crops but also of the land itself. For the same reason, he
is even inclined to regard himself as responsible—creatively as
maker—for the produce itself. The farmer is an audacious and self-
assertive character.

The shepherd, in contrast, lives a simple and by and large art-
less life. His work is mild and gentle; his rule requires no violence.
The sheep graze as they roam and produce wool and milk out of
their own substance, the shepherd contributing nothing but also
harming nothing. Though he wanders the earth as he pleases, the

---

2. Robert Sacks, "The Lion and the Ass: A Commentary on the Book of
Genesis (Chapters 1–10)," *Interpretation*, vol. 8, nos. 2/3 (1980), p. 68.

shepherd has no illusions of self-sufficiency; indeed, he is likely to
feel acutely the dependence of his entire life on powers not under
his control and processes not of his own creation.

In sum, Cain's way of life, like the man himself, is more complex: possessive, artful, potentially harmful, and dangerous, but with
the prospect of the higher achievements (and risks) of civilization.
Abel's way, like the man, is simple: open and permissive, harmless,
and certainly vulnerable (especially before craft, cunning, and tech-
nique) and, besides, incapable of accomplishing much of anything.
Abel's way is fragile, not to say impossible; Cain's way is problematic, not to say indecent—unless it can be educated and restrained.
Everything depends on whether the possession and the use of the
land are just and whether Cain's pride can be tamed by remembering that not he but God—a power beyond—is the source of his
farmerly success. The immediate sequel faces this question fron-
tally.

Sacrifice: Pride or Submission?

> In the course of time [*miketz yamim*; literally, "at the end
> of days"] it came to pass that Cain brought of the fruit of
> the ground an offering unto the Lord, and Abel, too,
> brought of the firstlings of his flock and of the fat thereof.
> (Genesis 4.3–4)

Sacrifice is of human origins. God neither commands nor requests
it; we have no reason to believe that He even welcomes it. On the
contrary, we have reason to suspect—and will soon give ample evidence to defend this suspicion—that the human impulse to sacrifice
is, to say the least, highly problematic, especially from God's point
of view. To be sure, God will eventually command sacrifices, though
then only under the strictest rules. As in so many other matters,
the problematic is permitted but only if regulated. Because He will
not, or cannot, extirpate the dangerous impulses in men, God makes
concessions to them, while, at the same time, containing them under explicit and precise commandments. The present story, which
begins the reader's education regarding the questionable nature of
sacrifices, should arouse our suspicion because it is Cain who is
their inventor and founder.

Competing yet deep-seated passions lie beneath the human impulse to give a share or to pay tribute to the divine, to offer gifts and oblations to God or gods. To begin with, there are fear and gratitude—fear that, unless appeased with presents, the powers that be will thwart (or ignore) our hopes and wreck our plans; gratitude for experienced good results and good fortune, interpreted as divine favor directed at us. Less "rational" are "the ecstatic passions," associated with bloody and orgiastic sacrifice (in Greece, the province of Dionysus); these appear to play no part in the present offering, but they will figure in Noah's sacrifice after the flood and in many later and equally questionable biblical sacrifices.[3]

The impulse to sacrifice need not be at all impulsive. It is frequently a matter of rational calculation, not to say cunning manipulation. Man may seek to put the gods in his debt, or, more nakedly, to bribe them into delivering benefits and withholding harms. Any human being, conscious of being at the mercy of powers not under his command, will attempt to do something to improve, or avoid, his fate. For primitive man, in the wide open spaces—and especially for farmers, eager for rain—the powers of concern were the powers aloft, including the sun and the moon, the wind, and the rain. It is perfectly fitting that the primordial farmer be the first to think of sacrifice—even before he knows anything at all about who the gods really are.

Indeed, ignorance of the divine—and the wish to dispel that ignorance—is itself another powerful motive for bringing sacrifice. Men intuit the presence of higher powers, perhaps first through the experience of awe and wonder before the spectacles and phenomena of nature: sunrise and sunset, new and full moons, thunder and lightning, and the fall of water out of the sky. Natural piety gives rise to the desire to close the gap between the human and the divine, to mediate the distance, to establish ties, to gain a close and firm connection to the whole and its ruling forces. This, too, is an appropriate enough desire for the first truly human earthlings.

---

3. One might even argue that it is these ubiquitous wild impulses that are being excited only to be repulsed in the story of the binding of Isaac, which shows, once and for all, that the God of Abraham—unlike the deities worshipped by others—does not want child sacrifice.

But it is no simple matter to act on this desire. For how can and ought one communicate with what is so remote, unknown, or inscrutable? Unless man knows *who* God is and *what* (if anything) He wants, communicating will be strictly a shot in the dark. Curiously, however, human beings do not behave as if God were mysterious and inscrutable. On the contrary, both the fact of offering sacrifice and the particular gift offered bespeak certain clear—and clearly presumptuous—assumptions about the divine: (1) God is (gods are) the kind of being(s) that does (do) or could care for me; (2) He (or they) would be more likely to care for me—do me good and not evil—if I could please Him (them); (3) I could please Him (them) with gifts. Why? Because *I* am pleased by gifts. Unspoken premise: the gods are just like me; (4) He (they) must like what I like (same premise of similitude).

The deep ambiguity at the heart of the human impulse to sacrifice now stands revealed: all the underlying assumptions—even in the best case, a sacrifice from pure gratitude—are in fact expressions of human pride and presumption, masquerading as true submission. Any deity worthy of the name must, no doubt, see this for what it is worth.[4]

Cain, the initiator, addresses the divine as eater. He brings before the (to him unknown) god or gods "of the fruit of the ground," *his* produce, but produce—he must be aware—that depends on the gods' sending rain. In what spirit Cain brings his gift we cannot be sure. But the text hints at possible halfheartedness: he waited until "the end of days" to offer; and, unlike his brother Abel, who (though

---

4. God will, later, *reluctantly* command and institutionalize sacrifice, once it becomes clear that the children of Israel need sensuous experience in coming closer to God. The crucial text is Exodus 24, describing the wild sacrifice and then the sensualist experience of the elders on Mount Sinai, following which God immediately lays down the law for the building of the tabernacle, the place of sacrifice. Finding a mean between absolute remoteness and absolute nearness, and between absolute inscrutability and complete knowledge, God permits man "to approach" by practices *already familiar to human beings.* The human and the humanly ambiguous are brought under law and sanctified by God's commandments. But one must first see—as we begin to see in the present story—why the unregulated and unsanctified human impulse is so troubling.

LEON R. KASS   121

merely a follower) brought the *best* portions (the fat) of the *first-lings* of the flock, Cain's gift was indifferent or worse.[5] But, as we have shown, the sacrifice itself is ambiguous enough—especially when not commanded, especially when coming from a farmer like Cain.

> And the Lord had respect unto Abel and to his offering;
> but unto Cain and to his offering He had not respect.
> And Cain was very wroth and his countenance fell.
> (Genesis 4.4–5)

The economy of the text leaves big questions unanswered. Hidden are God's *reasons* for respecting Abel's offer and not Cain's. Did He discern a difference in intent and disposition, along the lines hinted at above? Does God simply prefer Abel's way of life to that of Cain, a difference that might be reflected in different attitudes toward the world and the divine? We do not know. We are, it seems, meant to focus on the outer fact alone.

Looking only at what we do know, we must avoid a common misperception. As Robert Sacks has pointed out, "Cain's sacrifice was not rejected but merely not yet accepted . . . . From Cain's reaction it appears as though he understood God's disregarding his sacrifice as a simple rejection, but this is not necessarily the case."[6] The sequel will bear this out. But we must first face Cain's anger—the first human display of this crucially human and ever-dangerous passion—and also his shame ("his countenance fell").

Anger, Shame, and Justice

Both the shame and the anger have their roots in pride, wounded pride. Cain, the firstborn, the proud farmer proud of his own produce, first also in his relation to God as the "inventor" of sacrifices, desires to be first and best and to be so recognized. His younger brother, a lazy shepherd, a mere follower in gift-giving, has surpassed him in God's respect. Cain feels the sting of shame, as the world does not affirm his lofty self-image. But, still proud, he takes the loss as a slight or insult; he not only hangs his head in disgrace,

---

5. In a famous Greek tale, Prometheus, who first taught men to sacrifice, showed them how to save the best portions for themselves.

6. Sacks, *The Lion and the Ass,* p. 69.

he fills his heart with rage, for he believes that he has been not only harmed but injured. Though it isn't pretty, Cain's anger carries the world's first (outraged) sense of (in)justice.

The intrinsic connection between anger and justice has been noted since antiquity. Aristotle calls anger "an impulse . . . to revenge . . . caused by an obvious *unjustified* slight," and slight, "an active display of opinion about something one takes to be worthless." A man feels especially slighted—unjustly—by "those to whom he looks for good treatment—persons, that is, who are indebted to him for benefits, past or present, which they have received from him." Cain's display of anger reveals retroactively his state of soul in making the sacrifice. Because he had sought to place God in his debt by means of his gift, Cain feels slighted by what he takes to be God's unjustified rejection of his offering. If indeed part of Cain's anger is directed at the divine, it shows how presumptuous and hubristic were his expectations.

More likely, however, Cain's anger is directed mainly at his brother. God, after all, is invisible and (up to this point) silent; for all Cain truly knows of divinity, there may not even be a being capable of bestowing slights and favors. And, be this as it may, it is surely safer to displace (not necessarily by a conscious process) his anger at God onto his human rival, in whose absence God would not have found him to be merely second best. The bitterness of not having his own gift respected is nothing compared with that of seeing the greater success of his (lesser) brother. Cain treats Abel's success in sacrifice as if Abel had been trying to outdo him.

Rousseau has captured this essentially human (all too human) phenomenon, showing the evils that lurk in the otherwise reasonable and fruitful concern for self-esteem:

> Everyone began to look at everyone else and to wish to be looked at himself, and public esteem acquired a value. The one who sang or danced the best, the handsomest, the strongest, the most skillful, or the most eloquent came to be the most highly regarded, and this was the first step at once toward inequality and vice: from these first preferences arose vanity and contempt on the one hand, shame and envy on the other; and the fermentation caused by these new leavens eventually produced compounds fatal to happiness and innocence.

As soon as men had begun to appreciate one another, and the idea of regard [*consideration*] had taken shape in their mind, *everyone claimed a right to it,* and one could no longer with impunity fail to show it toward anyone. From this arose the first duties of civility even among Savages, and from it any intentional wrong became an affront [or "outrage"] because, together with the harms resulting from the injury, the offended party saw in it contempt for his own person, often more unbearable than the harm itself. Thus everyone punishing the contempt shown him *in a manner proportionate to the stock he set by himself, vengeance became terrible,* and *men bloodthirsty and cruel.*[7]

Cain, not treated as he thought he deserved, smoldered with resentment at Abel, who was treated better than Cain thought he deserved, who had in fact usurped—de facto—his pride of place. No wonder he was angry.

God enters the picture in an attempt to assuage Cain's fury; indeed, He expresses (feigned?) surprise that Cain should be angry at all:

And the Lord said unto Cain: "Why art thou wroth? and why is thy countenance fallen? If thou doest well, shall there not be a lifting? But if you do not do well, sin shall be couching [*rovetz*] at your door; its desire shall be for you, but you shall rule over it." (Genesis 4.6–7)

Trying to comfort and encourage Cain, God makes clear that his sacrifice has not been rejected. Rather, acceptance will come provided Cain "does well." We must now try to put ourselves in Cain's place.

No doubt Cain ought to be pleased by God's attention and interest in him. (Though He respected Abel's offering, God speaks only to Cain; Cain seems to hold more interest, being both more promising and more problematic.) The promise of a lifting—of his sacrifice, of his countenance, and of his fallen dignity and standing—ought to

7. Jean-Jacques Rousseau, "Discourse on the Origin and Foundations of Inequality among Men," *The First and Second Discourses and the Essay on the Origin of Languages,* Victor Gourevitch, trans. and ed. (New York: Harper & Row, 1986), pp. 175–76, emphasis added.

be encouraging. Yet God's counsel is surely puzzling, not to say Delphic. Indeed, this part of God's speech (Genesis 4.7) is regarded as one of the most difficult passages in the entire Bible. One must not assume that Cain found it less obscure than we.

God's counsel, whatever it finally means, seems to assume that notions of "doing well" and "not doing well" are present and clear to human beings, without further instruction; for human beings do indeed have some kind of knowledge of good and bad. True, there has been no given law; there are as yet no well-defined crimes or punishments. Still, human beings act, moved by their own perceptions of better and worse. "Do well," exhorted the Lord; and even if you don't do well, and thus even if sin is in your way, ready to pounce like a wild animal, you will be able to rule over it. If God intended to warn Cain of the dangers lurking in his own heart, he might have found a clearer way to do so; and, clear or not, the overall message—"Do well; you can master the obstacles"—was not, on balance, a teaching of self-restraint. Cain, still angry, now put his mind to "doing well."

Those who wonder why God might not have produced a more powerful and successful antidote to Cain's anger might wish to consider God's speech as if it were (rather) the voice of reason and goodness—such as these might exist in "natural man"—manifesting itself (as if coming "from the outside") against a soul filled with rage (like the appearance of Athena, who suddenly appears and prevents Achilles from drawing his sword on Agamemnon in Book I of the *Iliad*). "Be reasonable," says the voice, "bide your time, you'll get your position back. Do well." The voice of reason is, first of all, concerned with our own good; otherwise, we will not listen. Absent very *specific* instructions and delineations, rationality is experienced not as counseling the other fellow's good, but as promising my own—not now, but later, that is, if I "do well" and "overcome sin,"[8] which threatens to get in my way and drag me down. The sequel shows how little availing are such vague instructions in the face of vengeful passions. They might even be understood to *counsel* revenge—only not impulsively, but with due calculation and premeditation. Primordial human knowledge of good and bad may be used self-

---

8. The word for sin, *chatath*, comes from a root, *chata*, which means "to miss the mark." To the morally uninstructed, like Cain, it might mean simply "failure."

righteously, but it is a far cry from righteousness. This we readers quickly learn from the ensuing events.

Fratricide

> And Cain appointed a place where to meet Abel his brother [literally, "And said (*vayomer*)[9] Cain to (*el*) Abel his brother"], and it happened when they were in the field, that Cain rose up against [*el*] Abel his brother, and killed him. (Genesis 4.8)

Cain uses his reason to help take his revenge. He plans the event, employs speech to arrange Abel's presence, and picks a place out in the fields where no one will see and where no one can come to Abel's rescue. But if reason is the instrument, jealousy remains the likely motive: the hated rival is removed. But gain might also have been on Cain's mind; with Abel out of the way, his flocks would belong to Cain, who might then be able to offer a respectable sacrifice (or who might now flourish, despite the bad harvest). And, to stretch the point perhaps beyond what is reasonable, Cain may even have thought this is precisely what was meant by "doing well." For how was he to know that murder is bad, it not having been forbidden? Because the deed was committed not in heat but with premeditation, we must assume Cain believed that he was doing good—at least for himself.

Whatever he may have thought beforehand, he soon learns, painfully, the wrongness of his deed—and so do we.

> And the Lord said unto Cain: "Where is Abel thy brother?"
> And he said: "I know not [*lo yodati*]; am I my brother's keeper [*hashomer achi onokhi*]?"
> And He said: "What hast thou done? the voice of thy brother's blood cries unto me from the ground."(Genesis 4.9–10)

---

9. In this expansive rendering of *vayomer,* I follow U. Cassuto's reading in *A Commentary on the Book of Genesis, Part One: From Adam to Noah* (Jerusalem: Magnes Press, 1964, p. 213), though little is lost to the argument by leaving the text in its original opacity. It is important that Cain *said something* to Abel, indicating premeditation; it is not important to know exactly what he said.

God does not begin with an accusation or an assertion, but, like both a good teacher and a good investigator, with a question, and with a question that requires Cain to confront himself in his brotherliness: Your brother Abel, your young playmate, out of the same womb: Why is he not at your side? Where is he?

Cain denies knowledge of Abel's whereabouts. Though an analytic philosopher might try to argue that Cain's speech is true—for where indeed is the soul of Abel now?—Cain, to protect himself, lies to God (or, if you prefer, to his newly aroused conscience), but not to himself. Indeed, to keep the inquisitive voice from forcing him to confront fully the meaning of his deed, he answers the question with a question, no doubt tinged with indignation and even mocking: Why are you asking *me*? Am *I* supposed to be his guardian? *You*, you who liked his sacrifice, you who made him prosper—aren't *you* his keeper? Why don't you know where he is? And (implicitly), what kind of a guardian are *you*?

God (or "conscience") is not deceived. Taking Cain's counteroffensive to be a tacit admission of guilt, He puts the well-timed question to Cain: What have you done?! Of course I know where Abel is. I have heard *your* brother's spilled blood crying out unto Me from the earth. How could you have done such a thing to your *brother*?

The enormity of his deed is now borne in on Cain, thanks to the awesome intervention of the transcendent voice. The image of the screaming blood of his brother awakens Cain's horror; a "protoreligious" dread accompanies this picture of violent death. Very likely, guilt wells up in response to the accusation implied by the screams, as does pity for his fallen brother. Even the murderer cannot but be moved. Not just the will of Abel, but the cosmos itself has been violated; the crime is a crime against "blood"—against both life and kin; the whole earth, polluted and stained with bloodshed, cries in anguish and for retribution. We anticipate precisely God's next remarks.

"And now cursed art thou from the ground, which hath opened her mouth to receive thy brother's blood from thy hand. When thou tillest the ground, it shall not henceforth yield unto thee her strength; a fugitive and a wanderer shalt thou be in the earth." (Genesis 4.11–12)

The earth that supports life, now defiled by life's wanton destruction—watered not by (the wished-and-sacrificed-for) rain but by blood, shed by the farmer's hand—becomes an alien place for the murderer. The world is arranged so that murder will not go unnoticed; it will also not go unanswered. The earth shall resist the murderer's plow; nowhere on earth shall he find a comfortable place to settle, both because no one else will welcome him and because his conscience and his fears will give him no rest. A man who has once shed blood knows in his marrow that his own life hangs by a thread, that he lives, as it were, by the grace of God. Despite the fact that God does not exact the fitting specific (capital) punishment for his murder—as there is yet no law against it, there can be no exact punishment (see Genesis 9.6, Exodus 21.12)—Cain is nonetheless thrown into despair.

> And Cain said unto the Lord, "My punishment [*avoni*; or "my sin"] is greater than I can bear. Behold, Thou has driven me out this day from the face of the earth; *and from Thy face shall I be hid*; and I shall be a fugitive and a wanderer in the earth; and it shall come to pass that *everyone that findeth me shall slay me*." (Genesis 4.13–14, emphasis added)

Cain's fears lead him to exaggerate the "punishment." He understands—mistakenly—that he is banished from the whole earth, and that, in wandering, he will be out of sight of the (a merely local god's?) divine protection, exposed to predators not unlike himself, men who will kill him for gain or for sport. Cain, the farmer, the man who sought security in settlement and possession of a portion of the earth, feels utterly bereft at the prospect of wandering—of living an open life such as that of his brother Abel. Believing that God defends only those who are settled and established—after all, God was apparently not able to protect Abel out in the fields—Cain fears for his life once he is forced to roam about among uncivilized men.

God addresses Cain's fear of violent death:

> And the Lord said unto him, "Therefore, whosoever slayeth Cain, vengeance shall be taken on him sevenfold." And the Lord set a mark upon Cain, lest any finding him should slay him. (Genesis 4.15)

The mark of Cain—wrongly regarded as the sign of murderous guilt—is, in fact, meant to protect Cain's life in the wilderness, and to obviate the need for settled defense. Reassured but only temporarily, Cain sets out on his travels.

> And Cain went out from the presence of the Lord, and
> dwelt in the land of Nod, on the east of Eden. (Genesis 4.16)

Heading backward toward the Garden, longing perhaps for its safety and comfort, Cain comes to the land of Nod—literally, the land of "wandering"—and he *settles* there! Though he is in the place of wanderers, Cain refuses to wander. He lacks trust—in nature, in God, and in his fellow human beings. He would rather rely on his wits and his own flesh and blood to sustain and defend him. These he trusts because these he knows.

Cain's Second Sailing: A City of One's Own

> And Cain knew his wife,[10] and she conceived, and bore
> Enoch; and he builded a city, and called the name of the
> city after the name of his son Enoch. (Genesis 4.17)

Having broken his ties to his origins, now alone, vulnerable, and without refuge, Cain deals with his predicament by looking to the future. Aware of the prospect of violent death, he takes out insurance. Knowing his wife, Cain fathers a son, whom he names Enoch, meaning "to initiate or discipline; to dedicate or train up." Cain initiates a family to which he will dedicate himself, and which he will discipline and train up in the ways of dedication. Unlike the later (and precociously modern) builders of the city of Babel, who seek a

---

10. On a literalist-historical reading of the text, there is no woman (other than Eve) mentioned who might be eligible to be the wife of Cain. This silence leads to unpleasant inferences, the most palatable of which is brother-sister incest with (unmentioned) daughters of Eve. Silently, the text may be hinting that, at the human beginning, incest may be unavoidable. (My wife was kicked out of Sunday school at age six for asking about the wife of Cain.) But read anthropologically, rather than historically, Cain is the human prototype: farmer, fratricide, and founder of the first city, in defense of his own. *That* he had a wife (and descendants), not where she came from or who she was, is what we here need to know.

name for themselves here and now, the city Cain builds is dedicated
to the name of his son. The city is almost certainly founded on the
fear of death and with a view to safety.

The Hebrew word for city, *iyr*, comes from a root meaning "to
watch" and "to wake." In the first instance, a city is a place guarded
by a wakeful watch; it is not the market or the shrine but the watch-
tower or outpost that first makes a city a city. Though Cain retains
his pride (in his son), his confidence has been tempered by fear. But
civilization as it comes into being starting from his founding act is
tainted: the city is founded in fear of violent death, but first, in
fratricide. This taint, one must believe, is, from the Bible's point of
view, inherent in civilization as such. We follow its emergence in
the hope of learning why and how it may be defective.

> And unto Enoch was born Irad [meaning "fugitive"];
> and Irad begot Mehujael [meaning "smitten of God" or "seer
> of God"];
> and Mehujael begot Methushael [meaning "man who is of
> God"];
> and Methushael begot Lamech [meaning is obscure].
> And Lamech took unto him two wives:
> the name of one was Adah [meaning "ornament"],
> and the name of the other Zillah [meaning "shadow" or "de-
> fense"].
> And Adah bore Jabal [from a root meaning "to flow," "to lead,"
> "to bring forth"]:
> he was the father of such as dwell in tents and of such as
> have cattle.
> And his brother's name was Jubal [same root as for Jabal]:
> he was the father of all such as handle the harp and pipe.
> And Zillah, she also bore Tubal-Cain [meaning unclear; per-
> haps "Tubal the smith"], the instructor of every artificer
> in brass and iron;
> and the sister of Tubal-Cain was Naamah [meaning "pleas-
> antness"]. (Genesis 4.18–22)

Our attention is focused on Lamech, the seventh—the completed or fulfilled—generation of the line (through Cain) begun by
Adam. It is in this generation that civilization flowers. With one
wife an ornament, the other a shadowy protector, Lamech has chil-

dren who teach men how to protect and adorn themselves: they introduce tents, fixed habitations against the elements and for protection of privacy; cattle, a new form of wealth; music, the arts of memory and song; and metallurgy, the transformative art of forging tools and also weapons. Human beings, now externally well equipped, undergo coincident changes in their souls. In particular, vanity—the desire to be well regarded by those around—grows to dangerous proportions.

> And Lamech said unto his wives: "Adah and Zillah, Hear my voice; ye wives of Lamech, hearken unto my speech; For I have slain a man to my wounding, and a young man to my bruising. If Cain shall be avenged sevenfold, truly Lamech seventy and sevenfold." (Genesis 4.23–24)

Lamech combines poetry and prowess in his own person; he sings (the Hebrew is in high poetic style) of his own exploits in fighting, and boasts of his great superiority, ten times greater than Cain's, greater even than God in vengeance.[11] Lamech, a combination Achilles-and-Homer, belongs to the heroic age, made possible by the arts, especially music and metallurgy; he seeks nothing less than immortal fame, not to say apotheosis itself, by being master of life and death.

Founding and Fratricide

We are now in a position to pull together some threads, connecting the deeds of Cain and the civilization that rests upon them. Concerned with his position as number one, eager to establish himself as lord and master of his domain, Cain (like Romulus, the mythic founder of Rome) commits the paradigmatic crime of the political founder: fratricide. For the aspiration to rule entails necessarily the denial and destruction of radical human equality, epitomized in the relationship of brotherhood. To wish to rule, to dominate, to be in command, means—by its very nature—the wish not only to re-

---

11. Lamech's claims are not quite clear. Most translators have him taking fatal revenge on men who merely wounded or bruised him. But Cassuto, in his usual careful analysis of the precise wording, argues that it is Lamech who is doing the wounding and bruising; but so great is his strength, his mere taps proved fatal: "A man I slew, as soon as I bruised (him)." In either case, Lamech boasts in song of his prowess in killing his enemies.

move all rivals, but also to destroy the brotherly relation with those under one's dominion. The ruler, as ruler, has no brothers.

The more that rude and ambitious men have to do with one another, the more they both have to fear and seek to outdo one another. For both reasons—safety and pride—they cultivate prowess in fighting. And the city begun in fear proudly begets one of heroic ambition. There is a direct line from the plowshare to the sword.

But the context here is not simply political. Cain was jealous over a matter of *divine* favor. Cain was the first to be interested in bridging the gap—in his case, by gifts—between the human and the divine, an impulse we have shown to be largely *hubristic*. This prototypical human being begets a line leading to civilization, the arts, and the heroes—all manifestations of an impulse that culminates in a desire to jump the gap entirely, in a wish to *become* a god. Lamech, the hero, acts as if he has succeeded; but we, readers prepared by what has come before, know that he is self-deceived.

The present story—of Cain and Abel, and the line of Cain to Lamech—does not explicitly give the reasons for rejecting paganism; but it surely paints a vivid picture of the bloody indecency connected with the way of Cain and the pursuit of self-sufficiency and heroism. The elements of the human soul that lead in this direction are shown to be, to say the least, problematic. So too our much vaunted "knowledge" of good and bad. Seeing something of himself in the mirror of this story, the reader is stimulated to hope that there is an alternative to the human-all-too-human way of Cain.

Another Beginning

The menacing outcome of the line of Cain—the line of pride, presumption, violence, the arts of death, and the desire for apotheosis—begs for another way. We are not disappointed. The story ends as it began, with a new birth.

And Adam knew his wife again; and she bore a son, and called his name Seth: "for God hath appointed me another seed instead of Abel; for Cain slew him." And to Seth, to him also there was born a son; and he called his name Enosh; *then began men to call upon the name of the Lord*. (Genesis 4.25–26, emphasis added)

Though the description echoes closely the birth of Cain, there are crucial differences. No longer boastful, Eve is, instead, subdued. The death of Abel hangs heavily upon her, as does the fact that it was Cain, her pride and joy (but now also lost to her), who slew him. Chastened regarding also her own pride in Cain's birth, she feels only gratitude in the birth of Seth. She feels the beneficence of powers beyond her, here manifested in the birth of a much-wanted replacement. Seth, unlike Cain, is received as a gift—from beyond, precious, unmerited. Seth, unlike Cain, will be less likely to suffer from excessive parental expectations. Tragedy has humbled parental pride; woman and man no longer stand as creators and claimants upon the world, but as grateful recipients of the blessings of new life.

To Seth also is born a son, whom he names Enosh, a name that means "man, understood as *mortal*"—a meaning less dignified than that of *adam* ("man," understood as "from the earth," *adamah*). Enosh, mortal man, in the line of Seth corresponds to Enoch, disciplined dedication, in the line of Cain: the greater modesty of the new beginnings is evident in the names. No longer disciplined in trying to jump the gap between man and god, the line of Seth is marked near its start by the memory of death—Abel's—and by the recognition of the difference between mortal man and immortal God.

In keeping with this new recognition, "men began to call upon the name of the Lord." How they called or what they said the text keeps inaudible—in sharp contrast to the loud vauntings of Lamech, or even to the explicit report of the goods brought in sacrifice by Cain and Abel. True, there remains a more than residual presumption in calling upon God—as if He should care for me—and, even more, in the familiarity of calling Him *by name*. But, at the same time, we have what seems like a spontaneous calling out—springing from the heart without calculation—probably out of need and fear, perhaps also out of love or respect. Recognizing the gap between man and God, Seth, Enosh, and their kin call out across it, hoping someone will listen. Of God's response, we know nothing. But we cannot help but think that some progress has been made: the new approach to the divine proceeds through speech and hearing, not through gifts of food that we hope God might fancy. Someone seems to have divined that it is not through material means—nor through pride of place or acquisition—that man can hope to stand in fitting relation to God. Someone seems to have divined that—

more than the arts and sciences, power, and prosperity—decent human life and human relations require just such a reverent and attentive orientation to the divine.

Even a civilized and sophisticated reader, late in the twentieth century, cannot help but agree. Chastened by this profound tale that mirrors the dark recesses of our own souls and that exposes the shady and violent origins of the human city, we are ready to read on and to receive further instruction.

13

Culture and Kristol

Robert H. Bork

> *[W]hat began to concern me more and more were the clear signs of rot and decadence germinating within American society—a rot and decadence that was no longer the consequence of liberalism but was the actual agenda of contemporary liberalism. . . . [S]ector after sector of American life has been ruthlessly corrupted by the liberal ethos. It is an ethos that aims simultaneously at political and social collectivism on the one hand, and moral anarchy on the other.*
>
> IRVING KRISTOL
"My Cold War"

Equivocation has never been Irving Kristol's long suit. About the fact of rot and decadence there can be no dispute, except from those who deny that such terms have meaning, and who are, for that reason, major contributors to rot and decadence. We are accustomed to lamentations about American crime rates, the devastation wrought by drugs, rising illegitimacy, the decline of civility, and the increasing vulgarity of popular entertainment. But the manifestations of American cultural decline are even more widespread, ranging across virtually the entire society, from the violent underclass of the inner cities to our cultural and political elites, from rap music to literary studies, from pornography to law, from journalism to scholarship, from union halls to universities. Wherever one looks, the traditional virtues of this culture are being lost, its vices multiplied, its values degraded—in short, the culture itself is unraveling.

These can hardly be random or isolated developments. A degeneration so universal, afflicting so many seemingly disparate areas, must proceed from common causes. That supposition is strengthened by the observation that similar trends seem to be occurring in all or at least most Western industrialized democracies. The main features of these trends are vulgarity and a persistent left-wing bias, the latter being particularly evident among the semi-skilled intellectuals—academics, bureaucrats, and the like—that Kristol calls the New Class.

But why should this be happening? The short answer is the one Kristol gives: the rise of modern liberalism. (The extent to which he would agree with the following argument about the sources and future of modern liberalism, I do not know.) Modern liberalism grew out of classical liberalism by expanding its central ideals—liberty and equality—while progressively jettisoning the restraints of religion, morality, and law even as technology lowered the constraint of hard work imposed by economic necessity. Those ideals, along with the right to pursue happiness, are what we said we were about at the beginning, in the Declaration of Independence. Stirring as rallying cries for rebellion, less useful, because indeterminate, for the purpose of arranging political and cultural matters, they become positively dangerous when taken, without very serious qualifications, as social ideals.

The qualifications assumed by the founders' generation, but unexpressed in the Declaration (it would rather have spoiled the rhetoric to have added "up to a point"), have gradually been peeled away so that today liberalism has reached an extreme, though not one fears its ultimate, stage. "Equality" has become radical egalitarianism (the equality of outcomes rather than of opportunities), and "liberty" takes the form of radical individualism (a refusal to admit limits to the gratifications of the self). In these extreme forms, they are partly produced by, and partly produce, the shattering of fraternity (or community) that modern liberals simultaneously long for and destroy.

Individualism and egalitarianism may seem an odd pair, for liberty in any degree produces inequality, while equality of outcomes requires coercion that destroys liberty. If they are to operate simultaneously, radical egalitarianism and radical individualism, where they do not complement one another, must operate in different areas of life, and that is precisely what we see in today's culture. Radical egalitarianism advances, on the one hand, in areas of life and society where superior achievement is possible and would be rewarded but for coerced equality: quotas, affirmative action, income redistribution through progressive taxation for some, entitlement programs for others, and the tyranny of political correctness spreading through universities, primary and secondary schools, government, and even the private sector. Radical individualism, on the other hand, is demanded when there is no danger that achievement will produce inequality and people wish to be unhindered in the pursuit of pleasure. This finds expression particularly in the areas of sexuality and violence, and their vicarious enjoyment in popular entertainment.

Individualism and egalitarianism do not always divide the labor of producing cultural decay. Often enough they collaborate. When egalitarianism reinforces individualism, denying the possibility that one culture or moral view can be superior to another, the result is cultural and moral relativism, whose end products include multiculturalism, sexual license, obscenity in the popular arts, the unwillingness to punish crime adequately and, sometimes, even to convict the obviously guilty. Both the individualist and the egalitarian (usually in the same skin) are antagonistic to society's traditional hierarchies or lines of authority—the one because his pleasures can be maximized only by freedom from authority, the other because he resents any distinction among people or forms of behavior that suggests superiority in one or the other.

The universality of these forces is indicated by the fact that they are prominent features of two institutions at opposite ends of the cultural spectrum: the Supreme Court of the United States and rock music.

The Court reflects modern cultural trends most obviously when it invents new rights of the individual against the decisions of the political community, but it also does so in the expansion of rights expressed in the document beyond anything the drafters and ratifiers could have intended. Radical individualism surfaced when the Court created a right of privacy, supposedly about the sanctity of the marital bedchamber, which soon explicitly became a right of individual autonomy unconnected to privacy. Four justices subsequently pronounced it a "moral fact that a person belongs to himself and not others nor to society as a whole"—a "fact" which means that a person has no obligations outside his own skin. The same tendency is seen in the Court's drive to privatize religion, as when a girl is held to have a First Amendment right not to have to sit at graduation through a short prayer because it might offend her sensibilities. The list could be extended almost indefinitely. The autonomy the Court requires, of course, is necessarily selective, almost invariably consisting of the freedoms preferred by modern liberalism.

The Court's commitment to egalitarianism is so strong that it overrode the explicit language and legislative history of the 1964 Civil Rights Act to allow preferences for blacks and women. The Court usually argued that the preferences were for past discrimination, discrimination not against the individuals now benefited but against other members of their race or sex in the past. Even that requirement was dropped when the Court allowed preferences for minorities in the grant of station licenses by the Federal Communications Commission, despite the lack of any evidence that such grants had ever been tainted by discrimination. In these ways, the Court reflects, and hence illegitimately legitimates, the thrusts of modern liberal culture.

To point the parallel: in a book appropriately titled *The Triumph of Vulgarity*, Robert Pattison points out that rock music celebrates the unconstrained self: "The extrovert, the madman, the criminal, the suicide, or the exhibitionist can rise to heroic stature in rock for the same reasons that Byron or Raskolnikov became romantic heroes—profligacy and murder are expressions of an emotional intensity that defies the limits imposed by nature and society."[1] Rock culture teaches egalitarianism as well, not only in its frequent advocacy of revolution, but in its refusal to make distinc-

1. Robert Pattison, *The Triumph of Vulgarity: Rock Music in the Mirror of Romanticism* (Oxford: Oxford University Press, 1987), p. 122. He notes that "within its mythology rock does glorify sex, drugs, revolution, and mayhem in general as legitimate avenues of self-expression," which would seem, to put it mildly, radically individualistic, yet continues, "but if rock's myths were invariably translated into actions, the West would long since have sunk into an anarchy that would make the reign of Elagabalus look like the age of reason." Ibid., p. 176. This is the familiar the-world-has-

tions about morality or aesthetics based upon any transcendent principle. There is no such principle, only sensation, energy, the pleasure of the moment, and the expansion of the self.

Vulgarity and obscenity are, of course, rife in popular culture. Rock is followed by rap; television situation comedies and magazine advertising increasingly rely on explicit sex; such cultural icons as Roseanne Barr and Michael Jackson can be seen on family-oriented television clutching their crotches. The prospect is for more and worse. Companies are now doing billions of dollars' worth of business in pornographic videos, and volume is increasing rapidly.[2] They are acquiring inventories of the videos for cable television, and a nationwide chain of pornographic video and retail stores is in the works. One pay-per-view network operator says, "This thing is a freight train."

It is likely to become a rocket ship soon if, as George Gilder predicts, computers will soon replace television, allowing viewers to call up digital films and files of news, art, and multimedia from around the world.[3] He dismisses conservatives' fears that "the boob tube will give way to what H. L. Mencken might have termed a new Boobissimus, as the liberated children rush away from the network nurse, chasing Pied Piper pederasts, snuff-film sadists, and other trolls of cyberspace." Gilder concedes, "Under the sway of television, democratic capitalism enshrines a Gresham's law: bad culture drives out good, and ultimately porn and prurience, violence and blasphemy prevail everywhere from the dimwitted 'news' shows to the lugubrious movies." But he blames that on the nature of broadcast technology, which requires central control and reduces the audience to its lowest common denominator of tastes and responses.

But the computer will give everyone his own channel: "The creator of a program on a specialized subject—from Canaletto's art to chaos theory, from GM car transmission repair to cowboy poetry,

---

not-come-to-an-end defense, but Pattison neglects to claim that our culture has not been adversely affected by the attitudes that rock and its myths inculcate. The point here, however, is not that rock is deleterious, only that it both reflects and urges radical individualism and the breaking of restraints.

2. John R. Wilke, "A Publicly Held Firm Turns X-Rated Videos into a Hot Business," *Wall Street Journal*, July 11, 1994, p. 1.

3. George Gilder, "Breaking the Box," *National Review*, August 15, 1994, p. 37.

from Szechuan restaurant finance to C++ computer codes—will be able to reach everyone in the industrialized world who shares the interest."

Perhaps. But there seems little reason to think there will not also be an enormous increase in obscene and violent programs. Many places already have about fifty cable channels, including some very good educational channels, but there are still MTV's music videos, and the porn channels are coming on line. The more private viewing becomes, the more likely that salacious and perverted tastes will be indulged. That is suggested by the explosion of pornographic film titles and profits when videocassettes enabled customers to avoid going to "adult" theaters. Another boom should occur when those customers don't even have to ask for the cassettes in a store. The new technology, while it may bring the wonders Gilder predicts, will almost certainly make our culture more vulgar and violent.

The leader of the revolution in pornographic video, referred to admiringly by a competitor as the Ted Turner of the business, offers the usual defenses of decadence: "Adults have a right to see [pornography] if they want to. If it offends you, don't buy it." Modern liberalism employs the rhetoric of "rights" incessantly to delegitimize restraints on individuals by communities. It is a pernicious rhetoric because it asserts a right without giving reasons. If there is to be anything that can be called a community, the case for previously unrecognized individual freedoms must be thought through, and "rights" cannot win every time.

The second notion—"If it offends you, don't buy it"—is both lulling and destructive. Whether you buy it or not, you will be greatly affected by those who do. The aesthetic and moral environment in which you and your family live will be coarsened and brutalized. There are economists who confuse the idea that markets should be free with the idea that everything should be on the market. The first idea rests on the efficiency of the free market in satisfying wants; the second raises the question of which wants it is moral to satisfy. The latter question brings up the topic of externalities: you are free not to make steel, but you will be affected by the air pollution of those who do make it. To complaints about pornography and violence on television, libertarians reply: "All you have to do is hit the remote control and change channels." But, like the person who chooses not to make steel, you and your family will be affected by the people who do not change the channel. As Michael Medved put it, "To say that if you don't like the popular culture then turn it off, is like saying, if you don't like the smog, stop breathing. . . . There are Amish kids in Pennsylvania who know about Madonna." And their parents can do nothing about that.

Can there be any doubt that as pornography and violence become increasingly popular and accessible entertainment, attitudes about marriage, fidelity, divorce, obligations to children, the use of force, and permissible public behavior and language will change, and with the change of attitudes will come changes in conduct, both public and private? The contrary view must assume that people are unaffected by what they see and hear. Advertisers bet billions the other way. Advocates of liberal arts education assure us those studies improve character; it is not very likely that only uplifting culture affects attitudes and behavior. "Don't buy it" and "change the channel" are simply advice to accept a degenerating culture and its consequences.

Modern liberalism also presses our politics to the left because egalitarianism is hostile to the authorities and hierarchies—moral, religious, social, economic, and intellectual—that are characteristic of a bourgeois or traditional culture and a capitalist economy. Yet modern liberalism is not hostile to hierarchy as such. Egalitarianism requires hierarchy because equality of condition cannot be achieved or approximated without coercion. The coercers will be bureaucrats and politicians who will, and already do, form a new elite class. This is the political and social collectivism that Kristol condemns. Political and governmental authority replace the authorities of family, church, profession, and business. The project is to sap the strength of these latter institutions so that individuals stand bare before the state, which, liberals assume with considerable justification, they will administer. We will be coerced into virtue, as modern liberals define virtue: a ruthlessly egalitarian society. This agenda is, of course, already well advanced.

Both diminished performance and personal injustice are accomplished through radically egalitarian measures. Quotas and affirmative action, for example, are common and increasing not only in the workplace but in university admissions, faculty hiring, and promotion. The excuse is past discrimination, but the result is that individuals who have never been discriminated against are preferred to individuals who have never discriminated, regardless of their respective achievements. Predictably, the result is anger on both sides and an increasingly polarized society. After years of struggle to emplace the principle of reward according to achievement, the achievement principle is being jettisoned for one of reward according to birth once more.

Remarkably little thought attends this process. The demand is always for more equality, but no egalitarian ever specifies how much equality will be enough. And so the leveling process grinds insensately on. The *Wall Street Journal* recently reprinted a Kurt Vonnegut story, which the paper retitled "It Seemed Like Fiction" because it was written "in 1961, before the passage of the Equal Pay Act (1963), the Civil Rights Act (1964), the Age Discrimination in Employment Act (1967), the Equal Employment Opportunity Act (1972), the Rehabilitation Act (1973), the Americans with Disabilities Act (1990), the Older Workers' Benefit Protection Act (1990), and the Civil Rights Act (1991)." At the time of reprinting, Congress was preparing hearings on "The Employment Nondiscrimination Act of 1994" and was considering additional amendments to the Civil Rights Act.[4] Even before all this, Vonnegut saw the trend and envisioned the day when Americans would achieve perfect equality: persons of superior intelligence required to wear mental handicap radios that emit a sharp noise every twenty seconds to keep them from taking unfair advantage of their brains, persons of superior strength or grace burdened with weights, those of uncommon beauty forced to wear masks. Why not?

Modern liberalism is most particularly a disease of our cultural elites, the people who control the institutions that manufacture or disseminate ideas, attitudes, and symbols—universities, some churches, Hollywood, the national press (print and electronic), much of the congressional Democratic party and some of the congressional Republicans as well, large sections of the judiciary, foundation staffs, and almost all the "public interest" organizations that exercise a profound if largely unseen effect on public policy. So pervasive is the influence of those who occupy the commanding heights of our culture that it is not entirely accurate to call the United States a majoritarian democracy. The elites of modern liberalism do not win all the battles, but despite their relatively small numbers, they win more than their share and move the culture always in one direction.

This is not a conspiracy but a syndrome. These are people who view the world from a common perspective, a perspective to the left

---

4. *Wall Street Journal*, July 29, 1994.

of the attitudes of the general public. Two explanations for this phenomenon have been advanced. Both seem accurate. One is a heretical version of Marxism, a theory of class warfare; the other might
be called a heretical version of religion, a theory of the hunger for
spirituality, for a meaning to life.

Joseph Schumpeter first articulated the idea that capitalism
requires and hence produces a large intellectual class. The members of that class are not necessarily very good at intellectual work;
they are merely people who work with or transmit ideas at wholesale or retail, the folks referred to above as our cultural elites. Irving Kristol, who elaborated on this theme, calls them the New Class.
Others call them the "knowledge class," the "class of semiskilled
intellectuals," or the "chattering class."

Why should the New Class be hostile to traditional or bourgeois society? The answer, according to the class warfare theory, is
that capitalism bestows its favors, money, and prestige on the business class. The New Class, filled with resentment and envy, seeks
to enhance its own power and prestige by attacking capitalism, its
institutions, and its morality. It is necessary to attack from the Left
because America has never had an aristocratic ethos and because
the weapons at hand are by their nature suited to the Left. The
ideas are held not for their merit but because they are weapons.

There is probably a good deal to this, but it seems not quite
sufficient. For one thing, it does not account for the Hollywood Left.
These are folks with no need whatever to envy the CEO of General
Motors his prestige or financial rewards. And no one, to my knowledge, has ever classified Barbra Streisand, Jane Fonda, Ed Asner,
and Norman Lear as intellectuals.

There is, however, an additional theory. Max Weber noted the
predicament of intellectuals in a world from which "ultimate and
sublime values" have been withdrawn: "The salvation sought by an
intellectual is always based on inner need . . . . The intellectual
seeks in various ways, the casuistry of which extends to infinity, to
endow his life with a pervasive meaning." The subsidence of religion leaves a void that must be filled. As Richard Grenier observes:
"Among intellectuals . . . most subject to longings for meaning, Max
Weber listed, prophetically: university professors, clergymen, government officials . . . 'coupon clippers,' . . . journalists, school teachers, 'wandering poets.'" By "coupon clippers," I take it Weber meant

the generations that inherit the wealth of the men who made it, which would explain why so many foundations created by wealthy conservatives become liberal when the children or grandchildren take over. And for "wandering poets," read the likes of Robert Redford and Warren Beatty. The epitome of Weber's university professors is John Rawls, whose egalitarian theory of justice swept the academy. Among other odd notions, Rawls laid it down that no inequalities are just unless they benefit the most disadvantaged members of society. There is, of course, no good reason for such a rule, and it is a prescription for permanent hostility to actual societies, and most particularly that of the United States, which can never operate in that fashion. No vital society could.

What we are seeing in modern liberalism is the ultimate triumph of the New Left of the 1960s. The New Left collapsed as a unified political movement and splintered into a multitude of intense, single-issue groups. We now have, to name but a few, radical feminists, black extremists, animal rights groups, radical environmentalists, activist homosexual groups, multiculturalists, People for the American Way, Planned Parenthood, the American Civil Liberties Union, and many more. In a real sense, however, the New Left did not collapse. Each of its splinters pursues a leftist agenda, but there is no publicly announced overarching philosophy that enables people to see easily that the separate groups and causes add up to a general radical Left philosophy. The groups support one another and come together easily on many issues. In that sense, the splintering of the New Left made it less visible and therefore more powerful, its goals more attainable, than ever before.

In their final stages, radical egalitarianism becomes tyranny and radical individualism descends into hedonism. Those translate as bread and circuses. Government grows larger and more intrusive in order to direct the distribution of goods and services in an ever more equal fashion, while people are diverted, led to believe that their freedoms are increasing, by a great variety of entertainments featuring violence and sex. David Frum argues that the root of our trouble is big government, but the root of big government is the egalitarian passion, which intimidates even many conservatives. So long as that passion persists, government is likely only to get bigger and more intrusive.

We sometimes console ourselves with the thought that our current moral anarchy and statism are merely one phase of a pendulum's swing, that in time the pendulum will swing the other way. No doubt such movements and countermovements are often observable, but it is entirely possible that they are merely epiphenomena that do not affect the larger movement of the culture. After each swing the bottom of the pendulum's arc is always further to the cultural and political Left. Certainly, in the United States, we have never experienced a period of cultural depravity and governmental intrusiveness to rival today's condition.

The prospects look bleak, moreover, if we reflect on the sources of modern liberalism's components. The root of egalitarianism lies in envy and insecurity, which are in turn products of self-pity, arguably the most pervasive and powerful emotion known to mankind. The root of individualism lies in self-interest, not always expressed as a desire for money but also for power, celebrity, pleasures, and titillations of all varieties. Western civilization, of course, has been uniquely individualistic. Envy and self-interest often have socially beneficial results, but when fully unleashed, freed of constraints, their consequences are rot, decadence, and statism.

Because they arise out of fundamental human emotions, it is obvious that individualism and egalitarianism were not invented in the 1960s. They have been working inexorably through Western civilization for centuries, perhaps for millennia, but they have only recently overcome almost all obstacles to their full realization. These forces were beneficent for most of their careers; they produced the glories of our civilization and, freed of the restraints of the past, became malignant only in this century. We are delighted that the restraints that afflicted men in the classical world, in the Middle Ages, even in the last century and much of this have been weakened or removed. Our names for particular events and eras celebrate that movement: the Renaissance, the Reformation, the Enlightenment, our own Declaration of Independence and Bill of Rights, the civil rights movement. Though they had other complex effects, all involved the loosening of restraints: religious, legal, and moral. But any progression can at last go too far.

The constraints that made individualism and egalitarianism beneficial included economic necessity, which channeled individualism into productive work, and religion (with its corollaries, morality and law), which tempered self-interest and envy. It is only in this century, and particularly in the years since World War II, that Americans have known an affluence that frees many of us from absorption with making a living, and it is in that same period that the decline in religion, which began centuries ago, reached its low point. Religious belief remains strong but seems to have a diminishing effect on behavior. And only lately have we developed the technologies that not only make work easier but also make the opportunities for sensation almost boundless. We have always known that unfettered human nature does not present an attractive face, but it is that face that is coming into view as modern liberalism progresses. It is difficult to imagine the constraints that could now be put in place to do the work that economic necessity and religion once did.

If the drive of modern liberalism cannot be blunted and then reversed, we are also likely to see an increasingly inefficient economy. The hedonism of radical individualism is not consistent with the habits of work and saving that are essential to a vigorous economy. The quotas and affirmative action that are growing in our educational institutions and in our corporations, the dilution of the achievement principle, coupled with the government's determination to intervene in the economy through manifold regulations, mandates, and taxes, will place additional burdens on productivity. Despite all we have learned from watching other economies, perhaps we are fated to repeat the socialist mistakes and suffer the inevitable consequences.

This is a picture of a bleak landscape, and there are many who disagree. Optimists point out, for example, that American culture is complex and resilient, that it contains much that is good and healthy, that many families continue to raise children with strong moral values. All that is true. I have been describing trends, not the overall condition of the culture, but the trends have been running the wrong way, dramatically so in the past thirty years. It would be difficult to contend that, the end of racial segregation aside, American culture today is superior to, or even on a par with, the culture of the 1950s.

Others might argue that the elections of 1994 are an indication that a cultural swing is taking place, that Americans have rejected huge, regulation-happy government. That may be so, but I remember thinking the same thing in November 1980 when the electorate chose Ronald Reagan and defeated a clutch of the most liberal senators. But little long-term improvement occurred. Government now regulates more than it did then. It was fifteen years between Reagan's first inauguration and the Republican domination of Congress. We will know that a sea change has happened if, fifteen years from now, government is smaller, less expensive, and less intrusive.

Modern liberalism, moreover, maintains its hold on the institutions that shape values and manipulate symbols. Hollywood and the network evening news will not change their ways because of Republican majorities. Political correctness and multiculturalism will not be ejected from the universities by Newt Gingrich. If the reaction of the Left to Reagan's elections is any guide, modern liberalism will become more aggressive and intolerant. In any event, even a persistently conservative government can do little to deal with social deterioration other than stop subsidizing it through welfare, and it remains to be seen whether Republicans have the will to overcome the constituencies that want welfare. Moral decay is evident, moreover, among people who are not on welfare and never will be.

No one can be certain of the future, of course. Cultures in decline have, unpredictably, turned themselves around before. Perhaps ours will too. Perhaps, ultimately, we will become so sick of the moral and aesthetic environment that is growing in America that stricter standards will be imposed democratically or by moral disapproval. Perhaps we will reject a government that is controlling more and more of our lives. But then again, perhaps not. Merle Haggard, a social philosopher with a perspective like Kristol's, said, "[The decade of the 1960s] was just the evening of it all. I think we're into the dead of night now."[5] Chances are, that is too optimistic and the dead of night still lies ahead. For the immediate future, in any event, what we probably face is an increasingly vulgar, violent, chaotic, and politicized culture and, unless the conservative resurgence of 1994 is both long-lasting and effective, an increasingly incompetent, bureaucratic, and despotic government. Kristol refers to himself as a cheerful pessimist. If the argument here is even close to the mark, we had all better start working on the cheerful part.

---

5. *New York Times*, July 29, 1993, p. C1.

14

Justice versus Humanity in the Family

James Q. Wilson

> *[O]ur popular culture, having spent years disassembling the family as a sociological institution, is now trying to reconstitute it as a purely voluntary association based on personal feelings. But the family in real life is based on impersonal feelings. We do not honor our father and mother because of the kinds of persons they are, but because they are our mother and father. We do not recognize their authority because they, in any sense, "deserve" it. We do so—and we are pleased to do so—out of a natural sense of piety toward the authors of our being.*
>
>

IRVING KRISTOL
"Reflections on Love and Family"

There is no more radical a cultural division in all of history than that between the attachment ordinary people have for the family and the hostility intellectuals display toward it. Not, of course, all people or all intellectuals: just as there are men and women who want neither marriage nor children, so also there are intellectuals who praise the family and analyze its virtues. But the profamily intellectuals must contend with some powerful opponents, among them Plato, Jesus, St. Paul, Marx, and Engels. If defenders of the family manage to survive an encounter with those heavyweights, they must run a gantlet of lesser but still formidable writers who either attack the family outright (for example, novelists such as André Gide, aesthetes such as Cyril Connolly, anthropologists such as Edmund Leach, and radical feminists such as Shulamith Firestone) or describe it as a relatively recent social invention that can, presumably, be uninvented (for example, historians such as Philippe Aries, Lawrence Stone, and Edward Shorter).

Ferdinand Mount, in his splendid book, *The Subversive Family*,[1] supplies the reader with a convenient sample of the more important attacks on the family. Let me mention a few.

Plato, in his discussion of those people who in *The Republic* are to be members of the guardian class, argues that a "community of wives and children among our citizens is clearly the source of the greatest good of the state."[2] To achieve that, the law shall decree that "the wives of our guardians are to be in common, and their children are to be in common, and no parent is to know his own child, nor any child his parent."[3]

Jesus is reported by St. Luke to have said that "if anyone comes to me without hating his own father and mother and wife and children and brothers and sisters, and his very life too, he cannot be a disciple of mine."[4] Though Jesus said that he had come to enforce the laws of the prophets, among which was the obligation to honor one's father and mother, he also described his mission on earth to be, as St. Matthew put it, "to turn a man against his father, and a daughter against her mother. . . . No one who loves father or mother more than he loves me is worthy of me."[5]

In carrying Jesus' message to the Corinthians, St. Paul urged people who were already unmarried to remain that way:

To all who are unmarried and to widows, I would say this:
It is an excellent thing if they can remain single as I am.
. . . An unmarried man is concerned about the Lord's work,
and how he can please the Lord. A married man is con-

1. (New York: Free Press, 1992).
2. Plato, *Republic 5*, p. 477.
3. Ibid., p. 467.
4. Luke 14.26.
5. Matthew 10.35–38.

cerned about worldly affairs, and how he can please his wife, and so his interests are divided.[6]

It is hard to imagine Jesus or his disciples agreeing with Karl Marx and Friedrich Engels about anything, but they come closest with respect to the family. All of them thought the family an impediment to a higher goal. In a famous passage in *The Communist Manifesto,* Marx and Engels predict that "the bourgeois family will vanish as a matter of course . . . with the vanishing of capital." And a good thing, too, because

> the bourgeois claptrap about the family and education, about the hallowed co-relation of parent and child, becomes all the more disgusting . . . by the action of modern industry. . . . Bourgeois marriage is in reality a system of wives in common and thus, at the most, what the communists might possibly be reproached with is that they desire to introduce . . . an openly legalized community of women.

When the great British anthropologist, Sir Edmund Leach, delivered the Reith Lectures in 1967, he spoke for many intellectuals when he said that "far from being the basis of the good society, the family, with its narrow privacy and tawdry secrets, is the source of all our discontents."

The examples could be multiplied endlessly; for many more, see Mount's book.

Yet virtually every study of the sources of human happiness among ordinary people reveals that family life, though filled with problems and tensions, is the greatest source of human satisfaction, at least among people living in societies that have achieved a reasonable level of economic affluence. For the very poor, becoming not-so-poor is an overriding concern; but people who are already not poor look for happiness in a good family life.[7]

It is tempting to say that when intellectuals are hostile to the family, it is because they come from unhappy homes or have been

---

6. 1 Cor. 7.9, 32–34.

7. Robert E. Lane, "Does Money Buy Happiness?" *The Public Interest,* no. 113 (Fall 1993), pp. 56–65.

unable to contract good marriages. Though that might explain some cases, this form of psychological reductionism does an injustice to the arguments that they are making. Those who speak out against the family make arguments that we ought to take seriously. I find three main reasons for their hostility to the family.

First, the family subverts the claims of higher loyalties. The stronger the bond to parents and siblings, the weaker the commitment to a religious vocation, the leadership of the state, the solidarity of the working class, or service to one's fellow man. Jesus and St. Paul did not oppose the family for most people, only for those who wished to follow them as committed disciples. Plato thought that in the ideal state family life was suitable for artisans but not for warriors or guardians, each of whom had a higher calling for which the most rigorous (and nonfamilial) training was necessary. Marx did not attack all families, but only bourgeois ones, and he suggested that capitalism had already made true family life among the proletariat impossible. Engels was later to claim that the modern family, with its emphasis on sexual fidelity, male dominance, and private property, was neither natural nor inevitable but the result of class-based economic necessity. Primitive man, he believed, enjoyed sexual freedom amid group marriages. (We now know that this view is false.) Even among those who do not believe in divine or revolutionary missions, the family is a barrier to "public life." Stephanie Coontz and others have argued that efforts to celebrate the family are, in effect if not by design, efforts to encapsulate people in a private sphere and thus discourage them from participating in the (presumably more important) public realm in which government policy is determined.[8]

Second, the family as it has been glorified in the West represents a form of cultural intolerance. The two-parent family is only one of several alternative living arrangements. In the words of Coontz, single-parent families are not pathological or disorganized but "alternative family forms" that are "flexible, effective ways of

---

8. Stephanie Coontz, *The Way We Never Were: American Families and the Nostalgia Trap* (New York: Basic Books, 1992), pp. 96–98. Not only do family values undercut public commitments, but they are responsible, in her eyes, for "racism." Coontz writes that "the new emphasis on family relations and private morality led easily to scapegoating and victim blaming. Poverty was attributed not to unemployment or low wages but to lack of middle-class family norms. . . . The triumph of family moralism thus coincided with an outburst of nativism and racism" (p. 111).

pooling resources and building community." We should not berate these alternative forms for "failing to conform to an idealized white model."[9]

Finally, family life as it now exists perpetuates inequalities. Susan Moller Okin has given the fullest and most careful statement of this view: "The gendered family radically limits the equality of opportunity of women and girls of all classes. . . . There is no way to alleviate the continuing inequality of women without more clearly defining and also reforming marriage."[10] The highest virtue is justice, and it is as applicable to families as to other social institutions.[11] The inequality of power relations in the family reinforces inequality in the larger society.[12] Working wives still have to do a disproportionate share of child-care work; as a result, they cannot play an equal role in the affairs of the economy, the community, and the government.[13]

What these critiques have in common is, first, the view that the family is a social construction and, second, the assumption that people have a higher obligation—to justice, to themselves, to the socialist order, to the prospect of eternal life—to which family obligations ought to be subordinate.

The Origins of the Family

There is no doubt that family systems and family life are shaped by social circumstances. There are nuclear and extended families, private and clan-linked families, happy and unhappy families. But admitting that they are shaped by society is not the same as saying they are constructed by it. They are not entirely or even largely a matter of convention or artifice. The natural, fundamental, and irreducible unit of human society is that of the mother and child. It is natural in that the child requires a mother and until very recently could not be fed without her. It is fundamental in that the maternity of a child is indisputable, though its paternity may not be. It is irreducible in that there is no smaller social unit that can be imagined.[14]

---

9. Ibid., p. 242.

10. Susan Moller Okin, *Justice, Gender, and the Family* (New York: Basic Books, 1989), pp. 134, 139–40.

11. Ibid., p. 135.

12. Ibid., p. 147.

13. Ibid., p. 153.

14. Robin Fox, *Kinship and Marriage* (Cambridge: Cambridge University Press, 1983), chap. 1, esp. pp. 31, 36.

Men can have varying relationships with this unit. They can be casual impregnators, monogamous husbands, or polygamous husbands, or they can alternate among these roles as their interests and opportunities permit. For several thousand years, the preferred relationship in virtually every civilization has been one that requires the husband to acknowledge and support the woman he has impregnated and the child he has fathered. The reasons for this preference are not hard to understand. A child not supported by its father will either die (unless the woman has easy access to abundant nearby food) or become a burden on others (which is a bothersome expense). A child not acknowledged by the father becomes a matter of dispute. This dispute affects claims to property and status, and it feeds the flames of sexual jealousy.

Requiring males to acknowledge paternity and provide support is not easily accomplished, for it runs counter to the preferences of many men—for sexual adventure, for personal independence, or for the maximization of their progeny. To overcome this tendency of men to be either unattached Don Juans or polygamous husbands, societies have developed a variety of methods. Women behave coyly, requiring courtship before sex. During courtship, a woman and her family test the man's likelihood of making a commitment to her that will last beyond the appearance on the scene of the next attractive woman. Society defines rules for the inheritance of property in ways that give special advantage to legitimate offspring. Cultural and religious codes stigmatize philandering and proscribe adultery.

The monogamous contract, as William Tucker has put it, is a fragile institution because it represents an imperfect reconciliation of partially competing interests.[15] Moreover, it is often and to some degree a one-sided contract. Men often obtain disproportionate advantages from it. They frequently control the disposition of property, exercise unchecked authority in the household, and hold their wives to higher standards of sexual fidelity than those they are prepared to observe.

When a bargain is struck between two parties and one is weaker than the other, the weaker party is often forced to make the greater concessions. In marriage arrangements, the woman has usually been

---

15. William Tucker, "Monogamy and Its Discontents," *National Review,* October 4, 1993, pp. 28–38.

the weaker party: weaker not only physically, but also in having fewer alternatives. She requires a husband to sustain her during pregnancy and early child rearing, but he does not need her. Though weak, however, she gets something in exchange for her dependency: support and protection. And he also gets something in exchange for the constraint on his independence: a reduction in the struggle for access to women. He has ensured access to one woman, which is denied to all other men. His wife's child is indisputably his offspring. There need not be as much fighting among men, and so life is a bit more tranquil, especially for relatively weak men.

I apologize for describing in such blunt and biological language what many regard as romance, a sacrament, or a television sitcom. But it is best to understand the fundamental biological and evolutionary significance of the family before we attempt to modify it to suit our political or philosophical preferences. If the origins of the monogamous family are something like what I have sketched, we ought to be clear what the real, as opposed to imaginary, alternatives are.

One alternative can be dismissed out of hand. From time to time someone comes up with the notion that we can divorce sex entirely from family formation and create a utopian commune in which "free love" is practiced. Invariably, the participants learn that free love is a contradiction in terms: sex is never free. The nonmonetary price is fierce competition, feelings of jealousy, and demands for commitment. As the price rises, the commune collapses. No such experiment has ever lasted more than a few years.

There are only two realistic alternatives. First, men may take several wives, either at one time (we call that polygamy) or one at a time (we call that serial monogamy); or, second, women may depend on some larger collective to support them and their children (we call that welfare). Neither is very attractive.

We have experimented with these alternatives. Elijah Anderson has published extraordinary accounts of life among underclass men.[16] Young male gangs control neighborhoods and demand sexual access to the women who live there. There are fights among the men and wars with rival gangs. Making babies is a sign of virility but carries with it no corresponding obligations. Women turn to communal sources—families or welfare—to support the resulting

16. See Elijah Anderson, *A Place on the Corner* (Chicago: University of Chicago Press, 1978), and *Streetwise: Race, Class, and Change in an Urban Community* (Chicago: University of Chicago Press, 1990).

children. There are frequent quarrels. The children suffer from both poverty (single women cannot command the resources that married couples can) and inadequate parenting (children are not good at raising other children).

One would think that by now all this would be common knowledge. But no. Recently, on the occasion of the selection of a new chancellor of the New York City public school system, a member of the board of education, Victor Gotbaum, derided his fellow board members for selecting Ramon Cortines: "The majority members are enamored of middle-class, two-parent families with children who don't have sex. Their values are not representative of the school system."[17]

Even more recently, a flier issued by an office of the U.S. Senate announcing a seminar on single-parent families told the reader that "many Americans assume that the normal American family has two biological parents and that all other combinations are abnormal." The seminar, sponsored by the Senate, was designed to talk people out of this assumption.

What does it mean to say that a preference for a two-parent family with decent children is a "value"? Does Mr. Gotbaum or the Office of Senate Health Promotion think we have chosen it as we might choose whether to vote for a Democrat or a Republican—a choice made because it seemed the right thing to do at the moment, and which can be unmade when circumstances change? The monogamous family is not in the least a value in that sense; it is the product of millenniums of trial and error, a product designed, however imperfectly, to achieve two of the highest desires of mankind: to care for children and to preserve a modicum of social peace.

The Family and Loyalty

Let us evaluate the evidence bearing on each of the three major criticisms of the conventional family. The first is that family ties impede the formation of higher loyalties. In this view, the family and family values are parochial; by contrast, the aspirations of men and women are cosmopolitan and their obligations universal.

The evidence supports exactly the opposite conclusions. Though there are countless examples of people content to live and act within the confines of the family, those who act altruisti-

17. *New York Daily News,* August 13, 1993.

cally on behalf of people outside their families came dispropor-
tionately from strong family backgrounds and have close relations with their parents.

Those European gentiles who, at great risk to themselves, rescued Jews in Nazi-occupied countries from the horrible prospect of
a trip to a death camp were the product of exceptionally strong and
loving families.[18] European gentiles who were like the rescuers in
all respects save their willingness to rescue victims were the products, on average, of less strong families.

Note, I say that *truly* altruistic people have strong families.
There are many who claim to act on behalf of "humanity," "the
people," or "the poor" who, in fact, act only to foster grand theoretical or ideological schemes—communes, utopias, revolutions—in preference to actually helping any living, breathing person. And such people,
from Rousseau to Mao, do indeed attach little value to family life.

It may be true that family attachments prevent some people
from forsaking family life in favor of a religious vocation or an ideological crusade. There might be more saints and revolutionaries if
those persons disposed to undertake a mission cared less about
spouses, parents, or children. (There might also be more criminals
if those persons greedy for material possessions cared less for their
families.) But among that great number of people who are neither
saints nor revolutionaries, the likelihood of having a strong conscience, a clear sense of duty, and a willingness to act on one's principles goes up, not down, as the strength of the bond to one's parents
increases.

The Family and Snobbery

The second criticism, that of cultural snobbery, is based on the assumption that there are alternatives to the traditional two-parent
family that, if not superior to it, are at least as good. Supporters of
this criticism often claim that people who deny the criticism are
revealing their sentimental and unrealistic attachment to an out-
dated "Ozzie-and-Harriet" model of the family, one that belongs in
the dust heap of 1950s memorabilia along with saddle shoes, balle-

18. Samuel P. Oliner and Pearl M. Oliner, *The Altruistic Personality*
(New York: Free Press, 1988), pp. 214–20, 297–98. See also James Q. Wilson,
The Moral Sense (New York: Free Press, 1993), pp. 37–39, 108–109, 145–48.

rina skirts, ducktail haircuts, and black-and-white television.

No. The evidence, for a while equivocal, is now clear: single-parent families at almost every income level and for all races create deeper problems for their children than do two-parent families. I have elsewhere reviewed the evidence;[19] it is by now so compelling that even the administration of President Clinton, many of whose members felt rather differently before, now speaks unanimously about the dangers (and even the wrongness!) of out-of-wedlock births.

Let me mention two of the better studies. Deborah Dawson has reported the results of a survey of the family arrangements and personal well-being of 60,000 children living in households all over the country. The results, published by a unit of the U.S. Department of Health and Human Services, showed that at every income level save the very highest (more than $50,000 per year), for both sexes and for whites, blacks, and Hispanics alike, children living with a never-married or a divorced mother were substantially worse off than those living in two-parent families. The former were twice as likely to have been expelled or suspended from school, to display emotional or behavioral problems, and to have trouble getting along with their peers. This gap was about as wide in households earning more than $35,000 a year as it was in those making less than $10,000.[20] These findings should make it clear that the problems of the mother-only family do not afflict just black families. They afflict *all* such families.

Sara McLanahan and Gary Sandefur have examined virtually all the available data on the effect of family structure on children's prospects. Though poverty, an especially acute problem for female-headed households, hurts the children, just being in such a household, independent of its earnings, hurts them also. Single mothers exercise less control over their children than do mothers in two-parent families, and such differences in parenting practices account for more than the difference in high-school dropout rates between children from broken and those from intact families. Parenting (not income) also accounts for most of the difference in idleness of boys.[21]

19. James Q. Wilson, "The Family-Values Debate," *Commentary* (April 1993), pp. 24–31.

20. Deborah A. Dawson, "Family Structure and Children's Health: United States, 1988," *Vital and Health Statistics*, series 10, no. 178 (June 1991).

21. Sara McLanahan and Gary Sandefur, *Growing Up with a Single Parent: What Hurts, What Helps* (Cambridge: Harvard University Press, 1994).

By now it should be evident that those, like Coontz, who maintain that it is simply poverty and not family structure that hurts children are wrong.

The Family and Justice

The third criticism is that families, especially two-parent ones, are unjust as they are presently constituted because they subordinate women. Okin says that a just society requires just families, and just families are ones in which all parties have equal rights and roles. Society cannot be made more just without making family members more equal. By equal she means having an equal allocation of roles and duties between husbands and wives, and in particular equal time spent on child care.

One can certainly concede the force of that argument in the extreme case. It is hard to imagine and impossible to find a society based on equal political liberties for all and government by popular consent that has a family system based on tribal clans, arranged marriages, the denial of property rights to women, and the existence of a caste system by which some families are assigned in perpetuity to an inferior social and political status. Indeed, the chief reason why political liberty and popular rule are almost exclusively features of Western societies is precisely because it has been in the West that there arose some centuries ago consensual and companionate marriages and the individual ownership of property, both free of clan control.[22]

But I am aware of no evidence in contemporary Western cultures suggesting that variations in the degree of justice in society as a whole are caused by variations in the degree of justice within the family. Okin has argued that justice is the fundamental and most essential virtue of both the polity and the family. I certainly agree that justice is *a* standard by which family should be judged. That standard would prohibit, among other things, familial violence against women and would ensure property rights to wives. In the West, familial violence and the ancient doctrine of coverture have long been illegal. But I disagree that justice is the most essential standard, such that it must govern the assignment of roles.

---

22. James Q. Wilson, *The Moral Sense,* chap. 8.

To begin with, that is not how the vast majority of people see the matter. The opinion studies that Okin herself cites reveal husbands and wives readily acknowledging conventional distinctions between housework and wage work and endorsing by large—though perhaps shrinking—majorities the desirability of mothers with small children staying at home.[23]

But we need not rely on social science data, because more compelling evidence is all about us in songs, stories, novels, talk shows, and daily conversation: marriage is chiefly about companionship, nurturance, and affection. The complaints that people—and if I may say so, especially women—have about their marriages is that their spouses are inattentive, uncommunicative, unromantic, and insensitive. There are to be sure some complaints about role sharing: he won't help me with the baby, he expects me to work during the day and cook every evening, and so on. But there are remarkably few ballads that lament husbands who won't wash the dishes; there are thousands that lament husbands who are silent or unfaithful. Loneliness and jealousy, not injustice or role separation, are the timeless themes of every generation's sorrows about unhappy marriages.

It may be objected that the people who repeat these complaints are suffering from false consciousness: culture has induced them, especially women, to accept the false or unjust idea that women are the primary caretakers of children. The idea that the family is a social construction is an essential component of the argument that the family is unjust. If the different roles of men and women are the result of something more profound than social convention, then the possibility of insisting on the absolute interchangeability of those roles is much reduced.

How can we determine if the rules are purely social constructs? We can look at those few but important attempts to redefine gender roles inside the family along more egalitarian lines. The most important of these has been the Israeli kibbutz, or collective farm. Every major study of this extraordinary effort at modifying familial roles has demonstrated how resistant they are to planned change.

The most impressive demonstration of that resistance—impressive because of both the quality of the research and the initial sup-

---

23. Okin, *Justice, Gender, and the Family,* pp. 140–41; Philip Blumstein and Pepper Schwartz, *American Couples* (New York: William Morrow, 1983), pp. 52, 115, 118–25, 324.

positions of the author—comes from the studies of a kibbutz by Melford E. and Audrey Spiro. When the Spiros first studied it in 1951, the kibbutz was already thirty years old; when they returned in 1975, it had been in existence for nearly sixty years. It thus represented a mature example of a bold experiment: to achieve on a farm a wholly egalitarian society based on collective ownership, cooperative enterprise, a classless society, and the group rearing of children in an atmosphere that accords no significance to difference in gender. Within a week after birth, infants were brought to a communal nursery; at one year of age, they moved into a toddlers' house; at five years of age, they entered kindergarten; and so on through grammar school and high school, living always with other children and never with their parents, except for daily, brief visits.

Although there were slight differences in dress, in general male and female children were treated in exactly the same way: they dressed together, bathed together, played together, and slept together. They were given the same toys and the same chores. Men and women married and lived together, but the family as a parent-child unit was abolished, as were sex-differentiated roles within the family—not only in the assignment of rights, duties, and opportunities, but also in dress. Communal facilities—the kitchen, laundry, dining room, nursery, and school—were to be staffed without regard to gender, and women, who wore pants, avoided cosmetics, and retained their maiden names, were encouraged to work the fields alongside the men.

The communal nursery was successful in discouraging clear sex-role identifications among the children. In their fantasy play, boys rarely assumed adult male roles. Some boys chose to wear ribbons and dresses during their games, and boys and girls played together rather than in same-sex groups. But from the first, some gender differences in behavior appeared, despite efforts to discourage them. Just as in conventional families, boys played more strenuous games than girls. Boys were more likely to pretend they were driving vehicles and girls more likely to play with dolls and baby buggies; girls engaged in more artistic games and boys in more mechanical ones. As they got older, the formal sexual equality of life continued: boys and girls lived together, took showers together, and could indulge their sexual curiosity without adult interference or guidance. But the signs of sexual identification continued to appear. At parties girls spontaneously sang, danced, and initiated activity; boys increasingly sat on the sidelines and watched. Girls be-gan assisting the nurses, boys the farmers. Teachers began to re-mark that the girls were socially more sensitive, the boys more egotistical.

By the time the children were adults, something akin to tradi-tional role assignments had emerged. The family had reasserted itself: sabra women sought renewed contact with their children (though not at the expense of abandoning collective education), the children's living quarters were increasingly staffed by women, and men began to do most of the major agricultural jobs and to domi-nate the leadership roles and discussion in the communal meetings. Women returned to feminine styles in clothing and opened a beauty parlor. This is not to say that there was now sexual inequality in the kibbutz, only that there was sexual diversity—in roles, preferences, styles, and modes of thought—within a structure of legal and for-mal equality.

When conflict arose in the children's houses, the girls tended to handle it by supplying assistance, by sharing, and through coop-eration, while the boys more often relied on initiating activities, applying rules, or issuing directives. Boys were, predictably, the most aggressive children. Both boys and girls would attempt to control the aggression, but only the girls would console the victims of it.

It is hard to imagine that a free society will ever make a more determined effort to eliminate gender differences in social roles than did the Israeli kibbutzim. It is also hard to imagine that such an effort would be studied by anyone more sympathetic to its goals than Melford and Audrey Spiro. As the former wrote in 1979:

> As a cultural determinist, my aim in studying personal-ity development in Kiryat Yedidim [the pseudonym of the kibbutz] was to observe the influence of culture on hu-man nature or, more accurately, to discover how a new culture produces a new human nature. In 1975 I found (against my own intentions) that I was observing the in-fluence of human nature on culture.[24]

---

24. Melford E. Spiro, *Gender and Culture: Kibbutz Women Revisited* (Durham: University of North Carolina Press, 1979), p. 106. See also Spiro, *Children of the Kibbutz*, rev. ed. (Cambridge: Harvard University Press, 1975).

The special attachment that exists between a mother and her child is a fact of nature that cannot be altered by social engineering or legal reform. What can be reformed, of course, are the legal barriers that confront women in playing roles outside the family and the legal rules that result, in this country, in the impoverishment of divorced women. Okin reminds us, accurately, of how the formal equality of the divorce laws often leads to actual inequality. The divorce court may divide property equally between husband and wife, but since the wife retains custody of the children while the husband is free to pursue his career, the woman is often left economically much worse off. Solving that problem is both important and feasible; other nations have done it. But solving it does not require, as Okin supposes, imposing in the name of justice an obligation on all families that roles be shared equally.

Indeed, Okin herself shrinks from that implication of her own analysis. She does not insist that by law we require husbands and wives to spend equal time on household and child-rearing chores. It is odd that she does not. If justice is the "most essential" requirement of both society and family, then the laws we have passed to ensure justice in society (laws that require, for example, equal pay for equal work) ought to be applied in full force to the members of a family. Perhaps she shrinks from this implication because she senses that somehow the family is different from society. Indeed it is; that is precisely why the same criteria cannot be used to evaluate both institutions.

Turn the matter around. Suppose we were to agree that companionship, nurturance, and affection were the chief virtues by which family life should be judged. Would we think that these are the virtues by which society and its government should be judged? And if we thought that, would we insist that laws be passed mandating companionship, nurturance, and affection among all citizens? I think not.

Okin settles for a more modest implication of her position—namely, that the government ban sex discrimination and harassment in the workplace, require that employers offer parental leave to both husbands and wives on the occasion of the birth of children, and arrange child-support payments in the event of a divorce so that the child's caretaker (almost always the woman) is not impoverished. I have no principled quarrel with any of these recommendations, and I note that some have already become law. There are other family and women's support policies that could be put into place. But even if all were enacted and all fully enforced, none would lead to the equal sharing of household tasks. None, in short, would lead to Okin's definition of a just family.

What they might lead to can be observed by considering the case of Sweden. No nation, perhaps, has made a greater or more effective commitment to ensure the equal legal and social status of women. Women are on an equal legal and economic footing in marriage, have an equal right to inheritance, cannot be fired if they become pregnant, and are guaranteed equal pay for equal work. But beyond these protections, there has been a deep interest in sex roles in marriage and a major commitment to placing the woman on an equal footing in the family as well as in society at large.[25]

Parental leave was extended to one year, much of it paid. The joint tax return was abolished, thereby eliminating the deduction men could take for nonworking wives and so making it financially more advantageous for women to enter the work force. Divorce was made easy—in effect, on demand. Sweden has resisted the idea of paying families a child-care allowance, on the grounds that it might encourage the mother to stay at home and care for the child. This is in keeping with the language of a parliamentary report that might have been written by Okin: "Family policy must take as basic the principle that both parents have the same right and duty to assume breadwinning as well as practical responsibility for home and children."[26]

Okin would approve of many of the results of these policies and of the cultural changes that accompanied them. Sweden has a higher percentage of women in the workplace than any other industrialized nation, and women's wages are at least 90 percent of comparable male workers. Divorced women end up with 90 percent of their predivorce incomes.

But there have been some other consequences as well. Fathers are eligible for parental leave, but most do not take it. Women do. Sweden has an elaborate day-care system; most of the people who work in it are women. Sweden has a high rate of divorce. A high and growing proportion of children live in single-parent families. De-

---

25. This draws from David Popenoe, *Disturbing the Nest: Family Change and Decline in Modern Societies* (New York: Aldine de Gruyter, 1988), pp. 143–55, 176–77, and from information supplied by Dr. Elisabeth Langby of Stockholm.

26. Quoted in ibid., p. 149.

spite all the efforts to ensure gender equality in domestic roles, the vast majority of the single-parent families are headed by women.

Because of state-supplied benefits, being raised in a single-parent, female-headed household in Sweden is less likely to reduce a family to poverty than is the case in the United States. But despite this economic buffering, Swedish children suffer from living in a mother-only household. Sweden has for many years been experiencing a sharp increase in the rate of juvenile crime. One Swedish study found that a young person from a single-parent home was twice as likely to become delinquent as one from a two-parent home.[27]

Coping with Modernity

Working women have become an important and permanent feature of the modern world. It is not clear to me that this fact by itself puts the child at risk, although one must be careful to acknowledge that research on this matter is by no means consistent. Today, young men and women everywhere are struggling with the competing demands of child care and employment. There is no single solution suitable for each; under some circumstances and for some people, there is no solution at all. It is important that we help all who struggle with this problem to decide it under the best possible circumstances.

In helping them, however, we must remember that no good deed goes unpunished. Providing elaborate external support systems for individuals who happen to be married is not quite the same thing as providing support for marriages and families. Day-care centers, paid parental leave, no-fault divorce laws, favorable tax treatment for individuals, generous welfare benefits—all these make life easier for countless individuals, but they may also encourage the breakup or the nonformation of families organized around an enduring two-person commitment to the welfare of the child.

Every couple must define for itself the allocation of roles and duties within the family. This allocation has of late become more egalitarian, sometimes out of necessity (the wife must work) and sometimes out of principle. Anyone who suggests, as I have done, that there are limits to how far this egalitarianism can or should proceed risks being branded an enemy of both women and justice. I think such a reaction is a bit extreme. I have watched my own fam-

---

27. Ibid., p. 319; see also notes 30 and 31.

ily and those of my friends struggle to assign roles and duties in ways that strike them as reasonable. Different circumstances and different temperaments will lead to different assignments, but these differences in outcome are almost always far less than what is implied by the doctrine of strict gender equality. And they are less because, however equal the two sexes are legally and morally, they are different biologically and temperamentally. Just as men and women, and especially the latter, have discovered, contrary to what they were once told, that you can't "have it all," they are also discovering that whatever you have cannot be exactly what your mate has.

In coping with the tension between providing justice and opportunity for individuals and support and compassion for families, let us not delude ourselves into thinking that we can ever write on a blank slate. We can modify the roles that the two sexes play, but we cannot fundamentally alter them. The only thing as old as the love between the sexes is the war between them. We have wisely decided as a society to help the sex that is so often disadvantaged in that war—the female sex. But we cannot make and enforce a truce, change the nature of the combatants, or alter the needs of the child who is usually the product of the love and sometimes the casualty of the war.

15

Reflections of a Neoconservative Disciple

Mark Gerson

M y mother tells me that the Kristols left me on the doorstep one morning. I never really believed this, but it may help to explain why I have been given the honor of being asked to contribute to this volume. Certainly Irving Kristol and Gertrude Himmelfarb, without consciously volunteering to do so, have served as my intellectual godparents. And not only mine—in a passage especially favored by Gertrude Himmelfarb, Lord Acton wrote, "Ideas have a radiation and development, an ancestry and posterity of their own, in which men play the part of godfathers and godmothers more than that of legitimate parents." This is a role that the Kristols have served with particular distinction. Their work and the movement they spawned, neoconservatism, have molded the way in which I and many others view the world; a glance at a newspaper will inevitably call to mind a neoconservative argument, as will a professor's lecture, a politician's speech, or even a friendly discussion.

Since I am a recent college graduate, my age gives me a different perspective on Kristol's work from most of the other contributors. While accompanying Irving Kristol on the journey from alcove 1 to AEI would have made for a wonderful life of intellectual fulfillment, ideological excitement, and warm friendship, coming in at this late date has certain benefits as well. The first is the availability of the extensive Kristol *oeuvre*, which affords me the pleasure of being able to spend an evening with his work on any subject from any period. His penetrating wit alone guarantees a delightful experience. But the same can be said of Mel Brooks and Eddie Murphy, and there are no *Festschriften* for them.

Irving Kristol captures the imagination not only by the trenchant way in which he addresses social and political iss·ies, but also by the multifaceted education he provides along the way. There is a historical education, since a piece by him on any topic brings alive the polemical context in which it was written and, at the same time, has a historically informed depth of its own. Furthermore, there is an education in the uses and power of ideas; reading Irving Kristol teaches how ideologies develop, how intellectual movements evolve, how ideas affect culture, and how culture influences politics. Finally, there is an education in the largest questions of how politics should be conceived, how the diverse forces of society interact, and, ultimately, how men live together and can do a better job at it. For a young person trying to grasp the state of the American experiment at the end of the twentieth century, Kristol's work provides not only concrete guidance on a remarkable range of specific issues but also the inspiration of a coherent, yet flexible, theoretical and ideological sensibility shaped over decades of continuous intellectual engagement.

One exceptional feature of Irving Kristol's work is its staying power: his social commentary is brimming with insights and relevance decades after its specific subject passed from conversation. It is often said (or charged) that he has changed dramatically, from a liberal critic of liberalism to a conservative. Even though he has helped promote this impression with his famous comment that a neoconservative is a "liberal mugged by reality," the impression of sharp discontinuity is misleading. While his thinking has evolved in many respects over the decades (as has everyone's), his ideas have consistently emphasized the same fundamental lessons about the complex nature of man, the difficulty of politics, the importance of ideology, and the infinitely complicated relationship of modern man to the ideas that shape his world.

Examples are numerous. What can better describe the theological pollution that emanates when political liberalism infiltrates Judaism than the following comment of Irving Kristol in 1948?

What are we to make of a rabbi who claims for the Mishnah and the Talmud that they guarantee the right to strike—thereby providing Holy Writ with the satisfaction of having paved the way for the National Labor Relations Act?...What is this but an oblique way of saying that one of the merits of Judaism is that it permits its believers to read the *New Republic* with an untroubled soul?

Given that communism is dead, one might think that discussions of fellow travelers are dated—but not so in the work of Irving Kristol. His castigation of liberal professors who did not appreciate the ideological intensity of the Communists in the 1950s is the most revealing explanation I have come across of why liberal professors today allow their universities to be held captive by a bitter minority of postwhatevers. A 1964 *New Leader* article offers the most incisive definition of American conservatism penned to this day. And so on.

The continuing relevance of Irving Kristol's corpus is a testament to, but not a cause of, the great power of his work. What is it that makes him the foremost man of letters in America, and indeed one of the great public intellectuals of this century? Trying to answer that allows me to understand how Rabbi Hillel must have felt when he was asked to encapsulate the essence of Judaism while standing on one foot. With regard to Irving Kristol, the response would have to be, "Ideas rule the world; the rest is in *Commentary*." Even adding *The Public Interest,* that does not seem sufficient.

The first component of Irving Kristol's genius is his ability to clarify vague sentiments and common-sense observations and place them in the framework of piercing analyses and philosophic insights. There are few experiences more exhilarating than being told why one thinks the way one does and how those thoughts can be deepened—and Kristol provides that regularly. And in so doing, Kristol fulfills the ultimate duty of a social theorist, as he defined it in a 1958 *Commentary* review: "A social theory enlightens us with its very statement; it discovers the world we live in; we *see* the explanation of why things are happening the way they are." Do you sense that drugs invite a host of issues far deeper than the physiological ones often cited, but are not sure how? Witness "Urban Civilization and Its Discontents." Have a hunch that liberalism and its theology, secular humanism, are not good for Jews or Judaism? Be prepared for a sunburst: "The Future of American Jewry." Cannot figure out why conservatives win the arguments but remain on the defensive? Read "The Stupid Party" or "The Republican Future."

Nothing is incomprehensible for Irving Kristol because he sees social phenomena as products of an inner logic governed by the dynamics of culture. From his famous 1952 essay "'Civil Liberties,' 1952—A Study in Confusion" to *Wall Street Journal* columns in the early 1990s, he has consistently emphasized the power and importance of ideas. Ideas are not always translated clearly in debate, discussion, and lifestyle; they are at least drained of their purity when confronted by real-life situations. Mangled, confused, or even inscrutable, however, ideas determine the criteria and set the goals toward which even the most self-consciously pragmatic men strive. And this applies not only to "practical" ideas in the narrow sense, but to moral ideals as well. The principal function of ideologies is to define what makes a society moral, and the job of politics is to translate moral ideals (however imperfectly) into reality.

Absurdities that fill our newspapers and characterize our daily existence make perfect sense when viewed in this light. Take that common question: why are people so often drawn to schemes and systems that bring nothing but abjection, misery, and a breakdown of social bonds? Why do they shun that which clearly works, even fulfills their professed ideals, in exchange for something contingent on a thousand impossible transformations? Why, in essence, are some people never satisfied until they embrace what Kristol's mentor Lionel Trilling called "the adversary culture"? Irving Kristol explains that the adversary culture is not disappointed with society's progress but with what society is progressing toward. "For them," he has written, "as for Oscar Wilde, it is not the average American who is disgusting; it is the ideal American."

The question is often posed to Irving Kristol and his fellow neoconservatives: given that the adversary culture is, in nearly every setting, a rather small minority, why should it elicit such concern? Because certain worldviews can undermine and destroy valuable things, even if they are not capable of building up viable alternatives. Furthermore, ideas, unlike votes, respond to the depth of feeling behind them. Even the most eccentric ideas, passionately held by a minority, can have pervasive consequences if they are not contested in the right way. The prevalence of "multiculturalism" and quotas in ordinary American life is a sad testimony to the fact that an aberrant conception in the minds of a few intellectuals can, in not too long a time, dramatically alter the way a society gauges, judges, and operates itself. In order for a society to withstand this pressure, it must be buttressed by a self-confidence informed by a sense of its moral value. Human nature, Kristol tells us, demands no less:

> It is crucial to the lives of all our citizens, as of all human beings at all times, that they encounter a world that possesses a transcendent meaning, in which the human experience makes sense. Nothing, absolutely nothing, is more dehumanizing, more certain to generate a crisis, than experiencing one's life as a meaningless event in a meaningless world.

Socialists who maintain their anticapitalist faith long after the crashing failure of socialism, sociologists who (in the words of Daniel Patrick Moynihan and Charles Krauthammer) define deviancy up or down, privileged youth who declare, "You don't know what hell is like until you've grown up in Scarsdale"—these people, Kristol tells us, are certainly not stupid and probably not irrational. Actually, they are quite easy to understand. They are merely following a distinctive moral vision and, by virtue of possessing a vision, have an automatic claim on the imagination of men. As Kristol wrote in 1975, "You can't beat a horse with no horse," and the horses of modern politics are ideologies and the social visions they embody.

Irving Kristol has devoted his career to providing bourgeois society—that mixture of a market economy, a democratic polity, and a culture infusing virtue into both—with a horse. This has not been easy. First, bourgeois society is an open target for any utopian dreamer because, as Kristol writes, "bourgeois society is without a doubt the most prosaic of all possible societies." Aiming as it does for prosperity, liberty, and civilized coexistence within the constraints of human nature, bourgeois society has nothing to offer those who wish to transform man and his institutions radically. The bourgeois virtues, as defined by Kristol—"probity, diligence, thrift, self-reliance, self-respect, candor, fair dealing"—may be conducive to a prosperous economy and healthy community, but they are not going to satisfy those who yearn for heroic self-sacrifice, universal altruism, or any other romantic ends. And neither can a simple libertarianism or a narrow economism serve as an adequate counterweight. Statistics and arguments demonstrating that a particular philosophy or platform will not work are really beside the point; arguments from efficiency or even possibility cannot by themselves compete with a moral vision. "Efficiency," Kristol has written, "is not a moral virtue and by itself never legitimizes anything."

While the moral values of bourgeois society are noble if not glorious, bourgeois society has a terrible time showcasing them. This is inevitable, Kristol maintains, given that bourgeois society has forgotten not only its own ideological roots but the power of ideas to craft institutions and move men. Why is this so? Based on the assumption that culture is a private matter determined by personal tastes, contemporary bourgeois society has great trouble making the connections between ideas and the social realities that flow from those ideas. Consequently, bourgeois society has few defenses against the cultural ravages of an ideologically empowered adversary culture and new class. It simply does not take such forces seriously. Seeing, as Kristol charges, the adversary culture not as a mortal threat but as a business opportunity and a charity case, bourgeois society notices its enemy only when it creates that enemy's products or funds its causes.

Kristol's discussion of the ideological weakness of bourgeois society enables us to understand many of the most destructive aspects of our culture. I think back to my college graduation (Williams College, 1994), when the Phi Beta Kappa oration was delivered by a professor castigating the usual suspects: whites, capitalism, heterosexuals, the traditional family, men, etc. Given the state of our academic culture, there was nothing surprising about that, but the same cannot be said about the reaction of the audience of lawyers, doctors, professors, CEOs, bankers, brokers, and students: loud and persistent applause.

These intelligent and successful people can sit through a speech blasting the very ideas that order their lives and brought them to Williamstown on this beautiful weekend, and they cheer? Politeness is certainly a virtue, but.... Then, I remembered Kristol's 1970 discussion of the popularity of *The Graduate*. "There is something positively absurd in the spectacle of prosperous suburban fathers flocking to see—and evidently enjoying—*The Graduate*, or of prosperous, chic, suburban mothers unconcernedly humming 'Mrs. Robinson' to themselves as they cheerfully drive off to do their duties as den mothers." It is this same bourgeois inclination toward self-mutilation that led thriving professionals and prosperous businessmen at Williams to cheer a champion of the adversary culture castigating everything they presumably believe in, live for, and ask of their children.

If, as with the Phi Beta Kappa oration, all Kristol had done was to explain "why things are happening the way they are," *dayenu!* We would all be wiser for that. But he goes beyond translating the hieroglyphics of ideology. While he shows us why things are they way they are, he also tells us how they should be—and how we can make them that way. Irving Kristol's keen understanding of the social world allows him to craft ideas that both appeal to the moral imagination and actually work. Concerned with both philosophical integrity and practical possibility, he is one of the few who have been genuinely successful in developing what a different kind of thinker, Jurgen Habermas, has called "a theory of society conceived with practical intent."

Kristol the political thinker knows that democratic governance tempers ideology, and Kristol the social theorist provides a philosophical framework within which reasoned compromises can be made. The integration of these elements has been a great contribution of neoconservatism. Grounded in conviction yet attentive to social reality, recognizing the urgent importance of politics without treating politics as omnipotent, neoconservatism has flourished in that often haunted place—Lionel Trilling called it "the bloody crossroads"—where ideas and politics meet. Kristol and his neoconservative colleagues have shown how a political sensibility can avoid the uncritical acceptance of existing trends without simply rejecting the inevitable or mourning the irretrievable (an unfortunate stance Kristol calls "the politics of nostalgia"). The challenge of politics is to face the existing reality and mold it into something that is true to our principles and speaks to the better angels of our nature. Undergirding this approach to politics is Kristol's deep—and apparently unshakable—confidence in the continuing promise of American society and its capacity for decency and self-renewal.

I was not surprised to see a recent PBS interview in which the subject, Peggy Noonan, having distinguished between "old" and "young" conservatives, cited Irving Kristol as the prototypical young conservative. Now that we are celebrating his seventy-fifth birthday, it is appropriate that we pay homage to this man who—as Shakespeare said of the month of April—"hath put a spirit of youth in everything." For Irving Kristol has provided young thinkers, dreamers, and seekers of all ages with the intellectual vision needed to steer through the wonderfully complicated world. A realistic man with an impassioned moral imagination, Kristol demonstrates that our refusal to accept things the way they are no longer has to be channeled to the abyss of political religions. Bourgeois society can make good use of our most admirable visions and moral ambitions so long as it is sustained by traditional values and reinforced by a like-minded culture.

How will Irving Kristol's influence manifest itself in the future? Lord Acton's words apply here. All the godchildren of neoconservatism have not been born yet—and some may never know who their godparents are—but their influence, in one way or another, will perpetuate the legacy of Irving Kristol. How will we be able to identify these godchildren? Irving Kristol's godchildren will be the ones with an appreciation of ambiguity, an attachment to common sense, a commitment to reach the common good through genuine community, and a reverence for ideas. Perhaps most of all, they will champion the essence of what is the best in the American idea.

PART TWO

Passages and Epigrams

Passages and Epigrams

Introduction by Mark Gerson, compiler

M atthew Arnold wrote of Edmund Burke, "[He] is so great because . . . he brings thought to bear upon politics, he saturates
politics with thought." The same can be said of Irving Kristol.
Kristol saturates politics with thought, as he does economics, foreign policy, social institutions, and culture. Irving Kristol's work is
such a delight because it appeals to all the intellectual senses. He is
as dynamic as he is eclectic, as funny as he is wise, as accessible as
he is erudite. Consequently, one can read Kristol's work from any
period on any subject and experience the sensation that is gener-
ated when irony meets truth.

It is a rare thinker whose work could be as comfortable in a
scholarly journal as on a quote-of-the-day calendar, but that is the
case with Irving Kristol. The following section aims to provide a
glimpse into why the expression "as Irving Kristol wrote" has become part of the American political lexicon.

There is, however, a downside to all this. Given that Irving
Kristol has spent a half century as one of America's most prolific
writers, a compilation of his passages and epigrams is bound to be
incomplete. I have selected the quotations that I think best illus-
trate Kristol's major ideas with particular esprit. There are hundreds more that could just as easily fit: what follows is only part of
the best.

On Liberalism, Conservatism, and Neoconservatism

I am, for better or worse, a "neo-conservative" intellectual. *Newsweek*, *Time* and the *New York Times* have all identified me as such, and that settles the matter. As with the original Adam, theirs is the power to give names to all the political creatures in the land, who in turn can only be grateful for having been rescued from anonymity.

"What Is a 'Neo-Conservative'?" *Newsweek,* January 19, 1976.

For me, then, "neo-conservatism" was an experience of moral, intellectual, and spiritual liberation. I no longer had to pretend to believe—what in my heart I could no longer believe—that liberals were wrong because they subscribe to this or that erroneous opinion on this or that topic. No—liberals were wrong, liberals are wrong, because they are liberals. What is wrong with liberals is liberalism—a metaphysics and a mythology that is woefully blind to human and political reality. Becoming a neo-conservative, then, was the high point of my cold war.

"My Cold War," *The National Interest,* Spring 1993.

A neoconservative is a liberal who has been mugged by reality.

Attributed in the early 1970s.

The essential purpose of politics, after all, is to transmit to our children a civilization and a nation that they can be proud of. This means we should figure out what we want before we calculate what we can afford, not the reverse, which is the normal conservative predisposition.

"A Conservative Welfare State," *Wall Street Journal,* June 14, 1993.

Much of the liberal-conservative quarrel in the United States has hardly anything to do with politics, strictly speaking. The locus of this debate is primarily in the sphere of education; it involves above all the image of man into which we should like to see the child mature. It is a clash of visions, of philosophies of life, loyalty and death—just the sort of thing that one would expect from a collision of ideologies. And in such a collison, the old truths of political philosophy—and political philosophy itself as a disinterested contemplation of *la condition politique de l'homme*—are crushed.

"Old Truths and the New Conservatism," *Yale Review,* May 1958.

But it is a fact that Communism today rules one-third of the human race, and may soon rule more; and that it is the most powerful existing institution which opposes such changes and reforms as liberalism proposes. Why, then, should not liberals, and liberals especially, fear and hate it?

"On 'Negative Liberalism,'" *Encounter,* January 1954.

For there is one thing that the American people know about Senator McCarthy: he, like them, is unequivocally anti-Communist. About the spokesmen for American liberalism, they feel they know no such thing. And with some justification.

"'Civil Liberties,' 1952—A Study in Confusion," *Commentary,* March 1952.

But above all American conservatism is loyal to what can be called, without paradox, a tradition of change. The American people have had, and largely still have, a fixed habit of mind as to how social change should come about. This habit of mind prescribes that such change should, wherever possible, be inaugurated, sustained and completed by the free activities of the citizens, rather than by the coercive activity of the government. To most Americans—and not so long ago to all Americans—this was the very essence and only true definition of free government.

"The Squares v. the Yahoos," *New Leader,* September 14, 1964.

I also regard the exaggerated hopes we attach to politics as the curse of our age, just as I regard moderation as one of our vanishing virtues.

Preface to *On the Democratic Idea in America* (New York: Harper, 1972).

What one calls "neoconservatism" among American intellectuals is distinguished above all by a keen sense of the incongruence between popular academic theories and what used to be called "the facts of life."

"What Ever Happened to Common Sense?" *Wall Street Journal,* January 14, 1984.

The trouble with traditional American conservatism is that it lacks a naturally cheerful, optimistic disposition. Not only does it lack one, it regards signs of one as evidence of unsoundness, irresponsibility: It has always felt more comfortable with a William Howard Taft than with a Theodore Roosevelt, and it is still inclined to think that history will judge Herbert Hoover to have been a much better president than Franklin Roosevelt.

"Congressional Right Has It Wrong," *Wall Street Journal,* November 18, 1985.

My instincts are—I have indeed come to believe that an adult's "normal" political instincts should be—conservative: I have observed over the years that the unanticipated consequences of social action are always more important, and usually less agreeable, than the intended consequences.

Preface to *On the Democratic Idea in America* (New York: Harper, 1972).

On the Politics of Ideas

What rules the world is ideas, because ideas define the way reality is perceived.

"On Conservatism and Capitalism," *Wall Street Journal*, September 11, 1975.

Ideological politics insists that the fulfillment of its ideals is the highest good, to which a mere civic equilibrium must be subordinate. . . . This radical commitment to ideals and its accompanying contempt for matter-of-factness in public affairs has given rise to the most disastrous assumption of 20th century politics: the assumption that one who espouses our values, only more aggressively and intransigently than we do, is closer to us than one who opposes them in the spirit of moderation. In light of the events of the past three decades, there should be little need to argue that, unless this premise is explicitly repudiated, the social and political order is ripe for catastrophic division.

"Vox Populi, Vox Dei?" *Encounter,* March 1957.

If politics is the art of the possible, then political thinking is the fusion of abstract idea with gross circumstance; it is directed and limited by political commitment. In contrast, political philosophy is (or ought to be) located at a distant remove from mere opinion: it is the contemplation of man as a political animal. It stands to political activity much as the philosophy of science stands to scientific activity: its comprehension is post facto, and when it is tempted to be prescriptive, it falls into presumption.

"A Treasure for the Future," review of *Between Past and Future: Six Exercises in Political Thought,* by Hannah Arendt, *New Republic,* July 10, 1961.

For two centuries, the very important people who managed the affairs of this society could not believe in the importance of ideas—until one day they were shocked to discover that their children, having been captured and shaped by certain ideas, were either rebelling against their authority or seceding from their society. The truth is that ideas are all-important. The massive and seemingly-solid institutions of any society—the economic institutions, the political institutions, the religious institutions—are always at the mercy of the ideas in the heads of the people who populate these institutions. The leverage of ideas is so immense that a slight change in the intellectual climate can and will—perhaps slowly, but nevertheless inexorably—twist a familiar institution into an unrecognizable shape.

"Utopianism, Ancient and Modern," *Imprimus,* April 1973.

Different gardeners will have different ideas, of course, but there will be a limit to this variety. The idea of a garden does not, for instance, include an expanse of weeds or of poison ivy. And no gardener would ever confuse a garden with a garbage dump.

"Thoughts on Reading about a Summer-Camp Cabin Covered with Garbage," *New York Times Magazine,* November 17, 1974.

Oh, yes one can cull "insights," as we say from their [the New Left] many thousands of pages. But the inmates of any asylum, given pen and paper, will also produce their share of such "insights"— only it doesn't ordinarily occur to us that this is a good way of going about collecting our insights.

"Utopianism, Ancient and Modern," *Imprimus,* April 1973.

Joining a radical movement when one is young is very much like falling in love when one is young. The girl may turn out to be rotten, but the experience of love is so valuable it can never be entirely undone by the ultimate disenchantment.

"Memoirs of a Trotskyist," *New York Times Magazine,* January 23, 1979.

For once a political ideology—whether liberal or conservative or radical—becomes unhinged from political reality, it will behave like a loose cannon, wreaking much mischief before its momentum expires.

"Unhinging of the Liberal Democrat," *Wall Street Journal,* March 29, 1984.

Politics is governed by circumstance, not by philosophy, and it becomes clear that, in our time, a nonideological politics cannot survive the relentless onslaught of ideological politics. For better or worse, ideology is now the vital element of organized political action.

"The New Republican Party," *Wall Street Journal,* July 17, 1980.

It requires strength of character to act upon one's ideas; it requires no less strength of character to resist being seduced by them.

"The Politics of Stylish Frustration," *New Leader,* April 1, 1963.

On Intellectuals and Academics

An intellectual may be defined as a man who speaks with general authority about a subject on which he has no particular competence.

"American Intellectuals and Foreign Policy," *Foreign Affairs*, July 1967.

Tell an American intellectual that he is a disturber of the intellectual peace, and he is gratified. Tell him he is a reassuring spokesman for calm and tranquillity, and he will think you have made a nasty accusation.

"American Intellectuals and Foreign Policy," *American Scholar*, Winter 1969–1970.

There are brilliant men at work in American sociology, but fewer sensible ones. The statistical ingenuity and dialectical subtlety which are so marked a characteristic of sociological writing (to say nothing of the invented rhetoric) tend toward a scholasticism whose self-contained world is ever more removed from the vulgar universe we inhabit.

"The Idea of Mass Culture," review of *The Political Context of Sociology*, by Leon Branson, *Yale Review*, February 1962.

It is all very well for the American Association of University Professors to state that a university "should be an intellectual experimental station, where new ideas may germinate and where their fruit, though still distasteful to the community as a whole, may be allowed to ripen." This is doubtless what a university should be. In some ways, it is a description of what the medieval university rather deviously was. But what has this ideal to do with the realities of American college life, where most of the students will get their diploma without knowing a hypothesis from a syllogism?

"The College and the University," *Encounter*, March 1956.

Our young radicals are far less dismayed at America's failure to become what it ought to be than they are contemptuous of what it thinks it ought to be. For them, as for Oscar Wilde, it is not the average American who is disgusting; it is the ideal American.

"'When Virtue Loses All Her Loveliness'—Some Reflections on Capitalism and 'the Free Society,'" *The Public Interest,* Fall 1970.

It is no accident that the major proponents of what we call "supply-side economics" have had their origins outside (or at the margin of) the academic profession. A Ph.D. in economics, as this subject is now taught in graduate schools, is only too likely to damage both one's perceptions and one's conception of economic reality.

"A New Look at Capitalism," *National Review,* April 17, 1981.

Who would ever have thought, twenty or even ten years ago, that we in the United States would live to see the day when a government agency would ask institutions of higher learning to take a racial census of their faculties, specifying the proportion of "Indo-Europeans" (traditionally, just another term for "Aryans")? And who could have anticipated that this would happen with little public controversy, and with considerable support from the liberal community? How on earth did this fantastic situation come about?

"How Hiring Quotas Came to the Campuses," review of *The Balancing Act and Anti-Bias Regulations of the University: Faculty Problems and Their Solution,* in *Fortune,* September 1974.

It is the self-imposed assignment of neoconservatism to explain to the American people why they are right, and to the intellectuals why they are wrong.

Introduction to *Reflections of a Neoconservative* (New York: Basic Books, 1983).

On Political Sentiments

We certainly do have it in our power to make improvements in the human estate. But to think we have it in our power to change people as to make the human estate wonderfully better than it is, remarkably different from what it is, and in very short order, is to assume that this generation of Americans can do what no other generation in all of human history could accomplish.

"A Foolish American Ism—Utopianism," *New York Times Magazine,* November 14, 1971.

When we lack the will to see things as they really are, there is nothing so mystifying as the obvious.

"'When Virtue Loses All Her Loveliness'—Some Reflections on Capitalism and 'the Free Society,'" *The Public Interest,* Fall 1970.

When in the grip of a countercultural passion, one can easily lose or repress the ability to distinguish the nutty from the sensible.

"Countercultures," *Commentary,* December 1994.

Every age is, in its own way, an "age of anxiety"—the title of a poem by W. H. Auden, written over twenty years ago. Every generation is convinced that its world is out of control, that "things are in the saddle" (Emerson), that the "centre cannot hold" (Yeats), that the past has lost its glory, the present its humanity, the future its hope. The premonition of apocalypse springs eternal in the human breast.

"Our Shaken Foundations," *Fortune,* July 1968.

There is, however, an older idea of democracy—one which was fairly common until about the beginning of this century—for which the conception of the quality of public life is absolutely crucial. This idea starts from the proposition that democracy is a form of self-government, and that if you want it to be a meritorious polity, you have to care about what kind of people govern it. Indeed, it puts the matter more strongly and declares that if you want self-government, you are only entitled to it if that "self" is worthy of governing. There is no inherent right to self-government if it means that such government is vicious, mean, squalid, and debased.

"Pornography, Obscenity and the Case for Censorship," *New York Times Magazine*, March 28, 1971.

"Permissiveness" and "authoritarianism" are indeed two possible poles of moral discourse—they are, both of them, the poles that come into existence when the center no longer holds. That center is authority, by which one means the exercise of power toward some morally affirmed end and in such a reasonable way as to secure popular acceptance and sanction.

"Thoughts on Reading about a Summer-Camp Cabin Covered with Garbage," *New York Times Magazine,* November 17, 1974.

First Law of politics: There are occasions where circumstances trump principles. Statesmanship consists not in being loyal to one's avowed principles (that's easy), but in recognizing the occasions when one's principles are being trumped by circumstances.

"When It's Wrong to Be Right," *Wall Street Journal,* March 24, 1993.

Nostalgia is one of the legitimate, and certainly one of the most enduring of human emotions; but the politics of nostalgia is at best distracting, at worst pernicious.

"From the Land of the Free to the Big PX," *New York Times Magazine,* December 20, 1964.

Evil may come by doing good—not merely intending to do good, but doing it. . . . Universal literacy has led to popular demagogy and mass mania; modern medicine finds unparalleled opportunities unleashed by the atomic bomb; the shortening of the working day goes hand in hand with the break-up of the family and the derangement of the sexual sentiment.

"How Basic Is 'Basic Judaism': A Comfortable Religion for an Uncomfortable World," *Commentary,* January 1948.

Compassion organized into a political movement is a very dangerous thing and, I think, a wicked thing. If you want to be compassionate, go out and be compassionate to people. If you want to give
people money, give people money. If you want to work with poor
people, go out and work with poor people. I have great respect for
people who do that. But when people start becoming bureaucrats of
compassion and start making careers out of compassion—whether
political, journalistic or public entertainment careers—then I must
say I suspect their good faith.

From Robert Glasgow, "An Interview with Irving Kristol," *Psychology Today,* February 1974.

Conformity, if we mean by that a profound consensus on moral and
political first principles, is the condition for a decent society; without it, blunt terror must rule.

"Liberty and the Communists," *Partisan Review,* no. 4, 1952.

I know the question of equality is something that many religious people are quite obsessed with. Here, I will simply plead
my Jewishness and say, equality has never been a Jewish thing.
Rich men are fine, poor men are fine, so long as they are decent human beings. I do not like equality. I do not like it in
sports, in the arts, or in economics. I just don't like it in this
world.

"Spiritual Roots of Capitalism and Socialism," from *Capitalism and
Socialism: A Theological Inquiry,* ed. Michael Novak (Washington,
D.C.: American Enterprise Institute, 1981).

Put a bunch of Americans on a desert island and the first thing they
will do is enter into a new Mayflower compact, draw up a constitution, and form a PTA. The American West was exploited by rugged
individuals, but it was settled by communities that were more or
less identical in their legal and social structures. All of this is but
another way of saying that the instinct of American individualism
is also an instinct for voluntary community.

"Urban Civilization without Cities," *Horizon,* Autumn 1972.

On Culture and Morality

The liberal paradigm of regulation and license has led to a society where an 18-year-old girl has the right to public fornication in a pornographic movie—but only if she is paid the minimum wage. Now, you don't have to be the father of a daughter to think that there is something crazy about this situation.

"On Conservatism and Capitalism," *Wall Street Journal,* September 11, 1975.

In the end, when all has been said and done, the only authentic criterion for judging any economic or political system, or any set of social institutions, is this: what kind of people emerge from them?

"Republican Virtue v. Servile Institutions," *The Alternative: An American Spectator,* February 1975.

My impression of the American condition today can be summed up as follows: Our nation has just gone through a moderately severe nervous breakdown, and is in the process of making a shaky recovery. That breakdown is what the phrase "the '60s" means to me. Something important happened to us during that period—something which, even as we recover from it, will profoundly affect the rest of our lives. No one who has ever had a nervous breakdown is ever quite the same afterwards, no matter how pleased a doctor may be with his condition.

"Convalescing from the Frantic '60s," *Wall Street Journal,* February 16, 1976.

Our problem is not really political at all. It is cultural, in the largest sense of that term. It is not the case that our institutions are functioning badly; by all the familiar "objective" indices—increasing wealth, increasing education, increasing leisure—they are working quite well. What is happening to our institutions is that they are being inexorably drained of their legitimacy.

"The Old Politics, the New Politics, the New, New Politics," *New York Times Magazine,* November 24, 1968.

One wonders: how can a bourgeois society survive in a cultural ambiance that derides every traditional bourgeois virtue and celebrates promiscuity, homosexuality, drugs, political terrorism—anything, in short, that is in bourgeois eyes perverse?

"Our Shaken Foundations," *Fortune,* July 1968.

The moral code for all civilizations must, at one time or another, be prepared to face the ultimate subversive question: "Why not?" Our civilization is now facing that very question in the form of the drug problem, and, apparently, it can only respond with tedious, and in the end, ineffectual, medical reports.

"Urban Civilization and Its Discontents," *Commentary,* July 1970.

After all, if you believe that no one was ever corrupted by a book, you also have to believe that no one was ever improved by a book (or a play or a movie). You have to believe, in other words, that all art is morally trivial and that, consequently, all education is morally irrelevant. No one, not even a university professor, really believes that.

"Pornography, Obscenity and the Case for Censorship," *New York Times Magazine,* March 28, 1971.

A dionysiac music, celebrating the liberation of impulse and passion, is not easily assimilated to a bourgeois way of life whose fundamental principle is individual self-government sustained by individual self-discipline and self-control.

Introduction to *The Americans: 1976—An Inquiry into Fundamental Concepts of Man Underlying Various U.S. Institutions* (Lexington, Mass.: Lexington Books, 1976); cowritten with Paul Weaver.

Noise pollution in a New York slum! People are being mugged right and left, children are being bitten by rats, junkies are ripping out the plumbing of decaying tenements—and the EPA is worried about noise pollution! These same EPA officials, of course, go home at night and tranquilly observe their children doing their homework to the thumping, blaring, rock-and-roll music. And if the neighbors should complain, they get very testy.

"The Environmental Crusade," *Wall Street Journal,* December 16, 1974.

I am not unambiguously happy that the United States today has been so successful in exporting its popular culture to the world at large. Indeed, I am not happy that the United States even *has* this popular culture to export.

"All That Jazz," *The National Interest,* Summer 1992.

We have won the Cold War, which is nice—it's more than nice, it's wonderful. But this means that now the enemy is us, not them.

Response to "The End of History," by Francis Fukuyama, *The National Interest,* Summer 1989.

Multiculturalism is a desperate—and surely self-defeating—strategy for coping with the educational deficiencies, and associated social pathologies, of young blacks.

"The Tragedy of Multiculturalism," *Wall Street Journal,* July 31, 1991.

On Government and the Welfare State

I have not gone so far—I shall never be able to go so far—as to declare that the State is our Enemy. It is our ally—but a dubious, unreliable and occasionally even treacherous ally.

"Big Government and Little Men," *New Leader,* November 26, 1962.

Does it really make sense for the government to insist that no one has a legal right to work for a penny less than the minimum wage and for the government then to encourage us all to blow our week's wages at the betting cage? Does it really make sense for the government to enact a mountain of legislation—from SEC registration to the labeling of consumer products—which protects people from unwise expenditures while urging them to make the unwisest expenditure, a gambling bet?—Of course it is ridiculous. And dishonest. And corrupting, both of people and of government. But the urge to spend the people's money for the people's welfare is so powerful (and so mindless) that it actually comes to seem proper to cheat the people in order to spend on their welfare. This is paternalism run amok.

"Vice and Virtue in Las Vegas," *Wall Street Journal,* September 13, 1973.

In Mike Harrington's America [1964], there are 40–50 million people who are "maimed in body and spirit"—all because they have incomes under $4,000 a year. Well, that's not my America, and I don't believe it's the America of most of the 40 to 50 million, either.... They are...entitled not to be hectored, badgered, sermonized, psychoanalyzed, fingerprinted, Rorschached, and generally bossed around by a self-appointed body of self-appointed redeemers—who are, in any case, less interested in helping poor people than in satisfying some particular ideological passion.

"Poverty and Pecksniff," *New Leader,* March 30, 1964.

We easily forget that our extensive public services rely, to a degree not usually recognized, upon rather sophisticated individual cooperation: For garbage to be collected efficiently, it must first be neatly deposited in garbage cans.

"The Negro Today Is Like the Immigrant Yesterday," *New York Times Magazine,* September 11, 1966.

Practically all the founding fathers of *The Public Interest* had themselves risen from the ranks of the urban poor or near-poor, and they did not think much of this strategy. They saw jobs and education as still constituting the only effective passages out of poverty, and regard militant "community action" as likely to be counterproductive. But those who authored the War on Poverty were, of the most, upper middle-class graduates of elite universities who had been dazzled by trendy sociological theories to the effect that "empowering the poor" would so uplift the spirits of those living in poverty, would so quicken their incentives to move out of poverty, that the long, slow, traditional climb up the ladder of economic mobility could be circumvented.

"Skepticism, Meliorism and *The Public Interest*," *The Public Interest*, Spring 1979.

Incidentally, I cannot accept the notion that black Americans are a crippled people who cannot cope with the world except under "our" benevolent guidance. I doubt very much that they accept it, either.

"Irving Kristol Writes," *Commentary*, February 1973, in response to *Commentary* essay, "About Equality," November 1972.

The sociological evidence seems to be conclusive that the schools themselves have only a partial—maybe only marginal—impact on broad educational achievements. . . . Centering one's attention on the schools is an effective way of distracting one's attention from the far more important realities of poverty and discrimination."

"Decentralization for What?" *The Public Interest*, Spring 1966.

Just as anti-Semitism has been called the "socialism of fools," so New York's version of "environmentalism" can be fairly characterized as the socialism of upper-middle-class malcontents.

"The Mugging of Con Ed," *Wall Street Journal*, May 17, 1974.

The "new class" consists of scientists, lawyers, city planners, social workers, educators, criminologists, sociologists, public health doctors, etc.—a substantial number of whom find their careers in the expanding public sector rather than the private. The public sector, indeed, is where they prefer to be. They are, as one says, "idealistic"—i.e., far less interested in individual financial rewards than in the corporate power of their class. Though they continue to speak the language of "progressive reform," in actuality they are acting upon a hidden agenda: to propel the nation from that modified version of capitalism we call "the welfare state" toward an economic system so stringently regulated in detail as to fulfill many of the traditional anti-capitalist aspirations of the left.

"On Corporate Capitalism in America," *The Public Interest,* Fall 1975.

There can be no successful social program which does not take seriously, is not realistically attentive to, people's motivations.

"Human Nature and Social Reform," *Wall Street Journal,* September 18, 1978.

The greatest single cause, by far, of black poverty is the increasing number of female-headed households in the ghettos. . . . There is little doubt that it is our heedlessly constructed welfare system which has unwittingly created a set of perverse incentives for the proliferation of female-headed families as well as for the subsequent breakup of those families. Is it any wonder that so many blacks seem lacking in appreciation of that compassionate liberalism which has so savaged the black community?

"Jewish Voters and the Politics of Compassion," *Commentary,* October 1984, in reply to letters about "The Political Dilemma of American Jewry."

People today will simply not accept, as "natural" and "inevitable," the terrible sufferings their fathers and grandfathers experienced during the various steep recessions of the past one hundred years. Rather than placidly "going through the wringer" at the behest of orthodox economists, they will opt for wage and price controls, a vast expansion of "public service" jobs, the nationalization of major corporations to guarantee employment, etc. One may, if one wishes, lament the decline of moral fiber that this attitude represents. But such lamentations are for poets; not economists.

"A Guide to Political Economy," *Wall Street Journal,* December 19, 1980.

There will be a temptation, inevitably, for the Bush administration to exhaust its energies in simply coping with these issues as they arise, from day to day, week to week, month to month. That would be a terrible mistake, politically. The American people may have voted for prudent governance, but that does not mean they will for long be content with it. They do not like big government, but they do like their governments, at all levels, to be at least intermittently energetic.

"Bush Must Fight the GOP Energy Shortage," *Wall Street Journal,* December 21, 1988.

It would be helpful if our political leaders were mute, rather than eloquently "concerned." They are inevitably inclined to echo the conventional pap, since this is the least controversial option that is open to them. Thus at the recent governors' conference on education, Gov. Bill Clinton of Arkansas announced that "this country needs a comprehensive child-development policy for children under five." A comprehensive development policy for governors over 30 would seem to be a more pressing need.

"Educational Reforms That Do and Don't Work," *Wall Street Journal,* October 24, 1989.

On Capitalism and Its Discontents

A capitalist society does not want more than two cheers for itself. Indeed, it regards the impulse to give three cheers for any social, economic, or political system as expressing dangerous—because it is misplaced—enthusiasm.

Introduction to *Two Cheers for Capitalism* (New York: Basic Books, 1978).

Like most intellectuals, I have had certain clear and preconceived notions about how capitalism works in America. The economy is dominated by an interlocking directorate of Big Business which, while preaching competition and "free enterprise," manages things to suit its own convenience and, sometimes, the common good. Unlike my friends on the Left, I have not been outraged by this state of affairs, since it always seemed more reasonable to me that something as important as Big Business should be managed by hard-faced professionals than by, say, the editors of *The New Left Review*.

"An Odd Lot," *Encounter,* December 1960.

Why should anyone want to sing the praises of "the profit motive"? And who ever has? The Old Testament does no such thing, and the New Testament definitely does no such thing. Nor did the ancient philosophers, or the medieval theologians, or such founders of modern political thought as Thomas Hobbes, John Locke or James Madison. Nor, for that matter, did Adam Smith—though this may come as a surprise to many who have never really read that fine thinker, and whose understanding of him has come third-hand via some current exponents of "free enterprise."

"No Cheers for the Profit Motive," *Wall Street Journal,* February 20, 1979.

Meanwhile, a small businessman with a factory to establish would have to be out of his mind to locate it in New York City. The unions would cause him infinite trouble, the politicians would denounce him for polluting the atmosphere, the civil rights groups would picket him for trading with South Africa; SANE would excoriate him for producing war material—in short, he would be treated as a public nuisance rather than a public benefactor. Inevitably he asks himself: Who needs it?

"It's Not a Bad Crisis to Live In," *New York Times Magazine,* January 22, 1967.

The high taxes on large incomes may have some moral and political value, but they have little economic significance. The only class that would suffer if these taxes were reduced would be the tax lawyers.

"Keeping Up with Ourselves," *Yale Review,* June 1960.

After years of experience with New York's subway system, I am not at all averse to seeing it owned and operated by General Motors. Perhaps what is good for General Motors will be good for me. It couldn't be worse.

"Is the Welfare State Obsolete?" *Harper's,* May 1963.

The government grants me tax deductions for my two young children. Does that mean the rearing of my children is being subsidized by government money? I think not. It is being paid for by my money. . . . Many people seem to be under the impression that the government has original ownership of all the money in the country, and then in its wisdom decides to let the citizenry keep some part of it. The opposite strikes me as more in accord with both the real and the ideal.

"Taxes and Foundations," letter to the *New Republic,* February 15, 1964.

Witness how vulnerable our corporate managers are to accusations that they are befouling our environment. What these accusations really add up to is the statement that the business system in the United States does not create a beautiful, refined, gracious and tranquil civilization. To which our corporate leaders are replying: "Oh, we can perform that mission too—just give us time." But there is no good reason to think that they can accomplish this non-capitalist mission; nor is there any reason to believe that they have any proper entitlement to even try.

"'When Virtue Loses All Her Loveliness'—Some Reflections on Capitalism and 'the Free Society,'" *The Public Interest,* Fall 1970.

Our capitalists promote the ethos of the New Left for only one reason: they cannot think of any reason why they should not. For them, it is "business as usual."

"Capitalism, Socialism and Nihilism," *The Public Interest,* Spring 1973.

There are two requirements for the survival of any large institution in our society: The American people must feel it is somehow representative and somehow responsible, and this applies to big corporations, big universities, labor unions, the military, even the Post Office. Large institutions must be attentive to the public interest.

"Who Stands for the Corporation?" *Forbes,* May 15, 1974.

Not only don't we know who the chairman of General Motors is; we know so little about the kind of person who holds such a position that we haven't the faintest idea as to whether or not we want our children to grow up like him. Horatio Alger, writing in the era of pre-corporate capitalism, had no such problems. And there is something decidedly odd about a society in which a whole class of Very Important People is not automatically held up as one possible model of emulation for the young, and cannot be so held up because they are, as persons, close to invisible.

"Corporate Capitalism in America," *The Public Interest,* Fall 1975.

Since no society can be shown to live entirely up to its ideals, the greater the blind and mechanical stress on these abstract ideals, the smaller the possibility of what the Communists wish to avoid at all costs: any mere comparison of political realities—the reality of the life of an American worker, farmer, or intellectual with their Soviet counterparts, for instance.

"Flying off the Broomstick," review of *Witch Hunt: The Revival of Heresy,* by Carey McWilliams, *Commentary,* April 1951.

At the same time, precisely because the bourgeois-capitalist order is so "boring" from this "existential" point of view—what poet has ever sung its praises? what novelist was ever truly inspired by the career of a businessman?—the psychic needs are more acute. A dangerous dialectic is thereby created. Young people, no longer hard pressed to "better their condition," are all the more free to experience the limitations of their social world, to rebel against them, to participate in what Lionel Trilling called "the adversary culture."

Introduction to *Two Cheers for Capitalism* (New York: Basic Books, 1978).

Economic growth, after all, is not a mystery of nature like the black holes in distant galaxies. It is a consequence of purposive action by human beings very much like ourselves.

"The Economics of Growth," *Wall Street Journal,* November 16, 1978.

Common sense would suggest that, if you need the higher mathematics to analyze the issue of economic inequality, it really cannot be an issue worthy of such an effort.

"People Who Are S-S-ST," *Wall Street Journal,* July 24, 1978.

Meanwhile, liberal capitalism survives and staggers on. It survives because the market economics of capitalism does work—does promote economic growth and permit the individual to better his condition while enjoying an unprecedented degree of individual freedom. But there is something joyless, even somnambulistic, about this survival.

"The Adversary Culture of Intellectuals," *Encounter,* October 1979.

If you de-legitimize this bourgeois society, the market economy—almost incidentally, as it were—is also de-legitimized. It is for this reason that radical feminism today is a far more potent enemy of capitalism than radical trade unionism.

"The Capitalist Future," Francis C. Boyer Lecture, American Enterprise Institute, December 4, 1991.

In sum, the distribution of income under liberal capitalism is "fair" if, and only if, you think that liberty is, or ought to be, the most important political value. If not, then not.

"What Is Social Justice?" *Wall Street Journal,* August 12, 1976.

Efficiency is not a moral virtue and by itself never legitimizes anything.

"Horatio Alger and Profits," *Wall Street Journal,* July 11, 1974.

The enemy of liberal capitalism today is not so much socialism as nihilism.

"Capitalism, Socialism and Nihilism," *The Public Interest,* Spring 1973.

On American Foreign Policy

Power breeds responsibilities, in international affairs as in domestic—or even private. To dodge or disclaim these responsibilities is one form of the abuse of power.

"We Can't Resign as 'Policeman of the World,'" *New York Times Magazine,* May 12, 1968.

It is absurd and sickening to see this administration getting bogged down in congressional debates over whether we should place 55 military advisors there [in El Salvador] or 75. A great power that conducts its foreign affairs in this way loses all credibility in the world.

"Running like a Dry Creek?" *Wall Street Journal,* October 6, 1983.

In an era of ideological politics, which is ours, foreign policy tends to be a continuation of domestic policy by other means.

"Transatlantic 'Misunderstanding': The Case of Central America," *Encounter,* March 1988.

Our foreign policy is certainly less intelligent and imaginative than it ought to be; every foreign policy is; but this does not mean that more intelligence and imagination will in themselves provide a successful policy. Indeed, there are times when the seeming lack of these qualities has a peculiar suitability to, a correspondence with, even a flowing from, the recalcitrant facts of life.

"The Ideology of Economic Aid," *Yale Review,* Summer 1957.

There is no "community of nations" or any "world community" that shares certain essential values, as any authentic community does. The various international organizations to which the United States has subordinated its own foreign policy have become a playground for irresponsible or hostile governments to create mischief for the United States.

"Foreign Policy in an Age of Ideology," *The National Interest,* Fall 1985.

I just want to go on record as saying that I thoroughly deplore in this serious conversation on foreign policy, any mention of the UN Charter.

The Reagan Doctrine and Beyond, American Enterprise Institute Symposium, Washington, D.C., American Enterprise Institute for Public Policy Research, 1987.

But no one can seriously claim that the numerous authoritarian regimes now scattered all over the world constitute any kind of threat to liberal America or the liberal West. Totalitarian societies, on the other hand, are post-liberal realities—they emerge out of an explicit rejection of the Western liberal tradition, are the declared enemies of this tradition, and aim to supersede it.

"'Human Rights': The Hidden Agenda," *The National Interest,* Winter 1986–1987.

There are still some people around who think it wrong for the United States, under any conditions, to ally itself with nondemocratic regimes. But they are the kind of people who also think there is something immoral about comic books, and their voices do not resound in the land.

"The 20th Century Began in 1945," *New York Times Magazine,* May 2, 1965.

On Religion and Morality

It is such a moral endorsement that has always led Americans to believe that their constitutional order is not only efficient or workable, but also just. For such an endorsement to prevail, the "civil religion" must be at least minimally nourished by its religious roots.

"The Spirit of '87,'" *The Public Interest,* Winter 1987.

Moral codes evolve from the moral experience of communities, and can claim authority over behavior only to the degree that individuals are reared to look respectfully, even reverentially, on the moral traditions of their forefathers. It is the function of religion to instill such respect and reverence.

"The Future of American Jewry," *Commentary,* August 1991.

The kind of tension that is now building up between Jews and Christians has little to do with traditional discrimination and everything to do with efforts of liberals among whom, I regret to say, Jews are both numerous and prominent—to establish a wall between religion and society in the guise of maintaining the wall between church and state.

"Christians, Christmas and Jews," *National Review,* December 30, 1988.

It is crucial to the lives of all our citizens, as of all human beings at all times, that they encounter a world that possesses a transcendent meaning, in which the human experience makes sense. Nothing, absolutely nothing, is more dehumanizing, more certain to generate a crisis, than experiencing one's life as a meaningless event in a meaningless world.

"The Capitalist Future," Francis C. Boyer Lecture, American Enterprise Institute, December 4, 1991.

One need not have known a great deal about the theory of free-market economics to have been convinced that Soviet religious doctrine—described, somewhat redundantly but accurately enough, as "godless, atheistic materialism"—could never sink roots among the

Russian people. All people, everywhere, at all times, are "theotropic" beings, who cannot long abide the absence of a transcendental dimension to their lives. The collapse of Soviet Communism vindicates this truth.

"Countercultures," *Commentary*, December 1994.

William Stern reports that secular humanists are "leading exciting lives in quest of meaning and as part of the grand adventure of philosophy and science." Good for them. I just hope they have time to instill in their children such virtues as modesty, fidelity, probity, respect for their elders, and the other values found in the Jewish tradition specifically, and in religion generally.

"Is Secular Humanism Good for the Jews?" *Commentary*, December 1991—reply to letters responding to "The Future of American Jewry."

Beneath the priority that orthodoxy gives to right practice lies a basic, primordial intuition: that the world is meant to be a home for mankind. Leading a life according to virtue is therefore of metaphysical significance. In pursuing the ethical sanctification of the mundane, virtuous practice gains strength by linking the living to the dead to the unborn. In a traditional orthodox community, both the dead and the unborn have the right to vote.

"Countercultures," *Commentary*, December 1994.

After all, why should Jews care about the theology of a fundamentalist preacher when they do not for a moment believe that he speaks with any authority on the question of God's attentiveness to human prayer? And what do such theological abstractions matter as against the mundane fact that this same preacher is vigorously pro-Israel?

"The Political Dilemma of American Jewry," *Commentary*, July 1984.

One does get the impression that many American Jews would rather see Judaism vanish through intermarriage than hear the President say something nice about Jesus Christ.

"The Future of American Jewry," *Commentary*, August 1994.

The danger facing American Jews today is not that Christians want to persecute them but that Christians want to marry them.

Quoted in Jay Lefkowitz, "Romancing the State," review of *The Fatal Embrace: Jews and the State,* by Benjamin Ginsberg, *Commentary,* January 1994.

It is ironic to watch the churches, including large sections of my own religion, surrendering to the spirit of modernity at the very moment when modernity itself is undergoing a kind of spiritual collapse. If I may speak bluntly about the Catholic church, for which I have enormous respect, it is traumatic for someone who wishes that church well to see it modernize at this moment. Young people do not want to hear that the church is becoming modern. Go tell the young people that the message of the church is to wear sackcloth and ashes and to walk on nails to Rome, and they would do it. The church turned the wrong way. It went to modernity at the very moment when modernity was being challenged, when the secular gnostic impulse was already in the process of dissolution. Young people, especially, are looking for religion so desperately that they are inventing new ones. They should not have to invent new ones; the old religions are pretty good.

"Christianity, Judaism, and Socialism," in *Capitalism and Socialism: A Theological Inquiry* (Washington, D.C.: American Enterprise Institute, 1979).

PART THREE

*Bibliography of the Published Works
of Irving Kristol*

Books

Author

On the Democratic Idea in America. New York: Harper, 1972.

Two Cheers for Capitalism. New York: Basic Books, 1978.

Reflections of a Neoconservative: Looking Back, Looking Ahead. New York: Basic Books, 1983.

Editor

Encounters. Edited with Stephen Spender and Melvin Lasky. New York: Basic Books, 1963.

Confrontation: The Student Rebellion and the University. Edited with Daniel Bell. New York: Basic Books, 1969.

Capitalism Today. Edited with Daniel Bell. New York: Basic Books, 1970.

The American Commonwealth—1976. Edited with Nathan Glazer. New York: Basic Books, 1976.

The Americans: 1976—An Inquiry into Fundamental Concepts of Man Underlying Various U.S. Institutions. Edited with Paul Weaver. Lexington, Mass.: Lexington Books, 1976.

Essays

"Auden: The Quality of Doubt." Written under the name William Ferry. *Enquiry* (November 1942).

"Silone's Christian Experiment." Written under the name William Ferry. *Enquiry* (January 1943).

"Other People's Nerve." *Enquiry* (May 1943). Written under the name William Ferry.

"The Machiavellians." Written under the name William Ferry. *Enquiry* (July 1943).

"Koestler: A Note on Confusion." *Politics* (May 1944).

"Adam and I." *Commentary* (November 1946).

"British Labor Today." *New Leader* (February 15, 1947).

"A Labor Minister's Life Is Not a Happy One." *New Leader* (May 17, 1947).

"The Anti-Semitism of the Communists." *New Leader* (May 24, 1947).

"Bevin and the Left Wing Revolution." *New Leader* (June 14, 1947).

"The Myth of the Supra-Human Jew: A Theological Stigma. *Commentary* (September 1947).

"How Basic Is 'Basic Judaism': A Comfortable Religion for an Uncomfortable World." *Commentary* (January 1948).

"What the Nazi Autopsies Show." *Commentary* (September 1948). Reprinted as "The Nature of Nazism." In *The Commentary Reader*. Edited by Norman Podhoretz. New York: Atheneum, 1966.

"Who's Superstitious?" *Commentary* (December 1948).

"God and the Psychoanalysts." *Commentary* (November 1949). Reprinted as "God and the Psychoanalysts: Can Freud and Religion Be Reconciled?" In *Arguments and Doctrines: A Reader of Jewish Thinking in the Aftermath of the Holocaust*. Edited by Arthur Allen Cohen. New York: Harper and Row, 1970. Also reprinted in *Reflections of a Neoconservative*.

"Love Affair: Psychoanalysts and Religion." *Time* (November 14, 1949).

"Einstein: The Passion of Pure Reason." *Commentary* (September 1950). Reprinted in *Reflections of a Neoconservative*.

"Is Jewish Humor Dead?" *Commentary* (November 1951). Reprinted in *Mid-Century: An Anthology of Jewish Life and Culture in Our Times*. Edited by Harold Uriel Ribalow. New York: Beechhurst Press, 1955. Also reprinted in *Reflections of a Neoconservative*.

"'Civil Liberties,' 1952—A Study in Confusion." *Commentary* (March 1952).

"Ordeal by Mendacity." *Twentieth Century* (October 1952).

"McGranery and Charlie Chaplin." *New Leader* (November 24, 1952).

"Liberty and the Communists." *Partisan Review,* no. 4 (1952).

"Authors for 'Peace.'" *New Leader* (December 22, 1952).

"After the Apocalypse." *Encounter* (October 1953). With Stephen Spender.

"Men of Science—and Conscience." *Encounter* (October 1953).

"On 'Negative Liberalism.'" *Encounter* (January 1954). Reply to letters in *Encounter* (May 1954).

"The Simple and the True." *Encounter* (February 1954).

"Men and Ideas: Niccolo Machiavelli." *Encounter* (December 1954).

"Table Talk." *Encounter* (October 1955).

"Notes on Margate." *New Leader* (October 24, 1955).

"Trivia and History." *Commentary* (December 1956).

"Bandung Powers: Danger Zone for US Policy." *New Republic* (January 14, 1957).

"The Shadow of the Marquis." *Encounter* (February 1957).

"A Mixed Bag." *Encounter* (June 1957).

"The Ideology of Economic Aid." *Yale Review* (June 1957).

"Politics, Sacred and Profane." *Encounter* (September 1957).

"The Worst of Both Worlds." *Encounter* (October 1957).

"Class and Sociology: 'The Shadow of Marxism.'" *Commentary* (October 1957).

"Britain's Change of Life." *New Leader* (October 21, 1957).

"The Essence of Capitalism." *Encounter* (November 1957).

"'I Dreamed I Stopped Traffic.'" *Encounter* (December 1957).

"American Ambiguities." *Encounter* (January 1958).

"Old Truths and the New Conservatism." *Yale Review* (May 1958).

"Thoughts on the Bomb." *New Leader* (June 30, 1958).

"Class and Sociology: 'The Shadow of Marxism.'" *Commentary* (October 1958).

"...And a Reply." *Encounter* (March 1960). Reply to Richard Wollheim's "One Man, One Vote..." in same issue.

"Disagreeing on Fundamentals." *Encounter* (April 1960).

"Keeping Up with Ourselves." *Yale Review* (June 1960).

"High, Low, and Modern: Some Thoughts on Popular Culture and Popular Government." *Encounter* (August 1960).

"An Odd Lot." *Encounter* (December 1960).

"Machiavelli and the Profanation of Politics." In *The Logic of Personal Knowledge: Essays by Various Contributors Presented to Michael Polanyi on His Seventieth Birthday*. London: Routledge and Kegan Paul, 1961. Reprinted in *Reflections of a Neoconservative*.

"S. M. Levitas, 1894–1961." *New Republic* (January 16, 1961).

"Dead-End Streets." *Encounter* (February 1961).

"Explaining Ourselves." *Encounter* (May 1961).

"Civil Disobedience in the Algerian War." *Yale Review* (May 1961).

"Deterrence." *Commentary* (July 1961).

"God and Politics in America." *Encounter* (August 1961).

"Of G.E., T.V., J.F.K. and U.S.A." *Encounter* (September 1961).

"The Last Hundred Days." *New Republic* (November 20, 1961).

"Social Sciences and Law." In *The Great Ideas Today*. Edited by Robert M. Hutchins and Mortimer J. Adler. Chicago: Encyclopaedia Britannica, 1962.

"The Drift of Things." *Encounter* (February 1962).

"No Special Relation." *Spectator* (October 5, 1962).

"The Case for Intervention in Cuba." *New Leader* (October 15, 1962).

"Big Government and Little Men." *New Leader* (November 26, 1962).

"Of Newton Minow and Matthew Arnold." *New Leader* (January 7, 1963).

"A Case of Uneven Development." *New Leader* (February 18, 1963).

"The Politics of Stylish Frustration." *New Leader* (April 1, 1963).

"Is the Welfare State Obsolete?" *Harper's* (May 1963).

"Confessions of a Publisher." *New Leader* (May 13, 1963).

"Why the Welfare State Doesn't Work." *Atlantic* (June 1963). Reprinted in *Reader's Digest* (November 1963).

"One Man, One Vote." *New Leader* (June 24, 1963).

"Age of the Remittance-Man." *New Leader* (August 5, 1963).

"Facing the Facts about Vietnam." *New Leader* (September 30, 1963).

"My Friend, the Professor." *New Leader* (November 11, 1963).

"Jobs and the Man." *New Leader* (January 6, 1964).

"The Lower Fifth." *New Leader* (February 17, 1964).

"Poverty and Pecksniff." *New Leader* (March 30, 1964). Reprinted in *The Economics of Poverty: An American Paradox.* Edited by Burton Weisbrod. Englewood Cliffs, New Jersey: Prentice-Hall, 1965.

"Mythraking." *New Leader* (May 11, 1964).

"The Metaphysics of Journalism." *New Leader* (June 22, 1964).

"On Literary Politics." *New Leader* (August 3, 1964).

"The Squares v. the Yahoos." *New Leader* (September 14, 1964).

"From the Land of the Free to the Big PX." *New York Times Magazine* (December 20, 1964).

"Of Death and Politics." *New Leader* (January 18, 1965).

"A Few Kind Words for Uncle Tom." *Harper's* (February 1965).

"The Poverty of Equality." *New Leader* (March 1, 1965).

"The 20th Century Began in 1945." *New York Times Magazine* (May 2, 1965).

"Where Has the Money Gone?" *New Leader* (May 24, 1965).

"In Reply." Reply to Curtis Benjamin's "'Of Copyrights and Commissars': A Rejoinder." *New Leader* (June 21, 1965).

"Teaching In, Speaking Out: The Controversy over Vietnam." *Encounter* (August 1965).

"What Is the Public Interest?" *The Public Interest* (Fall 1965). With Daniel Bell.

"What's Bugging the Students." *Atlantic* (November 1965).

"The Troublesome Intellectuals." *The Public Interest* (Winter 1965–1966).

"A New Isolationism?" *Encounter* (June 1966).

"New Left, New Right." *The Public Interest* (Summer 1966). Reprinted in *The Radical Left: The Abuse of Discontent.* Edited by William Gerberding and Duane Smith. Boston: Houghton Mifflin, 1970.

"The Literary Intellectual." *Encounter* (August 1966).

"The Negro Today Is Like the Immigrant Yesterday." *New York Times Magazine* (September 11, 1966).

"The Pauper Problem." *New Leader* (December 5, 1966). Reply to letters in *New Leader* (January 2, 1967).

"It's Not a Bad Crisis to Live in." *New York Times Magazine* (January 22, 1967).

"Germany 1967." *Atlantic* (May 1967).

"American Intellectuals and Foreign Policy." *Foreign Affairs* (July 1967). Reprinted in *On the Democratic Idea in America.*

"The Negro and the City." In *A Nation of Cities.* Edited by Robert Goldwin. New York: Rand McNally, 1968. Reprinted as "Today's Negroes: Better Off than Yesterday's Immigrants?" In *U.S. News and World Report* (November 27, 1967).

"The Underdeveloped Profession." *The Public Interest* (Winter 1967).

"The Malcontent Professors." *Fortune* (January 1968).

"Memoirs of a Cold Warrior." *New York Times Magazine* (February 11, 1968). Reprinted in *Reflections of a Neoconservative.*

"Decentralization for What?" *The Public Interest* (Spring 1968).

"We Can't Resign as 'Policeman of the World.'" *New York Times Magazine* (May 12, 1968).

"Why I Am for Humphrey." *New Republic* (June 8, 1968).

"Our Shaken Foundations." *Fortune* (July 1968). Reprinted as "The Shaking of the Foundations" in *On the Democratic Idea in America*.

"A Fellow Can Be Civilized, Though Executive." *Fortune* (September 1, 1968).

"The Old Politics, the New Politics, the New, New Politics." *New York Times Magazine* (November 24, 1968). Reprinted as "The End of Liberalism?" In *Current* (January 1969).

"Paying for Protection." *New Leader* (December 2, 1968).

"A Different Way to Restructure the University." *New York Times Magazine* (December 8, 1968). Reprinted as "Toward a Restructuring of the University." In *On the Democratic Idea in America*. Response to letters as "Campus Confusion." *New York Times Magazine* (January 5, 1969).

"New York Intellectuals: An Exchange." *Commentary* (January 1969). With Irving Howe.

"Who Knows New York?" *The Public Interest* (Summer 1969). With Paul Weaver.

"A Bad Idea Whose Time Has Come." *New York Times Magazine* (November 23, 1969).

"American Historians and the Democratic Idea." *American Scholar* (Winter 1969–70). Reprinted in *On the Democratic Idea in America* and *Reflections of a Neoconservative*.

"Writing about Trade Unions." *New York Times Book Review* (February 1, 1970). Reply to letter as "Writing about Trade Unions (Continued)." In *New York Times Book Review* (March 1, 1970).

"What Business Is a University In?" *New York Times Magazine* (March 22, 1970). Reply to letters as "A University's Business." *New York Times Magazine* (April 19, 1970). Reprinted as "Toward Universities for Education." In *Current* (May 1970).

"Urban Civilization and Its Discontents." *Commentary* (July 1970). Reprinted in *On the Democratic Idea in America* and *Reflections of a Neoconservative.*

"'When Virtue Loses All Her Loveliness'—Some Reflections on Capitalism and 'the Free Society.'" *The Public Interest* (Fall 1970). Reprinted in *On the Democratic Idea in America* and as the epilogue to *Two Cheers for Capitalism.*

"'Capitalism' and 'the Free Society': A Reply." *The Public Interest* (Winter 1971).

"Is the Urban Crisis Real?" *Commentary* (November 1970).

"Pornography, Obscenity and Censorship." *New York Times Magazine* (March 28, 1971). Reprinted as "Censorship: Where Do We Draw the Line?" In *Reader's Digest* (July 1975). Also reprinted as "Is This What We Wanted?" In *The Case against Pornography.* Edited by David Holbrook. London: Tom Stacey Ltd., 1972. Also reprinted in *On the Democratic Idea in America* and *Reflections of a Neoconservative.*

"From Priorities to Goals." *The Public Interest* (Summer 1971).

"Welfare: The Best of Intentions, the Worst of Results." *Atlantic* (August 1971).

"A Foolish American Ism—Utopianism." *New York Times Magazine* (November 14, 1971). Reprinted as "Utopianism and American Politics." In *On the Democratic Idea in America.* Also reprinted under original title in *A Public Philosophy Reader*. Edited by Richard Bishirjian. New Rochelle, New York: Arlington House, 1978.

"Crisis for Journalism: The Missing Elite." From *Press, Politics and Popular Government*. Washington, D.C.: American Enterprise Institute, 1972. Reprinted as "The New Demagogic Journalism." In "The Press and American Politics." Ethics and Public Policy reprint 15 (December 1978).

"Urban Civilization without Cities." *Horizon* (Autumn 1972). Reprinted as "America's Future Urbanization." In *Current* (November 1972).

"About Equality." *Commentary* (November 1972). Reprinted in *Two Cheers for Capitalism*. Replies to letters in *Commentary* (February 1973).

"The American Revolution as a Successful Revolution." Distinguished Lecture Series on the Bicentennial of the United States of America. American Enterprise Institute, 1973. In *America's Continuing Revolution: An Act of Conservation,* with an introduction by Stephen J. Tonsor. Washington, D.C.: American Enterprise Institute, 1975. Reprinted in the following:
> *The American Revolution, Three Views*. New York: American Brands, 1975.
> *A Public Philosophy Reader*. Edited by Richard Bishirjian. New Rochelle, New York: Arlington House, 1978.
> "The Most Successful Revolution: The Leaders All Died in Bed." In *American Heritage* (April 1974).
> *Revista/Review Interamericana* (Winter 1975–1976).
> *Reflections of a Neoconservative*.

"Lag Found in Tempo of Reform." *New York Times* (January 8, 1973). Annual Education Review.

"Capitalism, Socialism and Nihilism." *The Public Interest* (Spring 1973). Reprinted in *Two Cheers for Capitalism*.

"Utopianism, Ancient and Modern." *Imprimus* (April 1973). Reprinted in *Vital Speeches* (June 1, 1973). Also reprinted in *The*

Alternative (June–September 1974). Also reprinted in *Two Cheers for Capitalism*.

"The Need for a Philosophy of Education." *The Idea of a Modern University*. Edited by Sidney Hook, Paul Kurtz, and Miro Todorovich. New York: Prometheus Books, 1974.

"Republican Virtue v. Servile Institutions." A Poynter pamphlet. The Poynter Center at Indiana University, Bloomington, Indiana (May 1974). Reprinted in *The Alternative: An American Spectator* (February 1975).

"Who Stands for the Corporation?" *Forbes* (May 15, 1974). Reprinted in *Think* (May–June 1975).

"Taxes, Poverty and Equality." *The Public Interest* (Fall 1974). Reprinted in *Two Cheers for Capitalism*.

"Thoughts on Reading about a Summer-Camp Cabin Covered with Garbage." *New York Times Magazine* (November 17, 1974).

"Furthermore: Is the Press Misusing Its Growing Power?" *More* (January 1975).

"On Corporate Capitalism in America." *The Public Interest* (Fall 1975). Reprinted in *Two Cheers for Capitalism* and *Reflections of a Neoconservative*.

"Libertarians and Bourgeois Freedoms." *National Review* (December 5, 1975).

"Adam Smith and the Spirit of Capitalism." In *The Great Ideas Today*. Edited by Robert Hutchins and Mortimer Adler. Chicago: Encyclopaedia Britannica, 1976. Reprinted in *Reflections of a Neoconservative*.

"What Is a 'Neo-Conservative'?" *Newsweek* (January 19, 1976).

"Socialism: An Obituary for an Idea." *Alternative* (October 1976). Reprinted in *The Future That Doesn't Work: Social Democracy's*

Failures in Britain. Edited by R. Emmett Tyrrell, Jr. Garden City, New York: Doubleday 1977. Rev. ed., New York: University Press of America, 1983. Also reprinted in *Reflections of a Neoconservative*.

"Post-Watergate Morality: Too Good for Our Good?" *New York Times Magazine* (November 14, 1976). Reprinted as "Post-Watergate Morality: A Dubious Legacy." In *Reader's Digest* (May 1977).

"Memoirs of a Trotskyist." *New York Times Magazine* (January 23, 1977). Reprinted in *Reflections of a Neoconservative*.

"A Regulated Society?" *Regulation* (July–August 1977).

"In Memory of Martin Diamond." *The Alternative: An American Spectator* (October 1977).

"Looking Back on Neoconservatism: Notes and Reflections." *American Spectator* (November 1977).

"The Measure of America." *Oklahoma Observer* (December 25, 1977).

"Thoughts on Equality and Egalitarians." In *Income Redistribution*. Edited by Colin D. Campbell. Washington, D.C.: American Enterprise Institute, 1977.

"Sense and Nonsense in Urban Policy." *National Cities* (February 1978).

"The Spiritual Roots of Capitalism and Socialism." In *Capitalism and Socialism: A Theological Inquiry*. Edited by Michael Novak. Washington, D.C.: American Enterprise Institute, 1979. Reprinted as "Christianity, Judaism and Socialism." In *Reflections of a Neoconservative*.

"The Disaffection of Capitalism." In *Capitalism and Socialism: A Theological Inquiry*. Edited by Michael Novak. Washington, D.C.: American Enterprise Institute, 1979.

"The Death of the Socialist Idea." *Saturday Evening Post* (March 1979).

"The Case for a Massive Tax Cut." *Reader's Digest* (April 1979).

"Does NATO Exist?" *Washington Quarterly* (August 1979). Reprinted in *Reflections of a Neoconservative*.

"Confessions of a True, Self-Confessed—Perhaps the Only— 'Neoconservative.'" *Public Opinion* (October–November 1979).

"The Adversary Culture of Intellectuals." *Encounter* (October 1979). Reprinted in *Reflections of a Neoconservative*.

"Some Personal Reflections on Economic Well-Being and Income Distribution." In *The American Economy in Transition*. Edited by Martin Feldstein. Chicago: University of Chicago Press, 1980. Reprinted in *Reflections of a Neoconservative*.

"Rationalism in Economics." *The Public Interest* (Special Edition, 1980). Reprinted in *Reflections of a Neoconservative*.

"The Goal." *Encounter* (March 1980).

"Ideology and Supply-Side Economics." *Commentary* (April 1981).

"A New Look at Capitalism." *National Review* (April 17, 1981).

"'No First Use' Requires a Conventional Build-Up." *The Apocalyptic Premise: Nuclear Arms Debated*. Edited by Ernest W. Lefever and E. Stephen Hunt. Washington, D.C.: Ethics and Public Policy Committee, 1982.

"Israel and Palestine: 'Some Plain Truths.'" *Encounter* (September–October 1982).

"Life with Sid: A Memoir." *Sidney Hook: Philosopher of Democracy and Humanism*. Edited by Paul Kurtz. New York: Prometheus Books, 1983.

"What's Wrong with NATO?" *New York Times Magazine* (September 25, 1983). Reprinted in *Current* (December 1983). Also reprinted as "NATO Needs Shock Treatment." In *Reader's Digest* (February 1984).

"The Political Dilemma of American Jews." *Commentary* (July 1984). Response to letters as "Jewish Voters and the Politics of Compassion." *Commentary* (October 1984).

"Reflections of a Neoconservative." *Partisan Review,* no. 4 (1984). Reprinted in *Partisan Review: The 50th Anniversary Edition.* Edited by William Phillips. New York: Stein & Day, 1985.

"A Transatlantic 'Misunderstanding': The Case of Central America." *Encounter* (March 1985). Reply to letter as "Kristol's NATO" (June 1985).

"Foreign Policy in an Age of Ideology." *The National Interest* (Fall 1985).

"Skepticism, Meliorism and *The Public Interest.*" *The Public Interest* (Fall 1985).

"Ideas Shape Every Generation." *American Business and the Quest for Freedom.* Ethics and Public Policy reprint 62 (February 1986).

"'Human Rights': The Hidden Agenda." *The National Interest* (Winter 1986–1987).

"Of Lords, Sirs, and Plain Misters: An Exchange between Irving Kristol and Max Beloff." *Encounter* (June 1987).

"Don't Count Out Conservatism." *New York Times Magazine* (June 14, 1987).

"Ideological Subdivisions." *Public Opinion* (November–December 1987).

"The Spirit of '87." *The Public Interest* (Winter 1987).

"Not the Deficits." *Forbes* (December 14, 1987).

"Why I Left." *New Republic* (April 11, 1988).

"Liberalism and American Jews." *Commentary* (October 1988). Published as "The Liberal Tradition of American Jews." In *American Pluralism and the Jewish Community*. Edited by Seymour Martin Lipset. New Brunswick, N.J.: Transaction, 1990.

"Christmas, Christians, and Jews." *National Review* (December 30, 1988).

"On the Character of American Political Order." In *The Promise of American Politics: Principles and Practice after Two Hundred Years*. Edited by Robert Utley. New York: University Press of America, 1989. Published jointly with the Tocqueville Forum.

"Second Thoughts: A Generational Perspective." *Second Thoughts: Former Radicals Look Back at the Sixties*. Edited by Peter Collier and David Horowitz. New York: Madison Books, 1989.

"The Way We Were." *National Interest* (Fall 1989).

"Defining Our National Interest." *The National Interest* (Fall 1990). Reprinted as "Our National Interest: Ideas That Define Us." In *Current* (February 1991).

Foreword to *Public Lives: 50 Figures of Public Consequence* by Paul Greenberg. Washington, D.C.: Ethics and Public Policy Center, 1991.

"Twelve Years and Out!" *American Legion* (February 1991).

"The Future of American Jewry." *Commentary* (August 1991). Reprinted as afterword to *American Jews and the Separationist Faith*. Edited by David G. Dalin. Washington, D.C.: Ethics and Public Policy Center, 1993. Response to letters as "Is Secular Humanism Good for the Jews?" In *Commentary* (December 1991).

"A New Age of Faith?" *Wilson Quarterly* (Autumn 1991).

"The Capitalist Future." Francis Boyer Lecture at the American Enterprise Institute, December 4, 1991. Reprinted as "The Cultural Revolution and the Capitalist Future." In *The American*

Enterprise (March 1992). Also reprinted as "Economic Success, Spiritual Decline, the Capitalist Future." In *Current* (June 1992).

"A Letter from Irving Kristol." *National Review* (March 16, 1992). Response to "In Search of Anti-Semitism" by William Buckley, *National Review* (December 31, 1991).

"Secular Rationalism Has Been Unable to Produce a Compelling, Self-Justifying Moral Code." *Chronicle of Higher Education* (April 22, 1992).

"America's Mysterious Malaise." *Times Literary Supplement* (May 22, 1992).

"All That Jazz." *The National Interest* (Summer 1992). Originally prepared for the conference "The New Global Popular Culture: Is It American? Is It Good for America? Is It Good for the World?" American Enterprise Institute, Washington, D.C., March 10, 1992.

Foreword to *Public Lives: 60 Figures of Public Consequence* by Paul Greenberg. Washington, D.C.: Ethics and Public Policy Center, 1993.

"My Cold War." *The National Interest* (Spring 1993). Reprinted as "Why I Am Still Fighting My Cold War." *Times* (London) (April 8, 1993).

"Why Religion Is Good for the Jews." *Commentary* (August 1994). Response to letters as "The Jewish Future: Judaism and Liberalism." *Commentary* (November 1994).

"Countercultures." *Commentary* (December 1994).

Newspaper Articles

The Wall Street Journal

"Why Jews Turn Conservative." September 14, 1972.

"The New Road for the Democrats." October 13, 1972.

"The Odd Distortions of TV News." November 16, 1972.

"Symbolic Policies and Liberal Reform." December 15, 1972.

"Convalescing from the Frantic '60s." February 16, 1973.

"The Misgivings of a Philanthropist." March 14, 1973.

"Social Reform: Gain and Losses." April 16, 1973. Reprinted in *Two Cheers for Capitalism.*

"The Nightmare of Watergate." May 17, 1973.

"What Comes Next after Watergate." June 14, 1973.

"The Frustrations of Affluence." July 20, 1973. Reprinted in *Two Cheers for Capitalism.*

"The Ironies of Neo-Isolationism." August 20, 1973.

"Vice and Virtue in Las Vegas." September 13, 1973.

"Notes on the Yom Kippur War." October 18, 1973.

"NATO: The End of an Era." November 16, 1973.

"Where Have All the Gunboats Gone?" December 13, 1973.

"The Credibility of Corporations." January 17, 1974. Reprinted in *Two Cheers for Capitalism.*

"The Corporation and the Dinosaur." February 14, 1974. Reprinted in *Two Cheers for Capitalism.*

"The Corporation: A Last Word." March 14, 1974.

"The Meaning of Henry Kissinger." April 11, 1974.

"The Mugging of Con Ed." May 17, 1974.

"Inflation and the 'Dismal Science.'" June 13, 1974. Reprinted in *Two Cheers for Capitalism.*

"Horatio Alger and Profits." July 11, 1974. Reprinted in *Two Cheers for Capitalism.*

"The Shareholder Constituency." August 14, 1974. Reprinted in *Two Cheers for Capitalism.*

"The Inexorable Rise of the Executive." September 20, 1974.

"Political Pollution in Washington." October 17, 1974.

"Secrets of State." November 14, 1974.

"The Environmentalist Crusade." December 16, 1974. Reprinted in *Two Cheers for Capitalism.*

"Food, Famine and Ideology." January 20, 1975. Reprinted as "Ideology and Food" in *Two Cheers for Capitalism.*

"The War against the Cities." March 13, 1975.

"Ethics and the Corporation." April 16, 1975.

"Business and 'The New Class.'" May 19, 1975. Reprinted in *Two Cheers for Capitalism*.

"The Conservative Prospect." June 13, 1975. Excerpted in *Current* (July–August 1975).

"The 'New Cold War.'" July 17, 1975.

"Nuclear Disturbances." August 18, 1975.

"On Conservatism and Capitalism." September 11, 1975. Reprinted in *Two Cheers for Capitalism*.

"Some Doubts about 'De-Regulation.'" October 20, 1975. Reprinted in *Two Cheers for Capitalism*.

"The New Forgotten Man." November 13, 1975.

"New York Is a State of Mind." December 10, 1975.

"'The Stupid Party.'" January 15, 1976. Excerpted as "GOP: The Stupid Party." In *Current* (March 1976). Reprinted in *Two Cheers for Capitalism*.

"On 'Economic Education.'" February 18, 1976. Reprinted in *Two Cheers for Capitalism*.

"Henry Kissinger at Dead End." March 10, 1976.

"Notes on the Spirit of '76." April 23, 1976.

"The Republican Future." May 14, 1976. Reprinted in *Two Cheers for Capitalism*.

"The Busing Crusade." June 17, 1976.

"The Poverty of Equality." July 12, 1976. Excerpted in *Current* (September 1976).

"What Is 'Social Justice'?" August 12, 1976. Reprinted in *Two Cheers for Capitalism*.

"Reforming the Welfare State." October 25, 1976. Reprinted in *Two Cheers for Capitalism*.

"'Morality, Liberalism and Foreign Policy.'" November 19, 1976. Reprinted in *Morality and Foreign Policy*. Edited by Ernest Lefever. Washington, D.C.: Ethics and Public Policy Center, 1977.

"The Economic Consequences of Carter." December 22, 1976.

"The Hidden Costs of Regulation." January 12, 1977. Reprinted in *Two Cheers for Capitalism*.

"The OPEC Connection." February 22, 1977. Reprinted in *Two Cheers for Capitalism*.

"On Corporate Philanthropy." March 21, 1977. Reprinted in *Two Cheers for Capitalism*.

"Détente and 'Human Rights.'" April 15, 1977.

"Toward a 'New' Economics." May 9, 1977.

"The Foxes v. the Hedgehog." June 14, 1977.

"Summer Notes and Footnotes." July 18, 1977.

"On the Unfairness of Life." August 16, 1977.

"President Carter's Coming Crisis." September 19, 1977.

"The Myth of 'Business Confidence.'" November 14, 1977.

"Sense and Nonsense in Urban Policy." December 21, 1977.

"Pumping Air into a Balloon." January 13, 1978.

"Of Oil and the Dollar." February 16, 1978. Reprinted in *Society* (September–October 1978).

"The Human Rights Muddle." March 20, 1978.

"The White House Virus." April 17, 1978.

"'Reforming' Corporate Governance." May 12, 1978.

"The Meaning of Proposition 13." June 28, 1978.

"People Who Are S-S-ST." July 24, 1978.

"Populist Remedy for Populist Abuses." August 10, 1978.

"Human Nature and Social Reform." September 18, 1978.

"Understanding Trade Unionism." October 23, 1978.

"The Economics of Growth." November 16, 1978.

"The Wrong War on Inflation." December 22, 1978.

"Foreign Policy: End of an Era." January 18, 1979. Excerpted as "End of an Era." In *Current* (March 1979).

"No Cheers for the Profit Motive." February 20, 1979.

"Business Ethics and Economic Man." March 20, 1979. Reprinted in *Reflections of a Neoconservative*.

"Can Carter Reap a Windfall?" April 13, 1979.

"The 'New Class' Revisited." May 21, 1979.

"'Business' vs. 'the Economy'?" June 26, 1979.

"Blame It on the People!" July 19, 1979.

"The Confusion over 'Inflation.'" August 22, 1979.

"NATO's Moment of Truth." September 24, 1979.

"Will 'Conservative' Economics Work?" October 22, 1979.

"The Worst Is Yet to Come." November 26, 1979.

"Mr. Carter and Iran." December 28, 1979.

"Our Foreign Policy Illusions." February 4, 1980.

"'Moral Dilemmas' in Foreign Policy." February 28, 1980. Reprinted in *Reflections of a Neoconservative*.

"The Panic over Inflation." April 1, 1980.

"The Trilateral Commission Factor." April 16, 1980.

"The Battle for Reagan's Soul." May 16, 1980.

"Two Economic Questions." June 26, 1980.

"The New Republican Party." July 17, 1980.

"The Quiet Death of the MAD Doctrine." August 15, 1980.

"Of Economics and 'Eco-Mania.'" September 19, 1980.

"Our Incoherent Foreign Policy." October 15, 1980. Reprinted in *Reflections of a Neoconservative*.

"The Shadow of '82.'" November 19, 1980.

"A Guide to Political Economy." December 19, 1980.

"False Principles and Incoherent Policies." January 13, 1981.

"A Letter to the Pentagon." February 20, 1981. Reprinted in *Reflections of a Neoconservative*.

"The Common Sense of 'Human Rights.'" April 8, 1981. Reprinted in *Reflections of a Neoconservative*.

"The Muddle in Foreign Policy." April 29, 1981.

"The Timerman Affair." May 29, 1981.

"NATO at a Dead End." July 15, 1981.

"The Trouble with Money." August 26, 1981.

"A Patch of Turbulence." September 25, 1981.

"Economic Policy: Trouble on the Supply Side." October 27, 1981.

"'The Truth about Reaganomics.'" November 20, 1981.

"The Key Question: Who Owns the Future?" January 11, 1982. Reprinted in *Reflections of a Neoconservative*.

"The Focus Is on the Fed." February 12, 1982.

"Exorcising the Nuclear Nightmare." March 12, 1982. Reprinted in *Reflections of a Neoconservative*.

"Diplomacy v. Foreign Policy in the United States." April 15, 1982. Reprinted in *Reflections of a Neoconservative*.

"The Self-Destruction of the Republicans." May 13, 1982.

"Notes for a Dismal Spring." June 16, 1982.

"The Question of George Shultz." July 23, 1982.

"Reconstructing NATO: A New Role for Europe." August 12, 1982. Reprinted as "Reconstructing NATO." In *Current* (December 1982).

"Why Reagan's Plan Won't Work." September 10, 1982.

"The Big Question." October 14, 1982.

"The Succession—Understanding the Soviet Mafia." November 18, 1982. Reprinted as "Understanding the Soviet Mafia." In *Reflections of a Neoconservative.*

"The Emergence of Two Republican Parties." January 4, 1983. Reprinted in *Reflections of a Neoconservative.*

"The Reagan Administration Bottoms Out." February 17, 1983.

"What Choice Is There in Salvador?" April 4, 1983.

"Mideast Peace Is the Most Elusive Catch." May 10, 1983.

"Fed Policy: Compromises We Can Live With." June 27, 1983.

"Bad Pollsters from the White House." July 27, 1983.

"Put Not Your Faith in Economic Soothsayers." August 30, 1983.

"Running Like a Dry Creek?" October 6, 1983.

"Toward a Moral Foreign Policy." November 15, 1983.

"There'll Never Be a '1984.'" December 16, 1983.

"What Ever Happened to Common Sense?" January 17, 1984. Excerpted in *Reader's Digest* (February 1990). Reprinted as "What Happened to Common Sense?" in the Canadian edition of *Reader's Digest* (March 1990).

"Try a Little Tenderness." February 29, 1984.

"Unhinging of the Liberal Democrat." March 29, 1984.

"'Fairness' and Income Equalizing." May 2, 1984.

"Our Four-Party System." June 15, 1984.

"Most Economists Ignore Reality." July 16, 1984.

"Dilemma of the Outside Director." September 11, 1984.

"Creative Coverage of Political News." October 11, 1984.

"The Honeymoon's Over, Mr. Reagan." November 15, 1984.

"An Automatic-Pilot Administration." December 14, 1984.

"Even in Israel, No Economic Miracles." January 25, 1985.

"A New Foreign-Policy Momentum." March 8, 1985.

"The Old World Needs a New Ideology." April 1, 1985.

"A White House in Search of Itself." May 13, 1985.

"International Law and International Lies." June 21, 1985.

"The New Populism: Not to Worry." July 25, 1985.

 "Reviewing Reagan's Reviewers." September 11, 1985.

"An Economy Too Good to Be True?" October 2, 1985.

"Congressional Right Has It Wrong." November 18, 1985.

"Coping with an 'Evil Empire.'" December 17, 1985.

"Three Economic Notes for 1986." January 9, 1986.

"'Global Unilateralism' and 'Entangling Alliances.'" February 3, 1986.

"Now What for U.S. Client States?" March 3, 1986.

"Why a Debate over Contra Aid?" April 11, 1986.

"The David I Knew." May 9, 1986.

"American Universities in Exile." June 17, 1986.

"The Background to a Sluggish Economy." July 31, 1986.

"Schools Can Do This Much." September 8, 1986.

"The Force Is with Reagan." October 24, 1986.

"Why Did Reagan Do It?" December 17, 1986.

"The Missing Social Agenda." January 26, 1987.

"Economic Notes and Footnotes." March 2, 1987.

"NATO Edges toward the Moment of Truth." April 14, 1987.

"The War of the Words." June 11, 1987.

"Nuclear NATO: A Moment of Truth." July 9, 1987.

"The New Liberal Isolationism." August 11, 1987.

"Ethics Anyone? Or Morals?" September 15, 1987.

"Look at 1962, Not 1929." October 28, 1987.

"Taking Glasnost Seriously." December 8, 1987.

"Foreign Policy Has Outlived Its Time." January 21, 1988.

"There's No 'Peace Process' in Mideast." February 19, 1988.

"The Reagan Revolution That Never Was." April 19, 1988.

"A Cure for Takeovers' Social Ills." May 13, 1988.

"The Bizarre Social Security Surplus." June 17, 1988.

"The Soviets' Albatross States." July 22, 1988.

"The Trouble with Republicans." August 22, 1988.

"The Question of Patriotism." September 16, 1988.

"Voodoo Economics or Voodoo Economists?" October 18, 1988.

"Bush Must Fight the GOP Energy Shortage." December 21, 1988.

"The War against the Corporation." January 24, 1989.

"Cries of 'Racism' Cow Crime Fighters." February 28, 1989.

"A Smug NATO Is Letting Germany Secede." May 2, 1989.

"Some Kindergarten Remediation." June 22, 1989.

"Friends of the Family." Excerpts from debut columns of columnists. In June 23, 1989.

"Who Needs Peace in the Middle East?" July 21, 1989.

"End Game of the Welfare State." September 11, 1989.

"Education Reforms That Do and Don't Work." October 24, 1989.

"Sometimes It's Over Before It's Over." December 1, 1989.

"The Map of the World Has Changed." January 3, 1990.

"Conservatives' Greatest Enemy May Be the GOP." February 20, 1990.

"Bush Is Right about Lithuania." April 11, 1990.

"Inflation: Almost Never What It Seems." May 16, 1990.

"In Search of Our National Interest." June 7, 1990.

"At Issue: Will the U.S. Reap a Large 'Peace Dividend' from the End of the Cold War?" With Seymour Melman. In *Editorial Research Reports* (June 8, 1990).

"It's Obscene but Is It Art?" August 7, 1990.

"Hoover, Nixon, Carter...Bush?" October 8, 1990.

"What Won, and What Lost, in 1990." November 16, 1990.

"The Challenge of a Political Reversal." December 17, 1990.

"After the War, What?" February 22, 1991.

"Tongue-Tied in Washington." April 15, 1991.

"The Conservatives Find a Leader." June 3, 1991.

"Reflections on Love and Family." January 7, 1992.

"What Shall We Do with the NEA?" March 16, 1992.

"Men, Women, and Sex." May 12, 1992.

"'Peace Process' That Heads Nowhere." June 18, 1992.

"AIDS and False Innocence." August 6, 1992.

"'Family Values'—Not a Political Issue." December 7, 1992.

"The Coming 'Conservative Century.'" February 1, 1993. Reprinted as the preface to *Disciples and Democracy: Religious Conservatives and the Future of American Politics*, edited by Michael Cromartie. Washington, D.C.: Ethics and Public Policy Center, 1994.

"When It's Wrong to Be Right." March 24, 1993.

"Two Parties in Search of Direction." May 12, 1993.

"A Conservative Welfare State." June 14, 1993.

"Clinton's Illusion—Spirit of the 60s." August 19, 1993.

"Too Clever by Half." October 12, 1993.

"From Perot to Buchanan." November 24, 1993.

"Russia's Destiny." February 11, 1994.

"The Inevitable Outcome of 'Outcomes.'" April 18, 1994.

"Sex, Violence and Videotape." May 31, 1994.

"The Tragic Error of Affirmative Action." August 1, 1994.

"Life without Father." November 3, 1994.

Other

"The Scandalous State of Human Rights." *Times* (London), May 5, 1981.

"Charity and Business Shouldn't Mix." *New York Times*, October 17, 1982.

"The Only Way for Reagan." *Times* (London), April 14, 1983.

"Soviet Intentions." *New York Times,* May 3, 1983.

"D'France de 'reaganomie' (Events of 'Reaganomics')." *L'Express* (Paris), July 20, 1984.

"America's Doomed Mideast Policy." *New York Times*, August 11, 1985.

"Room for Darwin and the Bible." *New York Times*, September 30, 1986.

"Should U.S. Withdraw from NATO? The Case For." *San Francisco Chronicle*, April 8, 1987.

"War on Drugs? Then Get Serious and Use the Military." *Washington Post*, March 28, 1988.

"Liberally Applied, It's Not Voodoo." *Los Angeles Times*, April 4, 1988.

"The Conservatives Have Better Ideas." *New York Times*, October 30, 1988.

"Forget Arms Control...Instead, Negotiate to Neutralize Eastern Europe." *New York Times*, September 12, 1989.

"There Is No Military Free Lunch." *New York Times*, February 2, 1990.

"12 Years and Out!" *Washington Post*, June 10, 1990.

"The G.O.P. Message: A State of Disunion." *New York Times*, January 27, 1991.

Reviews

"The Moral Critic." Review of *E. M. Forster*, by Lionel Trilling. *Enquiry* (April 1944).

Review of *Dangling Man*, by Saul Bellow. *Politics* (June 1944).

"In Hillel's Steps." Review of *In Darkest Germany*, by Victor Gollancz. *Commentary* (February 1947).

"Nightmare Come True." Review of *The Other Kingdom*, by David Rousset; *Smoke over Birkenau*, by Seweryna Szmaglewska, and *Beyond the Last Path*, by Eugene Weinstock. *Commentary* (October 1947).

"Christian Theology and the Jews." Review of *Christianity and the Children of Israel*, by A. Roy Eckardt. *Commentary* (April 1948).

"Boundaries of Belief." Review of *The Protestant Era*, by Paul Tillich. *Commentary* (March 1949).

"The Slaughterbench of History." Review of *Faith and History*, by Reinhold Niebuhr, and *Meaning in History*, by Karl Lowitz. *Commentary* (July 1949).

"Elegy for a Lost World." Review of *The Earth Is the Lord's*, by Abraham Joshua Heschel. *Commentary* (May 1950).

"American Humanist." Review of *Classics and Commercials* and *The Little Blue Light*, by Edmund Wilson. *Commentary* (November 1950).

Review of *The Gentleman and the Jew,* by Maurice Samuel. *New Leader* (December 25, 1950).

"Flying off the Broomstick." Review of *Witch Hunt: The Revival of Heresy,* by Carey McWilliams. *Commentary* (April 1951).

"In Power Begins Curiosity." Review of *The Irony of American History,* by Reinhold Niebuhr. *Partisan Review,* no. 3 (1952).

"The Indefatigable Fabian." Review of *Beatrice Webb's Diaries: 1912–1924,* edited by Margaret I. Cole. *New York Times Book Review* (August 24, 1952).

"Two Varieties of Democracy." Review of *The Rise of Total Democracy,* by J. L. Talmon. *Commentary* (September 1952).

"The Philosophers' Hidden Truth." Review of *Persecution and the Art of Writing,* by Leo Strauss. *Commentary* (October 1952).

Review of *Arrow in the Blue,* by Arthur Koestler. *New Leader* (October 6, 1952).

"The Web of Realism." Review of *The Web of Subversion: Underground Networks in the United States Government,* by James Burnham. *Commentary* (June 1954).

"American Ghosts." Review of *The Adventures of Augie March,* by Saul Bellow, and *Brothers to Dragons,* by R. D. Warner. *Encounter* (July 1954).

"The Judgment of Clio." Review of *Historical Inevitability,* by Isiah Berlin. *Encounter* (January 1955).

"The Family Way." Review of *Uncommon People,* by Paul Bloomfield. *Encounter* (December 1955).

"America: Mystery and Mystifications." Review of *American Government,* by Richard Pear; *History of the United States* (2 vols.), by R. B. Nie and J. E. Mopurgo; *The Great Experiment,* by Frank

Thistlethwaite; and *The Age of Reform: From Bryan to FDR*, by Richard Hofstadter. *Encounter* (January 1956).

"Bridge and the Human Condition." Review of *Theory of Games as a Tool for the Moral Philosopher*, by R. B. Braithwaite; *Aces All*, by Guy Ramsey; and *Sorry Partner*, by Paul Sterns. *Encounter* (February 1956).

"The College and the University." Review of *The Development of Academic Freedom in the United States*, by Richard Hofstadter and Walter Metzger. *Encounter* (March 1956).

"The Heterodox Conformist." Review of *Socialism and the New Despotism*, by R. H. S. Crossman. *Encounter* (April 1956).

"...And People Opening Veins in Baths." Review of *Tacitus on Imperial Rome*, translated by Michael Graves, and *Tiberius: A Study in Resentment*, by Gregorio Maranon. *Encounter* (May 1956). Reprinted in *Encounters: An Anthology*. Edited by Stephen Spender. New York: Basic Books, 1963.

"The Rock of Eden." Review of *The Dream of Success*, by Kenneth S. Lynn; *The Man in the Grey Flannel Suit*, by Sloan Wilson; and *The Exurbanites*, by A. C. Spectorsky. *Encounter* (June 1956).

"A Philosophy for Little England." Review of *Philosophy, Politics and the Soviet Union*, edited by Peter Laskett. *Encounter* (July 1956).

"Not One World." Review of *American Politics in a Revolutionary World*, by Chester Bowles. *Commentary* (August 1956).

"Socialism without Socialists." Review of *Twentieth Century Socialism*, by Socialist Union. *Encounter* (August 1956).

"Europe's Underground." Review of *Passion and Society*, by Denis de Rougemont. *Encounter* (September 1956).

"...A Condition of Mere Nature." Review of *The Anglo-American Tradition in Foreign Affairs*, edited by Arnold Wolfers and Lawrence W. Martin. *Encounter* (October 1956).

"India to Us." Review of *Conversations with Mr. Nehru*, by Tibor Mende. *Encounter* (November 1956).

"The New Forsyte Saga." Review of *Russia without Stalin*, by Ed Crankshaw. *Encounter* (December 1956).

"Trivia and History." Review of *The Crucial Decade*, by Eric F. Goldman. *Commentary* (December 1956).

"Vox Populi, Vox Dei?" Review of *Torment of Secrecy*, by Edward Shils; and *Freedom or Secrecy*, by James Russell Wiggins. *Encounter* (March 1957).

"On Boondoggling Democracy." Review of *The Affluent Society*, by John Kenneth Galbraith. *Commentary* (August 1958).

"The Shadow of a War." Review of *Every War but One*, by Eugene Kinkead. *Reporter* (February 5, 1959).

"Toward Pre-Emptive War?" Review of *War and the Soviet Union*, by H. S. Dinerstein. *Reporter* (May 14, 1959).

"The Conquistadors' Conscience." Review of *Aristotle and the American Indians*, by Louis Hanke. *Reporter* (September 17, 1959).

"Britain's Change of Life." Review of *They Are the British*, by Drew Middleton. *New Leader* (October 21, 1957).

"Strange Gods on Capitol Hill." Review of *Advise and Consent*, by Allen Drury. *Reporter* (November 12, 1959).

"On the Burning Deck." Review of *Up from Liberalism*, by William Buckley. *Reporter* (November 26, 1959).

"The Masculine Mode." Review of *The Spare Chancellor: The Life of Walter Bagehot*, by Alistar Buchan. *Encounter* (December 1959).

"D-a-v-y Da-vy Crockett." Review of *Mark Twain and Southwestern Humor*, by Kenneth S. Lynn. *Commentary* (February 1960).

"A Cool Sociological Eye." Review of *Political Man: The Social Basis of Politics,* by Seymour Martin Lipset. *Reporter* (February 4, 1960).

"Last of the Whigs." Review of *The Constitution of Liberty,* by F. A. Hayek. *Commentary* (April 1960).

"A Treasure for the Future." Review of *Between Past and Future: Six Exercises in Political Thought,* by Hannah Arendt. *New Republic* (July 10, 1961).

"New Books: Democracy and Its Discontents." *Harper's* (September 1961).

"The Idea of Mass Culture." Review of *The Political Context of Sociology,* by Leon Branson. *Yale Review* (February 1962).

"Learning to Live with the N.S.&N." Review of *New Statesmanship,* by Edward Hyams, and *The New Statesman,* by Edward Hyams. *Encounter* (August 1963).

"The View from Miami." Review of *Great Britain or Little England?* by John Mander; *A State of England,* by Anthony Hartley; and *The Outsiders: A Liberal View of Britain,* by James Morris. *Encounter* (November 1963).

"Murder in New Jersey." Review of *Doe Day: The Antlerless Deer Controversy in New Jersey,* by Paul Tillett. *New York Review of Books* (April 16, 1964).

"Professor Galbraith's New Industrial State." Review of *The New Industrial State,* by John Kenneth Galbraith. *Fortune* (July 1967).

"As Goes Demand, So Goes Invention." Review of *Invention and Economic Growth,* by Jacob Schmookler. *Fortune* (September 1, 1967).

"Common Sense about the Urban Crisis." Review of *Metropolitan Enigma,* by the United States Chamber of Commerce. *Fortune* (October 1967).

"Who's in Charge Here?" Review of *The Power Structure,* by Arnold Rose. *Fortune* (November 1967).

"Iron Mountain Lies beyond Credibility Gap." Review of *Report from Iron Mountain,* edited by Leonard Lewin. *Fortune* (January 1, 1968).

"Men on the Move." Review of *American Occupational Structure,* by Otis Dudley Duncan. *Fortune* (March 1968).

"Advice for Managers from a Florentine Consultant." Review of *Management and Machiavelli,* by Jay Anthony. *Fortune* (April 1968).

"The Strange Death of Liberal Education." Review of *Higher Education and Modern Democracy,* by Robert Goldwin. *Fortune* (May 1968).

"The New Regulators." Review of *Report of the Secretary's Advisory Committee on Traffic,* by the U.S. Department of Health, Education and Welfare. *Fortune* (June 15, 1968).

"Why It's Hard to Be Nice to the New Left." Review of *Permanent Poverty: An American Syndrome,* by Ben Seligman, and *Toward a Democratic Left,* by Michael Harrington. *Fortune* (August 1968).

"The New Era of Innovation." Review of *The Age of Discontinuity: Guidelines to Our Changing Society,* by Peter Drucker. *Fortune* (February 1969).

"Bilious Sermon from a Hero of the Moral Elite." Review of *American Power and the New Mandarins,* by Noam Chomsky. *Fortune* (May 1, 1969).

"The Crisis behind the Welfare Crisis." Review of *Multi-Problem Dilemma,* by G. E. Brown. *Fortune* (June 1969).

"The Improbable Guru of Surrealistic Politics." Review of *An Essay on Liberation,* by Herbert Marcuse. *Fortune* (July 1969).

"In Search of the Missing Social Indicator." Review of *Toward a Social Report*, by the U.S. Department of Health, Education and Welfare. *Fortune* (August 1, 1969).

"Barbarians from Within." Review of *Decline of Radicalism: Reflections on America Today*, by Daniel Boorstin. *Fortune* (March 1970).

"Cities: A Tale of Two Classes." Review of *The Unheavenly City*, by Edward C. Banfield. *Fortune* (June 1970).

"The Young Are Trying to Tell Us Something about Scarsdale." Review of *Movement toward a New America*, by Mitch Gooden. *Fortune* (August 1971).

"Does TV News Tell It Like It Is?" Review of *News Twister*, by Mitch Gooden. *Fortune* (November 1971).

"The Gang and the Establishment." Review of *Our Gang and How It Prospers*, by Richard W. Poston. *Fortune* (April 1972).

"I.Q. and a Professor's Nightmare." Review of *I.Q. and the Meritocracy*, by Richard J. Herrnstein. *Fortune* (May 1973).

"A College President Discusses America." Review of *Blue-Collar Journey*, by John R. Coleman. *Fortune* (April 1974).

"How Hiring Quotas Came to the Campuses." Review of *Anti-Bias Regulations of the University: Faculty Problems and Their Solutions*, by Richard A. Lester, and *The Balancing Act*, by George Roche. *Fortune* (September 1974).

"The High Cost of Equality." Review of *Equality and Efficiency: The Big Tradeoff*, by Arthur Okun. *Fortune* (November 1975).

"Urban Utopias v. the Real World." Review of *Urban Utopias in the Twentieth Century*, by Robert Fisher. *Fortune* (July 3, 1978).

"The Feminist Attack on Smut." Review of *Pornography and Silence*, by Susan Griffin. *New Republic* (July 25, 1981).

"The Dubious Science." Review of *Dangerous Currents: The State of Economics,* by Lester Thurow. *New Republic* (June 6, 1983).

"The State of the Union." Review of *The Good News Is the Bad News Is Wrong,* by Ben Wattenberg. *New Republic* (October 29, 1984).

"A Choice of Blind Allies." Review of *Politics and the Pursuit of Happiness,* by Ghita Ionesescu. *Times Literary Supplement* (November 1984).

Review of *The Good News Is the Bad News Is Wrong,* by Ben Wattenberg. *Hadoar* (November 30, 1984).

"What Every Soviet Leader Wants." Review of *The Soviet Paradox,* by Seweyn Bialer. *Fortune* (September 1, 1986).

"After New Models." Review of *The Trouble with America,* by Michael Crozier. *Times Literary Supplement* (December 6, 1985).

"The New York Intellectuals." Review of *Prodigal Sons: The New York Intellectuals and Their World,* by Alexander Bloom. *Washington Times* (April 7, 1986).

"Wills' America: A 'Sophisticate' Takes Revenge." Review of *Reagan's America,* by Garry Wills. *Washington Times* (February 9, 1987).

"Taking Political Things Personally." Review of *The American "Empire" and Other Studies of US Foreign Policy in a Comparative Perspective,* by Geir Lundestad; and *US Foreign Policy in the 1990s,* edited by Greg Schmergel. *Times Literary Supplement* (March 5, 1991).

"Standing Room Only." Review of *American Citizenship: The Quest for Inclusion,* by Judith Shklar. *Times Literary Supplement* (July 12, 1991).

Interviews, Symposiums, and Letters

"To Free Gold and Sobell." Letter to the *New York Times* (February 16, 1960). With Nathan Glazer, Sidney Hook, and Dwight MacDonald.

"Taxes and Foundations." *New Republic* (February 15, 1964), letter.

"A Talk-In on Vietnam." *New York Times Magazine* (February 6, 1966), symposium.

"Civil Disobedience Is Not Justified by Vietnam." *New York Times Magazine* (November 26, 1967), symposium.

"Irving Kristol: Interview with R. Emmett Tyrrell." *Alternative* (August–September 1969).

"Capital Dinner Guest." *New York Times* (April 15, 1970), letter.

Robert Glasgow, "An Interview with Irving Kristol." *Psychology Today* (February 1974).

"America Now: A Failure of Nerve?" *Commentary* (July 1975), symposium.

"What Is a Liberal—Who Is Conservative?" *Commentary* (September 1976), symposium.

Contribution to "Professors, Politicians and Public Policy." Edited by John Charles Daly. Washington, D.C.: American Enterprise Institute, 1977.

"How Equal Can We Be? An Interview with Irving Kristol." *Business and Society Review* (September 1977), symposium.

"Capitalism, Socialism and Democracy." *Commentary* (April 1978), symposium.

"Is America Moving Right? Ought It? A Conversation with Irving Kristol and Arthur Schlesinger, Jr." *Public Opinion* (September–October 1978). Reprinted in *Across the Board* (February 1979).

"Waste of Time." Contribution to "Is Dishonesty Good for Business?" *Business and Society Review* (Summer 1979).

Contribution to "William Baroody, Sr., Recipient of the 1980 Boyer Award." Washington, D.C.: American Enterprise Institute, 1981.

"Where Do We Go from Here? Directions from Stage Right." *Public Opinion* (December 1980–January 1981), symposium.

"Neo-Conservative Guru to America's New Order Q and A: Irving Kristol." *MacLean's* (January 19, 1981).

"If Conservatives Cannot Do It Now." Interview in *U.S. News & World Report* (July 20, 1981).

"Is Social Science a God That Failed?" *Public Opinion* (October–November 1981), symposium.

"Should the United States Stay in NATO?" *Harper's* (January 1984), symposium.

"Sex and God in American Politics: What Conservatives Really Think." *Policy Review* (Summer 1984), symposium.

"A Quarter-Century's Selection of Statements and Comments from Center Meetings, Symposia, and Convocations." Center for the Study of Democratic Institutions, *Center* (November–December 1984).

"What's Going On Out There?" *The State of the Nation: A Conference of the Committee for the Free World*. Edited by Steven C. Munson. Washington, D.C.: University Press of America, 1985.

"Why Europe Worries, and Why Washington Cares." *New York Times* (March 17, 1985), symposium.

"Beyond Containment: The Future of U.S.-Soviet Relations." *Policy Review* (Winter 1985), symposium.

"Has the United States Met Its Major Challenges since 1945?" *Commentary* (November 1985), symposium.

"Who Should Succeed Reagan: Some Preliminary Thoughts." *Policy Review* (Summer 1986), symposium.

"The U.S. Needs the Will to Be a Winner." *Insight* (December 29, 1986–January 5, 1987), symposium.

Contribution to symposium, "The Reagan Doctrine and Beyond." Washington, D.C.: American Enterprise Institute, 1988.

Contribution to the 1988 Francis Boyer Lecture on Public Policy, "Freedom and Vigilance: Ronald Reagan." Washington, D.C.: American Enterprise Institute, 1988.

"American Jews and Israel." *Commentary* (February 1988), symposium.

Contribution to *Our Country and Our Culture*, Committee for the Free World. New York: Orwell Press, 1989.

"This Is the Place to Be!" Interview with Ken Adelman. *Washingtonian* (July 1989).

Response to "The End of History and the Last Man," by Francis Fukuyama. *The National Interest* (Summer 1989).

"Books for Christmas." *American Spectator* (December 1990), symposium.

"A Chat with Irving Kristol." By Tom Bethell. *American Spectator* (December 1991).

"Does the Spread of American Popular Culture Advance American Interests?—A Response." Conference paper at American Enterprise Institute conference, "The New Global Popular Culture: Is It American? Is It Good for America? Is It Good for the World?" March 10, 1992. Reprinted as "All That Jazz." *The National Interest* (Summer 1992).

A NOTE ON THE BOOK

This book was edited by Ann Petty, Dana Lane, and
Cheryl Weissman of the publications staff of the American
Enterprise Institute. The text was set in New Century Schoolbook.
Lisa Roman of the AEI Press
set the type, and Automated Graphic Systems
of White Plains, Maryland, printed and bound the book,
using permanent acid-free paper.

The AEI Press is the publisher for the American Enterprise Institute for Public Policy Research, 1150 17th Street, N.W., Washington, D.C. 20036; *Christopher C. DeMuth,* publisher; *Dana Lane,*
director; *Ann Petty,* editor; *Leigh Tripoli,* editor; *Cheryl Weissman,*
editor; *Lisa Roman,* editorial assistant (rights and permissions).

www.ingramcontent.com/pod-product-compliance
Lightning Source LLC
Jackson TN
JSHW020016141224
75386JS00025B/555